How to Create and Maintain an Alien

How to Create and Maintain an Alien

An Insider's Look at Criminals and Their Culture

Arthur L. Mattocks, Ph.D.

Arthur L. Mattocks, Ph.D

VANTAGE PRESS
New York

Cover design by Susan Thomas

FIRST EDITION

Published by Vantage Press, Inc.
419 Park Ave. South, New York, NY 10016

Manufactured in the United States of America
ISBN: 978-0-533-15917-8

Library of Congress Catalog Card No.: 2007907308

0 9 8 7 6 5 4 3 2 1

Contents

Foreword

When I first received my copy of *How to Create and Maintain an Alien* I was slightly confused as I had never considered inmates to be aliens. In my mind an alien was either someone from outer space, or like myself, someone who was living in a foreign country. I was raised, and for the last twenty years have been working, in systems which at least gave lip service to the idea that inmates were like everyone else—they had just made a mistake somewhere along the way. Even in Britain there was a strong attempt to differentiate those who were "bad" from those who were "mad"; the former being incorrigibles who had undergone a decision not to conform and the latter those who were mentally ill and therefore not responsible for their actions.

It took very little time to begin to recognize the position Dr. Mattocks was taking and to change my way of thinking. I began to recognize that the term "alien" not only fits the group well, but also opens up a number of ways in which to formulate both policy and practice. It also allows the general public to begin to understand the difficulties faced by a person who has spent time in the penal system upon their release. It was something that I, a person who was raised in North America and who has been living in Britain for over twenty years, could relate to and recognize.

It also allowed me, a psychologist working in forensic settings and with forensic populations for much of that time, to look at those within the system in a different way. Not as someone vastly different from myself, but rather as someone who was facing or would face many of the same underlying concerns coming out of prison that I faced on coming to England. The advantages that I had, a place to live, a support system of family and caring people, and a position which would provide me with both respect and a sense of pride and accomplishment, are seldom in place for those leaving prison. For many of them being released is like being transported to a foreign country where the language and culture are different, given a minimal amount and being told to get on with it and make their own way. It is no wonder that the rate of return to prison is so high.

Dr. Mattocks takes us on a journey that few have encountered, or would wish to encounter. His experiences are related in a frank and forthright manner which is both compassionate and enlightening. By following in his footsteps, the reader will gain a far greater understanding not only of the processes by which such personalities are formed, but the extent to which both individuals and systems support and maintain the personality disorders which inhabit our world. The ongoing politization of the penal system is explored in depth along with the resultant effects of placing political appointees in charge of such institutions rather than professionals with a rehabilitation background. His insights into the need to intervene in a positive and rehabilitative manner are not just tied to California or North America, but apply across all cultures that view punishment as the intervention of choice. Having worked in both the U.S. and British systems, the similarities are clear both in the establishment of aliens as well as the manner in which they are viewed and treated or maintained.

The insights Dr. Mattocks makes and the interventions he has laid out are transferable and can be applied in both of the systems within which I have worked. I suspect they can be applied to many others as well. For those who take on board his concerns, there is hope; for those who ignore them there is the prospect of a world filled with an increasing number of aliens.

Dennis R. Trent, Ph.D.
Consultant, Clinical Psychologist

Preface

I feel that it is important to the reader to be aware of the factors that preceded my involvement in working with criminal offenders. This was not part of my early plans. A few months after graduating from high school I became the youngest theater manager in the state of California at the time. However, after two years, television began to make this a very questionable career, so I quit and returned to my hometown, where I started work as a psychiatric technician at a nearby state mental hospital. I also began to take classes at a community college. There I was required to declare a major upon registering for classes. I registered as a pre-med major and began to take the basic required classes and laboratory courses. Eight hours at my job and four to five hours of classes each day proved to be an arduous schedule. As a result I had to cut back on the number of classes I took each semester, which resulted in an extra year at the college. However, this in turn had allowed me to save up enough money to transfer to the University of California at Berkeley. This was very exciting to me!

My stint as a pre-med student soon ended at Berkeley. Fate, if you will, stepped in. One day I was browsing in the college bookstore when I spotted a book entitled, *Rebel Without a Cause.* Having seen the movie by that title, starring James Dean, I purchased the paperback with the goal of seeing how the book and the movie compared. I was very surprised, later back in my dorm, to find out that the book had no connection to the movie. Instead, the book I had purchased on impulse turned out to be written by a psychologist, Robert Lindner, and consisted of a detailed account of his therapy with an inmate of the Maryland State Penitentiary, including some sessions in which he utilized hypnotherapy. I found the book very fascinating.

So after reading the book, I went and consulted the college catalogs on different college majors and their requirements. I was most interested then in comparing psychiatry and psychology. At that time, the program to become a psychiatrist consisted of completing medical school and then selecting the speciality of psychiatry. This began with a year of related courses followed by a rotation of three month assignments each, consisting of a hospital for the mentally ill, a hospital for the mentally defective, a prison or jail facility, and finally a community mental health clinic. In the meantime, one had to complete a required reading list. Upon completion of all these requirements, the candidate underwent an oral exam for certification as a psychiatrist. All of this, including completion of the medical degree, was estimated to be eight years.

I then consulted the university catalog about becoming a doctor of psychology. Here I learned that I needed to begin immediately to take required courses in psychology. I also learned that there were a number of specialities, the two major being experimental or research psychology, and clinical or applied psychology. I began to give serious thought about where my real interests lay.

While I had enjoyed some of the laboratory courses in my pre-med preparation, I realized that the thought of diagnosing and treating physically ill people did not have great appeal to me. I also realized that I had always had a strong curiosity about why people behave the way they did, which was further enhanced by my work at the mental hospital. To pursue this interest, the curriculum for psychology doctorate degrees seemed much, much better than that for psychiatry. So in the middle of my junior year my major at the university changed, even though the catalog estimated nine to ten years for a doctorate in psychology. I decided that I was going to train to be the best psychologist I could by taking every course I could in psychology.

I should also mention that I had become fascinated by an earlier exposure to some cultural anthropology courses I had taken to fulfill some elective requirements. These courses had a powerful impact on my thinking about us humans. It made me deeply appreciative of the fact that people are often different, based upon the environments with which they have to learn to cope, and the customs developed to deal with their surroundings. I also was very fortunate to have been able to do two honors research projects under two very well-known visiting professors while in my undergraduate program at UC Berkeley. Dr. Benton J. Underwood had a profound impact on my future. I am sure that everyone has a teacher or mentor who influenced them greatly during their academic years. Dr. Underwood taught and encouraged critical thinking in his course. He encouraged my curiosity to the point that I expanded the research I did under him to a side project of my own. He later included my side research project in his book, *Meaningfulness and Verbal Learning*, thus giving me my first published credit. But he also was the one who encouraged me to take each academic degree from a different university in order to gain the widest exposure to different ideas and thinking. I followed his advice although this also meant another extra year of academia.

But the mysteries of academia insofar as time was concerned struck early. As I petitioned for my B.A. degree graduation, I was called into the Dean's office and informed that

I would have to take an extra semester of classes. Even though I had fulfilled all other requirements for graduation, it seems I was unaware that I had overlooked a restriction in the university catalog. While I had amassed more than enough units in science and all other required classes, I had exceeded the number of units I was allowed to take in my major field of psychology. To this day I remain mystified on why such a limit demanded that I take an extra semester of classes. According to the dean who informed me that I could not graduate until I did so. I could take any classes I wanted to, "including basketweaving," so long as I stayed away from the psychology department's offerings.

So I did complete my extra semester at UC Berkeley and stayed away from Psychology Department courses. Instead, I enrolled in courses such as "Culture and Personality." (Anthropology Department), "Crime Cause, Prevention, and Correction" (Criminology Department), and other related courses in these departments. One of the criminology courses I took was taught by Austin H. McCormack, who under Thomas Dewey had broken up and prosecuted Murder, Inc. years before, and who related these experiences to the class. All these extra semesters I spent in my undergraduate years made me more "mature," that is, older than many of my fellows graduates. This would have an impact later in my completion of the Master's of Science degree at California State University, San Francisco, and on my future career.

Acknowledgments

The author wishes to acknowledge the inmates of the California State Prison System who by sharing their life stories inspired him to write this book and impart his own opinions expressed therein. The names of those cited in the book have been changed in order to protect the innocent families of both the victims and the inmates.

A very special thanks to Maude Lund and her family for her hard work and their encouragement in getting this book published. The author also appreciates the support of a wonderful friend and scholar, Dr. Sandra Ratliff.

Last, but not least, appreciation is expressed to all the very skilled staff and co-workers with whom the author had the privilege to work over the years.

—Arthur L. Mattocks, Ph.D.

How to Create and Maintain an Alien

One

Entry into the World of Aliens

I was driving down a two-lane asphalt road lined with tall eucalyptus trees. The pavement was dappled by spots of sunlight filtering through the leaves of the trees. The road proceeded along the downslope of the hilly terrain. On the up-slope of the road were some small houses and occasionally one appeared on the down side slope of the road over which I was driving. Although it was a sunny early October day, the breeze coming off the waters of the San Francisco Bay made a warm jacket very welcome. As I continued driving down the road, I was experiencing a wave of emotions. First, there was the high anticipation related to an exciting new experience. I was about to enter my first clinical internship, a chance to put into actual practice my years of academic learning. Second, there was the anxiety about the very unusual and unfamiliar setting to which I had been assigned, the well-known and notorious San Quentin Prison, California's first and oldest prison.

Suddenly the trees lining the road came to an end. I approached some tall iron gates and maneuvered my car across a large expansive area of asphalt. Beyond, I could see the massive walls of the prison. As I slowly approached the high gates, two men in green uniforms stepped out of a small guardhouse. I stopped the car and identified myself and my purpose. One of them directed me to a small frame building

1

to the left of the gates, informing me that I would need to obtain a visitor's pass there. I thanked him for the information, backed up my car and pulled up to the curb in front of the small wooden building indicated by the guard. As I entered the building, it became apparent that part of the building was taken up by a large counter and a small waiting area. The rest of the area contained a large display of crafts and art objects made by prison inmates, which could be purchased by visitors.

I again identified myself and my purpose to the person behind the counter. "Oh yes," he replied, "here is your pass all ready for you. Just sign here. Show it to the officers at the gate and they will give you directions. Remember to keep this pass to show each time you pass through any security gates throughout the prison." When I returned in my car before those large iron gates and showed one of them my pass, he pointed through the gates and instructed me to continue on until I saw a turn off to the left, which would lead me down to a large parking area. The officer then signaled the other officer and the large gates opened before me.

I drove down to the parking area and after parking and locking my car, proceeded to some stairs at the far right corner which led up to the pedestrian gate. This gate accessed the area containing the prison itself, and what I came to know as the secondary security entrance. I now had a full view of the front of this imposing-looking prison. To the right of the pedestrian gate was another gate for entry of special permitted vehicles, and further up from that rose the two-story administrative building, separate from and outside of this secondary security area.

To the left of the pedestrian entrance, and looming high above the parking lot where I had parked my car, was a tall tower topped by a glass-enclosed octagonal room. I could see the form of a uniformed guard walking around inside, observing the area below. A long narrow catwalk extended out from ground level on the side nearest the prison to a door part way up the big concrete tower. The base of the tower extended downward to the level of the parking area, with a high chainlink fence topped with coiled barbed wire separating it and the prison from that parking area.

As I entered the small glassed-in building at the top of the stairs, I again showed my pass to an officer standing behind a low counter. He looked at it and indicated that they had been notified to expect me. I passed through a small metal detector and was then instructed to proceed through a small electrically operated gate, continue down the broad paved road to the left between the tower, and the outer wall of the prison. As I looked down the road I could see the second large tower near the end, where the guard said I would see a small guardhouse by another chainlink gate on my right. Just past the first tower was a flat-roofed building and a large broad catwalk leading from the road to its entrance. I was to learn later that this was a canteen type building where staff and approved visitors often went for coffee and light snacks.

Approaching the second tower, some distance down the long paved road, the towering wall of the prison itself made a 45-degree turn, and I came upon the high fenced area with a small gate and wooden guardhouse which I had been told to enter. Showing my pass to the officer there, he unlocked open the gate and beckoned me to enter. He introduced himself and indicated a sign-in logbook wherein I was to enter my name and the time I passed in or out of that gate. He was most helpful and directed me down the path from the gatehouse to the entrance of the large building jutting out from the high prison walls. This was called Neumiller Hospital. He further instructed me to enter there and proceed down the first corridor to the left after entering. To the left of the fence through which I had just entered, the paved road ended almost at the base of the second tall guard tower. The sparkling water of the bay lapped at the shore a few feet beyond. This was perhaps the most beautiful area around the prison, although I was told that the area around the warden's house contained some beautiful well-kept gardens. I could not comment on that since that was not open to visitors or employees. This area in front of Neumiller Hospital, however, was immaculately kept, with an expansive green lawn and well cared for roses and flowering shrubs. The officer informed me that the area was kept in its beautiful condition by a man dressed in blue denims standing a few yards away. Thus I was introduced to "Pineapple," the inmate gardener whom I would encounter there on all but the most inclement days over the coming several months of my intern placement. Down the concrete walk and a sharp turn to the right, I entered the door into the hospital. I faced another locked door, but it was quickly opened by another guard and I entered into the inner workings of the large prison.

I was at the far end of the first floor central corridor of the hospital. Almost immediately an exit appeared on the left into a narrow waiting room with simple benches bolted to the floor on both sides. The far end of the narrow waiting room gave way to a narrow hallway, which in turn took a sharp right down between small glassed-in offices. It finally ended in a large area of desks and file cabinets. As I approached, a neatly dressed man asked me if I was the new intern. "Let me inform your superiors that you are here," he replied to my acknowledgment. He went to a nearby office and tapped on the window. A youthful-looking man probably in his early forties emerged and walked toward me smiling. He was a very affable individual, confident in what he was doing, and skilled in getting along with a wide range of backgrounds. He was quick to assess situations and proved to be an excellent training supervisor. We spent the rest of the morning getting acquainted, he obviously evaluating my background and skills, while at the same time explaining the prison and the functions of the "Psych" department to me. As for myself, my level of anticipation and excitement regarding the new experience grew by the minute. Presently I was ushered out and introduced to the other staff of the San Quentin Psychiatric Department. The chief psychiatrist, I was informed, had been there since before most could remember, and was very proud to inform me he was a graduate of Stanford, my former alma mater's archrival in sports.

There were three staff psychiatrists, one of whom I had met when he was on the staff of the mental hospital where I had once worked. Besides my training supervisor, there was one other psychologist on the staff, a quiet, mild-mannered, somewhat self-effacing man (he referred to himself as "nobody but an old broken-down prison psychologist"). Though very pleasant, he usually deferred to other staff whenever I asked questions. Finally, the two female clerical staff and the man I encountered upon arrival were introduced.

The remainder of the day was taken up by orientation into the workings of the department, learning about the files on inmates and how to get information out of them, do's and don'ts of dealing with inmates, things to watch out for, and finally I was assigned to my office. It consisted of a small glassed-in cubicle opening directly off the main first floor corridor of the hospital. The glass windows were masked halfway up to provide some visual protection when seated from the diversions of the corridor. Space was at a premium and furnishings consisted of a desk and two chairs. Quickly I was to learn I would spend much of my time elsewhere in the prison. I had received my permanent pass and my book of meal tickets for the staff cafeteria (a consideration reserved only for interns and official visitors). At the end of the day I drove to the front gate through which I had entered that morning. Signs instructed one to stop the car, shut off the engine, and get out and open both the hood and the trunk of the car. Only after the gate officer checked to make sure I was the only occupant did the gate open, and I was allowed to start the car and proceed out the gate. I had just begun to learn the routines of prison. The following day I would enter the main prison, and the social structure within which I would be enmeshed for more years than I ever imagined at that point of my life.

The next day I showed my pass to the officers at the front gates, the gates opened, and I began the daily routine of entering and exiting a prison. As yet, I had not seen the interior of the prison proper. This morning my training supervisor informed me that he had arranged for a long-time experienced Sergeant of Custody to take me on a complete tour of the prison. I was introduced to my guide, a not too tall, older man with graying hair. Thus began my entry into a whole new world populated by people I had never encountered before, only heard about through occasional news media reports, my criminology classes, and movies about gangsters. I did recall when I was about twelve years old, my parents and I walking out on the Golden Gate Bridge to view the "Battle of Alcatraz," seeing occasional puffs of smoke as the Marines retook a cellblock that had been taken over by the inmates there. These very limited and sometimes distorted views of prison life provided me a naive concept of prison. This was the first day of a long but incredible learning experience for me that I hope to share with you, the reader.

The sergeant and I exited the hospital directly opposite the end I had entered that morning, and there we were in a wide passageway between the towering structures of the prison. He directed me to the left. "We'll take you through

West Block first so you can see what a cell block is like." While we passed out of the passageway into an open area with two small wooden barrack type buildings in it, he explained that this would be where I would be coming to conduct therapy groups. The structures looked like many of the typical temporary one-story barrack structures I had seen elsewhere. We walked past to the entrance of one of the large tan-colored buildings that composed most of the prison.

As we entered through the large concrete entry, he stopped and introduced me to the guard there and explained our presence. We were passed through a steel-barred gate into a prison cellblock itself. It was a big cavernous building with tall narrow barred windows climbing the full height of each wall. In the center were five tiers of barred cells fronted by wide steel catwalks. From an undergraduate criminology course I had taken at UC Berkeley, taught by Austin H. McCormack, I recalled that this type of prison design was referred to as "inside cell construction." That is, the cells were all in the center of the cellblock, away from the outside walls. About thirty feet from the steel catwalks in front of the cells ran a narrow catwalk on which stood an armed guard. I was informed by my guide that no weapons were allowed on the ground level. The weapons were confined to the towers, the catwalks, places inaccessible to inmates. Guards on the ground did not carry weapons because of the possibility that inmates could overcome a guard and thereby arm themselves. From the narrow catwalks, the guard had a clear view of the barred fronts of each cell.

On the vast expanse of smooth concrete floors of the cellblock was a lot of heavy metal tables with attached benches. This was where inmates could come down during scheduled unlocks and sit and talk or play dominos. We began climbing the metal stairs to the cells above. On the third tier, we stopped before an unoccupied cell. The electronically steel barred barrier suddenly slid back, giving us access. "Go ahead, step inside," said the sergeant. I slowly walked into the narrow cell. There was a steel cot on one side, bolted to the concrete wall. Opposite on the other wall stood a narrow steel locker, a steel toilet, and a small steel washbasin. The steel cot was covered with a thin mattress upon which lay a pillow, a folded blanket of dark gray, and some folded linen and a towel. In the ceiling was a small round recessed light with steel rods covering the opening. The lights were all controlled by guards in a central location. Within these gray concrete cubicles with the steel bar fronts men spent the major portion of their lives. I had seen "isolation cells" before, while working on the violent ward of a mental hospital, but they were larger and painted a light color that made them less gloomy. In addition, stays in isolation cells in the mental hospital were limited, according to the patient's behavior. But here, this was "home." Indeed, I subsequently heard inmates referring to their cells as "my house."

I stepped back out of the cell and we continued our climb up to the top-level tier. There we looked over the railing of the steel walkway to the concrete floor far below. Here I was told my first "horror story." Occasionally there have been incidents where inmates have either jumped or were thrown by other inmates over the guardrails to the floor below. I gazed thoughtfully down the four tiers below, knowing there was no chance of surviving a fall from that height to the concrete floor. We walked on around to the other side of the tier, an identical match to the side from which we had just come. Men were sitting or lying on the cots in their cells as we passed by, heading down the tier to the showers at the other end. "There is no privacy in prison," announced my guide.

We left West Block, which I was informed was the "honor block," and passed back the way we came, passing the inside entrance to the hospital, on into the "Main Yard" at San Quentin prison. The huge courtyard surrounded almost all around by the tall cellblocks of the prison was the main gathering place of most of the inmates. In the center were two long metal roofs supported by high steel pillars. Under these roofs were rows of steel tables with attached benches similar to those in the cellblock. The rattle of dominoes could be heard over the hum of voices. We walked slowly across the yard as the sergeant pointed out East Block, South Block, and North Block. Over in one corner of the yard he pointed to another stone-framed entry, "That takes you into where the elevator goes to the top floor, which is Death Row. You may get to see that sometime while you're here."

I realized I had not thought of the fact that San Quentin was indeed where the State of California carried out its executions. At that point I had not formed any opinion about death penalties. I wasn't even sure whether I wanted to see Death Row or not. We passed through the main yard. There was a small wooden structure on the left. It was the only wooden structure within the prison, other than the small barrack type buildings we had passed on the way to West Block. "That's called 'the Captain's Shack,'" my guide informed me. "The Captain of Custody has his office in there." Later I was to hear other stories about the "Captain's Shack." We passed on and turned down some steps to the "Old Cellblock," which I was informed now housed classrooms and the prison laundry. It was a two-story stone and concrete building, long and narrow. This was part of the old prison, built during the previous century as a cellblock. We entered the first floor since my guide informed me that this floor gave more of an idea of what it originally looked like.

Actually, this was now only the sorting area for the laundry, the old cell cubicles, with the bars removed, serving as bins into which to toss different items of laundry. The major difference, I observed to myself, from the present cellblocks I had seen, seemed to be that the cells lined the outer walls here. The old cubicles seemed smaller and the space outside the cells was not very large. Essentially the proportions were similar, but even gloomier, and evidently housed fewer inmates.

From there we resumed our tour. Not far, back up to the former ground level, we passed a newer building, a three-story building matching in color the older cell block building. "That is the Adjustment Center," said the sergeant. "That is the prison within the prison," he continued. "That is where the men who can't even get along in prison are housed so they don't hurt others. We won't go in there since no visitors are allowed in there, only approved custody personnel." We passed on without further comment to the prison chapel. There I was introduced to both the Protestant and the Catholic chaplains. Inside, the chapel was a contrast to and a relief from the stark severity of the rest of the prison. Next on our agenda was the main entrance building to the prison. I had seen it from the outside, but had been directed to enter the prison via the hospital gate, as previously mentioned. Inside were the visiting rooms. One resembled those I had seen in movies where visitors spoke through heavy mesh partitions. Visitors sat on wooden benches waiting to be called in to visit the inmate. All seemed controlled, very impersonal and not conducive to comfort. Years later I would get a much closer view of those who came to prison to visit sons, husbands, lovers, fathers, and friends.

Upstairs we went into some offices, then at the backside of the building we entered a large room. "This is where the disciplinary committee meets. When an inmate violates a prison rule, he is brought from lockup here before the committee to determine his guilt and punishment. You will probably have a chance to sit with the committee, since they have someone from the Psych Department sit in as a consultant if there is any question about the inmate's mental condition," the sergeant informed me. Indeed, this would turn out to be another one of my classrooms for learning about people in prison.

The morning had passed quickly and my current mentor, after asking if I had my meal tickets with me, took me downstairs and into a large dining room limited to employees of the prison. It was a pleasant room filled with tables with tablecloths, and comfortable chairs. Several inmates served as waiters. There you seated yourself and were presented with a menu by the inmate who then took your order. The food turned out to be good and well presented. I was told that the inmates who were assigned to work the staff restaurant were "short termers" with good behavior records who signed up for training in restaurant work. These inmates get good job training and the staff gets good meals, I was proudly informed.

After lunch I was told that we would be touring the "lower yard" and the industrial area. The "lower yard" consisted of a group of sports facilities. We walked over to a large flat area covered with a thin layer of sand. Metal benches anchored to concrete slabs were everywhere, along with racks of barbells and dumbbells with the weights welded on so the plates could not be removed. Men were busy groaning under huge poundage of weights and pumping biceps as large as most men's thighs. This was the "muscle beach" of the prison world. Below there was the baseball diamond and the track. I found out that occasionally outside teams would come in and play the champion inside team. Here a lot of excess energy was drained off in physical sports.

11

Next was another surprise. I was shown to a dock adjoining the bay side of the prison. Under some metal roofs were bales of cotton. A large industrial type building was inside the high fenced security area, again overlooked by a high guard tower. We entered the building wherein I was given explanations and viewed each step of the way from bolled cotton to various completed fabric products. From this "jute mill," as it was called, came the blue denims, sheets, towels, pillowcases for all the state hospitals and prisons. All the labor was provided by inmates with prison employees, referred to as "free staff," supervising each operation of the plant. For the inmates this was a glimpse into the "normal" world, as was the next prison industry I toured that day.

The furniture factory was in itself an amazement. Well laid out, organized and everything in its place. Here you could really see the pride in workmanship on the part of the inmate workers and their "free men" supervisors. The products were items of excellent quality, beautiful oak woods and wonderful craftsmanship. Since this furniture factory supplied office furniture for all state offices, I was to learn in future years to appreciate the products these men turned out more and more.

My final itinerary that day was up "on the walls." This was aimed at giving me an overview of the prison. Here my sergeant guide shared with me some anecdotes of his experiences at the prison, along with the admonition that there was lots to be learned here. He also pointed out that the only inmates we had spoken with were in the industrial areas, when we asked about their particular tasks. The rule at the prison was that there was no conversation between inmates and guards other than immediate giving of instructions to an inmate or addressing a relevant question by the inmate. There was no social conversation.

I had now seen the setting in which I would be working and learning for the next nine months. In my mind was the question of whether anything of a positive nature could be accomplished in a stark setting such as this, a question that would return after I began to get exposed first-hand to life inside those cold walls.

Besides the stark setting, I also wondered about the residents, inmates, many with cold stares as we passed by. I knew many were here because of terrible crimes they had committed. Judgment had been passed on all of them by the friends and families of their victims, by the courts and by society at large. I began to think about what could be accomplished trying to work with such people. That was it, I thought, they were people before they committed their crimes. What changed or what led them to the commission of crimes? I recalled from a past cultural anthropology class how early explorers often called the cultures they encountered as "uncivilized," "primitive," and "sub-human," their prejudgment preventing them from learning what those cultures had to offer. Thus, I resolved to myself that I would deal with each of the men I encountered as an individual human and try to learn what led him to prison. I was also aware there was a very important difference between *excusing* someone's behavior and *understanding* that behavior. My supervisor and others warned me, that many of these men were very skilled at "con games," manipulation, and excuses, so that checks and crosschecks were a natural part of sorting out the real person. I was here to learn and thanks to my earlier teachers of critical thinking, I eagerly began these new lessons about human lives and human behavior.

Two

First Task—Learning the Culture of Aliens

I had now been oriented to the prison itself, and told about the do's and don'ts, which gave me my initial glimpses of the culture within those prison walls. As to my duties, they began rapidly with inmates being assigned to me for evaluation and testing. On the top floor of the hospital were eight holding cells for the purpose of temporarily housing inmates who required more intense evaluation and initial treatment for severe mental illness. Each member of the staff was assigned these individuals on a rotational basis for evaluation and recommendations. Some of these men would be transferred to a state hospital with special housing for "criminally insane." Others would be treated with medications and returned to the prison "main line," that is, the prison's general population. After a couple of weeks, I began my rotational assignments there.

Also, you may recall, were those two barrack-type buildings the sergeant had pointed out during our tour. I was gradually given the lists of names of inmates that were to be seen in group therapy. These groups were based upon specific offenses. Thus I was assigned to conduct a child molester group, a robbery group, a burglary group, and a rapist group. Each group was assigned a number and I was cautioned not to reveal to anyone what the focus was for the

14

group. This is where I learned about the so-called "pecking order" within the prison culture. Top of that pecking order were the "lifers," those men doing life sentences for murder. Close second were robbers and men convicted of physical assault, battery, offenses looked upon by inmates as "stand up" confrontational types of offenses that proved manliness. Then came the burglars, crimes of theft, the property crimes. At the very bottom were the sex crimes. These offenders usually told their fellow prisoners that they were in prison for other crimes, such as burglary, or some non-sexual offense that carried a similar length of penalty. These men had been cautioned by prison officials to disguise their offense while in prison because these crimes were looked down upon in the prison culture as cowardly, something a real man would not do.

I was also given the opportunity to do some individual therapy with any inmate I felt to be motivated and capable of benefiting from the additional effort. Some of these men were men who were originally assigned to me for evaluation, but as time passed, I was approached by inmates or received written requests from inmates with whom I had had no prior contact, asking to talk with me. To my surprise I met individuals with whom I could relate. Their perspectives initially seemed strange and somewhat foreign to me, but as they began to trust me they began to share more and more long-denied and buried feelings. As I listened closer to the emotions that cautiously flickered through, they began revealing conflicts over past abuse, neglect, shame, resentment and angers that shaped their perspective of themselves and the world around them. Younger inmates sometimes would reveal feelings accompanied by tears, but to older convicts, therapy became very difficult and some wouldn't return for further sessions.

I soon learned another aspect of prison culture. It is a

very superficial culture, based upon the front you put before others. There was another social status distinction in the prison culture distinguishing between "inmates" and "convicts." The latter were the men who had years of confinement, either continuous or intermittent (that is, interrupted only by occasional parole), followed by re-offenders, "short termers," those who had not yet established themselves as trustworthy by convicts to be able to stand up for a cause (defend a fellow inmate or gang), and "hold his mud" (keep his mouth shut and not talk to the prison authorities). Minding your own business in prison meant that you saw or heard nothing that might get a fellow prisoner in trouble. "Snitching" to "the man" (custody personnel) could mean a severe beating or death at the hands of "regulars." Tender feelings and/or letting anyone know "your business" (sensitive information about yourself) was considered the ultimate show of weakness and also a sure sign you couldn't be trusted. Every day in prison, an inmate had to be wary of challenges that might put him at risk from other inmates.

The growing acquaintance with prison culture began to allow me to realize that many of these men revealed remarkably shallow, childlike thinking. Even experienced law enforcement personnel never cease to be amazed at the implausible, "the devil made me do it" types of explanations and excuses offered by offenders. The explanations would often boggle the mind with their naiveté, lack of mature logic, and incongruence. Nevertheless, these explanations are often given with such firm conviction from being repeated so many times that the teller often turns indignant and incredulous at the listener's disbelief. I would have numerous occasions over the years to look a man giving such a childish excuse or explanation in the eyes and ask, "Do you really believe the rest of the world is deaf, dumb and blind?" Once again, such self-serving naive explanations are fostered in the prison culture, which has as part of its code that you never question a fellow inmate's story about his crime.

I recall at a later time I added a new member to my child molester group. He was a man in his mid-twenties serving time for sexually molesting an eight-year-old girl. He was a husky six-footer who began explaining his offense to me and the group, how this little girl was all over him, and the only way he could get her away from him was to let her have her way with him sexually. The other group members, myself included, were incredulous that he would tell such a story, first of all, and then become so defensive and disappointed at the questioning of his story. The whole group session involved him defending his story against the questions and remarks of the other group members. I was happy to note that within the confines of the group, and the clearly stated rules of confidentiality, much of the prison culture "image code" was not questioned or closely adhered to by some of the group members.

When I began conducting these therapy groups, I didn't know how the men were going to react to me. The first misgiving was whether or not they would perceive me as just another version of "the man," just another authority figure that couldn't be trusted. This itself posed my major misgiving since therapy, to be effective, requires trust as a key element. Were my efforts to be an effective group therapist mere acts of futility? I realized I was working with society's most rejected population. Many had been so alienated from society's mores and values they committed heinous crimes most members of mainstream society could not even imagine. These men had been rejected and judged repeatedly, looked down upon as the "scum of the earth," and were reminded of this by their current situation. Thus would they react to me, as a representative of outside society, as just another authority figure there to "turn the screws" on them?

17

Much to my relief, I found that the inmates were direct and outspoken about their misgivings. This allowed me to share with them what I saw as my role and purpose, and clearly state the limits of confidentiality on my part. I was to tell them I expected them to keep whatever was said in the group within the group, not to be shared with anyone outside, thus emphasizing the importance of mutual trust. I told them that I knew trust was not an instant expectation, and that each of them would have to make decisions as the group progressed. I was relieved by the end of those first group sessions to see how the groups came together in moving towards the purposes I had outlined for them.

This group cohesion around the purpose of understanding their own behaviors were very impressively illustrated in the example cited above of the young man who tried to explain how an eight-year-old girl forced him into sexual intercourse. My response to him, as I recall, was merely commenting to him, "Some members of the group seem to have trouble with your story. Do you have any thoughts about why?" The group subsequently did a very effective job in eventually helping this man confront his own personal problems.

Listening to the childlike, self-serving reasoning of many felons is not the role for those given the tasks of arresting, charging, judging and confining those charged with crimes. However, the numerous errors made by our criminal justice system over the years clearly delineated the consequences of a rush to pass judgment, preventing search for the truth. My role I saw as different. As a therapist, I needed to listen to what the other person had to say in order to understand his reasoning, his perspectives, even his omissions that would reveal his beliefs about himself and others. My background in science seemed to always encourage that question, "Why?"—the question that always seems to lead to other questions. But listening and observing seems to result in answers, and better questions that result in even better answers. I recall an adage I had learned about scientific research that said when you had a clearly defined question, you were better than halfway to the answer.

There are clearly complexities in our laws that sometimes confuse those of simplistic thought. Some men in prison find these only more evident that they were "railroaded" to prison for something they don't think was their fault. I found that looking ahead at consequences of one's behavior is not characteristic of the reasoning of men who end up in prison. Again, I recall the story of a man in my robbery group who insisted he was wrongly convicted. In addition to his robbery conviction, he had also been convicted of second-degree murder, both convictions resulting from the same incident. In his story, he had decided to rob a small storeowner. He waited outside until there were no customers present. He then entered the store and observed the owner sitting in a small glassed-in office in the rear of the store, talking on the telephone. The robber walked up to the open door of the office, pulled out a gun, and ordered the storekeeper to hang up the phone, that this was a robbery. According to his story, the storekeeper remained remarkably calm, told whoever was on the other end of the telephone that he had to hang up and take care of some business. Meanwhile he stealthily opened a desk drawer as he hung up the phone and pulled a gun from the drawer. The startled robber responded by hitting the storekeeper with his gun, knocking the storekeeper backwards in his chair. In the process, the storekeeper's gun discharged. The bullet missed the robber and passed on through the front glass window of the store, resulting in the death of a person passing by. "The storekeeper should be sitting here, not me! I didn't kill anyone!" protested my group member. "If that storekeeper hadn't wanted to play hero, if he had just handed over the money like he was supposed to. I mean, the money was insured. He'd have got paid off by the insurance company and everybody would have been happy. None of this would have happened and I wouldn't be here. It's all because he wanted to be a hero."

I quietly tried to explain the cause and effect reasoning contained in the law under which he had been convicted. Simply stated, the law held that if you set up a situation (e.g. the armed robbery) in which someone can reasonably believe their life is at risk, then you are responsible for the consequences of any actions they might take to defend themselves. My explanation fell on deaf ears and most members of the group felt it was not the robber's fault that the passerby was shot and killed by the shopkeeper's gun. Only two in the group even mentioned the victim of the wayward bullet, and the fact that that person had paid the ultimate consequence. In the discussion that followed, the two same men were finally able to follow the reasoning behind the conviction. One even made another point regarding the storekeeper's actions, "Man, what do you mean, he was supposed to give you the money? He wasn't supposed to do anything you wanted. This wasn't a movie script. Man, this was reality!" From this discussion, I quickly learned several things. One, many men in prison are very impaired in their cause and effect reasoning, and two, some are unable to identify with victims of crimes as fellow human beings.

As I share with you more of my learning about criminal offenders, I will enlarge on both of these points.

The comment by the group member that the robber's crime was not a movie, but reality, also alerted me to another often occurring observation. I can tell you that during my internship at San Quentin in the early sixties, I heard men trying to mimic Edward G. Robinson, George Raft, and James

Cagney in their tough guy or gangster movie roles. In addition, I frequently encountered inmates, like the man in my robbery group, relate their crimes, placing the blame on the victim in some way, because the victim did not do like they were supposed to do, as if the victim didn't follow some script the criminal had in mind. Once again, these are observations that came to mean more to me later in understanding criminals.

As stated earlier, prison is a society, a culture, with its own mores and customs. From my courses in anthropology, I had learned that the customs and mores evolve in a culture as an adaptation to the environment. I mention this again because it is important in understanding some of the events I am about to describe. Generally, the first time in prison, individuals are often shocked and overwhelmed at this different culture. And like any society, it attempts to enculturate newcomers into its mores and unwritten rules.

Some of these unwritten rules sound a bit familiar, but violation of them can carry very heavy consequences. As an inmate you don't walk up and interrupt two men who are talking together, until they acknowledge your presence, or unless you are a friend of theirs. Or if you accidentally bump into another inmate, it is a standard rule to quickly apologize. And don't talk bad about another inmate to any inmate that is not your close friend. Word might get back to the inmate about whom you said something bad. These unwritten rules might strike you as just common courtesy, but in the prison culture, these are major affronts that can, and often do, result in a fight or other serious confrontations. Even more serious is talking to "the man" about anyone or anything happening in the prison. Even talking to a guard outside of the hearing of other inmates can bring suspicion upon you. "Snitching" or tattling is a major violation of the inmate code and can result in severe ostracizing and harassment, at the minimum, to severe physical beating and stabbing, usually resulting in death.

As you can imagine, showing "respect" to fellow inmates is of major importance in a culture desperate to preserve what little self-esteem they have been able to create for themselves. As mentioned earlier, it is very important that you do not "diss" (show any disrespect) anyone or allow anyone to disrespect you. One must stand up for themselves and get an apology or fight. In this society, you don't become a loner. In such a culture it is understandable why inmates band together in small groups, form gangs based on superficial things such as ethnicity, race, areas lived in when arrested, etc. It provides power and protection. But underneath the facade of taking care of your buddies, everyone knows it is everyone for himself in this walled society. These are the rules that the old "cons" teach the "fish" who are new in prisons.

I began to realize that most of the men who asked to see me individually were younger inmates, "fish," first termers. I began to understand why some were experiencing culture shock. A young man I had seen two or three times at his request to help him deal with his first time in prison, and his efforts to confront the realization of what led him to this place, provides a not untypical example. He appeared for his next scheduled appointment visibly upset. At first he seemed unsure whether he wanted to tell me what was upsetting him, but soon blurted out his situation. He was double-bunked in a cell with another inmate, a larger man who had seemed helpful to him in getting settled into prison life. He had offered him cigarettes and given him a couple of sodas purchased from the inmate canteen. However, this past week the man had begun demanding repayment for these favors. The young man insisted that he thought the guy gave him these things as a friend. Wrong! My young inmate was about to learn another lesson about prisons, not much different from the parental admonition to children to not accept gifts from strangers. The young man blurted out, "He is demanding sex from me! Last night he grabbed me and grabbed my butt, but I broke away from him and told him I didn't go for that sort of thing. But he said I was going to have to because he wasn't going to wait much longer, so I better get used to it. He is bigger than me and I don't know if I can keep him off me. I don't know what to do!" I told him I would talk to my supervisor and find out what could be done to help him out of his situation.

It was my turn, again, for some culture shock. I was advised to tell the young inmate to fight his cellmate the next time he made any sexual advances towards him. Even though he might receive a beating from the other inmate, the young man was to be further advised to put up a loud and vigorous fight so that the cellmate would be fearful the guards might hear and back off. Also, the inmates in adjoining cells, hearing his efforts, would tell the cellmate to back off, the kid has spirit. In prison culture, one has to make it clear that no one is going to push him around without a fight. I was told by my supervisor that most inmates will back off from fights if they can, since it means being sent to the "isolation unit." If the young inmate did not make it clear he would fight if pushed around, he would likely be "turned out," a term meaning he would be forced into becoming a sex toy, possibly not only by his bunkie but maybe by friends of his bunkie, should he want to share the young man's sexual favors. Also, his bunkie might decide to rent him out to other inmates in return for cigarettes and other canteen items.

I asked if there was any way prison staff could help the young inmate such as transferring him to another cell away from his tormentor. "No!" my supervisor replied. "That would put him in greater danger because inmates would be suspicious about a sudden housing transfer and suspect him as an informant or 'snitch,' a label that is life-threatening in prisons." I was to find out that rapes are not uncommon in prison. Only two weeks later I was to hear, upon my arrival one morning at the prison, of a suicide by an inmate. A young Mexican inmate had reportedly been raped the previous evening by five other inmates. This morning when the cells were opened to allow inmates out for breakfast, the young inmate threw himself off the tier to his death. I thought of my young inmate patient. He was fortunate, he did fight as advised. He informed me that it wasn't much of a fight and it didn't last long. His cellmate had grabbed him again and when he pulled away, the cellmate tried to hit him. The young man said he ducked and then started hitting the cellmate with all his might as fast as he could swing his fists, yelling at him. Someone in the next cell yelled "Knock it off, let the kid alone!" His cellmate then told him to back off and calm down, that he wouldn't bother him again, and that was it. The young inmate reported this to me with an attitude of relief and newfound confidence. He announced that he now had four other inmates that he hung around with when he was on the prison yard. He had passed his first major test for acceptance into the prison society.

Another lesson was that loners are vulnerable at times and it is better to form some associations so that you are not seen as easy prey.

There are times that avoiding hearing or seeing evil, even though you keep silent, is not insurance against danger from other inmates in gang-type groups. This became obvious that December I spent as an intern at San Quentin. It seems that a group of American Indian inmates had become involved in an argument with another group of inmates down in the lower sports yard area where the weight-lifting equipment was used. The result of the argument and ensuing fights was that one inmate was bludgeoned to death with a weight. There was tension in the prison about whether there would be any retaliation since custody staff suspected the incident might have been prison gang related. Those involved in the fray were locked up in solitary confinement and believed to be under control. Several days later an inmate was found stabbed to death with a homemade weapon. Tensions within the prison grew as the following days saw three more fatal stabbings. I recall seeing two of the bodies being rolled by my office toward the morgue. The "modus operandi," I was informed by staff, was referred to as "San Quentin style." That is, the intended target would be approached by two or more inmates, one from behind. The inmate would have his arms suddenly pinned behind him while the inmate in front stabbed him repeatedly and quickly with a prison-made "shiv." These prison-made weapons, I was later shown, were made out of a variety of materials, any kind of pieces of metal such as thick wire, tablespoons, etc. Plastic handles of toothbrushes or any piece of material including wood that was stiff enough to be rubbed on concrete floors of cells into sharp points and edges became formidable weapons.

After the fourth stabbing, the inmates were all locked in their cells and cold meals were being delivered to them in the cells. Custody staff was searching everywhere for weapons or any materials that could be made into shivs. No activity for me that day. This went down in the history of San Quentin as "Bloody December." After a few days the inmates were once again allowed out of their cells as custody ended the lockdown and the prison resumed its routine. A number of weapons were found during lockdown and search, and my supervisor and I were allowed to see the display of these weapons laid out on long tables in the administrative area. I believe there were inmates charged with new crimes as a result of their identification as possible participants, but not for the murders, as there were no witnesses. Inmate rumors were that two of the victims of the stabbings had been inmates thought by the perpetrators to have been accidental witnesses of the original murder, and were killed to make sure everyone else remained silent.

By this time I was wondering how any human could adapt to life in such an environment. In subsequent conversations with some of the more seasoned inmates, I began to pick up on their methods. The key, I was told, was to set up your own routine. This included getting a prison assignment such as working in prison industry (the jute mill or furniture factory), or jobs such as tier tender (clean up), kitchen aide, etc. This would minimize the amount of time spent with the general population of the prison. Choose a few friends to hang out with that you were sure were not involved in gang or illicit activities within the prison. When in the main yards, stay clear of large clusters of inmates. Stay away from any small areas within the prison of which custody personnel might not have a clear view. Keep your house (cell) clean, meaning, don't have any contraband materials in or around your bunk or locker. Don't purchase too many canteen items at a time. According to prison regulars, these general rules would minimize the chances of a man becoming involved in prison "craziness."

I was beginning to get a sense of the lives of the men for whom San Quentin was home. The majority of the population had experienced being in prison several times, or were serving life terms, so that prisons were their homes, the end of the road. However, there were two groups that I had yet to encounter. One of these groups was made up of the men on Death Row, those for whom this was indeed the end of the road. The chief psychiatrist asked me one day if I would care to join him on a visit to The Row. He had to go there to make a quick evaluation on the mental status of a man scheduled to be executed at the end of the week. He said he thought it would be a good opportunity for me to see the facility and get a feel of what it was like there. So off we went through the main yard and over to the heavily barred steel entry at one corner of the upper big yard, a corner where two of the high cellblock structures joined. We were greeted by a custody officer who guarded the entrance door. After greeting the Chief Psychiatrist and looking at my pass, he walked us from the locked steel door to the entrance of an elevator. He called into an intercom for the elevator and keyed us into it. The elevator went directly to the top floor. When the doors to the elevator opened we were greeted by two prison guards to whom I was introduced by my escort, and we then proceeded to a barred gate that opened to a long hall lined by steel barred cells with a clear view of the occupants. Another officer inside asked who we wanted to see. The doctor gave the man's name and we followed the officer down the row of cells. Unlike the other cellblocks I had seen, this one was quiet. Most of the inmates seemed to be reading or doing something in their cells. A few stood close to their doors and watched us pass with slight interest.

We reached the cell that housed the man the chief psychiatrist had come to examine. He greeted the man who acknowledged him in a subdued manner, and quietly nodded to me as I was introduced to him. In the ensuing conversation, the man spoke well. He denied any health problems and responded appropriately to the brief mental health questioning of the doctor. The man's attitude seemed resigned. He was cooperative and matter-of-fact. He was obviously aware of the purpose of the exam and the fact that the law prevented execution of a person who is determined to be physically or mentally ill at the time of scheduled execution.

The whole exam lasted less than twenty minutes. I said nothing, but listened to every sound around me. One of the guards brought something to the man two cells away from us. There was a humorous exchange between the two. It seemed very incongruous to me at the time. All these men were awaiting their turn to take the long walk to the gas chamber. I knew that most of them had already spent years confined to this small world, only on occasions receiving visits from outside such as family members, lawyers, and other approved visitors. On rare times when some medical procedure was required, they would be taken from The Row under heavy escort to the hospital wing. I had already seen this on a couple of occasions when crossing the upper main yard. The usually noisy yard suddenly became hushed and I would hear repeated calls, later made famous by a movie, *Dead Man Walking*. Immediately the inmates in the yard backed away, leaving a broad corridor as three officers, one on each side and one behind a man in cuffs and leg chains, passed through the big yard. All movement in the yard froze as the quartet moved through to their destination.

Again, standing on Death Row, it was hard to comprehend that these men had been here for years. The custody personnel, was rotated periodically through assignment to The Row. It was to me an amazing testimony of the adaptive capacity of humans. Of course, I had read accounts of Nazi concentration camps and methods those inmates of such camps utilized as efforts to adapt to the extreme conditions involving life and death. In this situation on Death Row, these men were supposedly aware of what they had done to end up facing death, and there seemed to me a sort of calm acceptance. However, this first impression was based upon my very brief and isolated exposure.

On our return to the hospital wing from Death Row, the chief psychiatrist and I discussed the irony that the State demanded that every man be in good mental and physical condition prior to being put to death.

"How would you like to witness this execution?" he asked. I admit that I was taken by surprise by his question. Such a possibility had never crossed my mind. However, at the moment the idea did not appeal to me and I expressed reluctance. "We can arrange it if you change your mind," he replied.

During the course of my stay at the prison, I would receive two more invitations to witness executions. However, I had firmly decided that such an experience would not enhance my learning more about criminals.

Nonetheless, during my internship at San Quentin I did have a very memorable experience associated with an execution. The Parole Board at that time requested that when they were seeing inmates regarding their readiness for parole, that a member from the psychiatric staff be present for consultation. On a few occasions I had the privilege of sitting with a panel of the Parole Board. On the particular day locked into my memory, one of the board members on the panel was Mr. Clinton Duffy, the illustrious former warden of San Quentin and a central figure in the book, *My Six Convicts*.

On that day an execution was scheduled. During the morning break, I walked with Mr. Duffy down the hall on the upper floor of the administration building, which sat just outside the main entrance to the prison. We stopped in front of a large window facing the front of the prison. As we chatted, I followed Mr. Duffy's gaze out the window. There, before the entrance to the gas chamber's witness door, stood a row of people obviously being addressed by the Associate Warden, and the uniformed Captain of Custody.

Mr. Duffy began to reminisce about his years past when he had been the prison's warden. He talked of the numerous times he had seen this ceremony of greeting and preparing the witnesses for what they were about to observe. He shared with me the fact that he had personally interviewed each man prior to his execution in an attempt to understand why the man committed a death penalty offense. Not one man, in all of his long career as Warden of San Quentin, ever admitted that he had considered any possibility of a death penalty, or given even a passing thought to such a penalty, prior to the commission of his crime. Mr. Duffy said that he very seriously doubted that the death penalty was a deterrent to crime. I was most impressed by our conversation, which was no doubt emotionally affected by what was soon to happen some yards away. I have never forgotten that talk with Mr. Duffy!

By this time I was fully oriented to the routines of the prison and was treated by both psychiatric and prison staff like a full-fledged staff member. I had received encouragement and some compliments on my work and my confidence was growing. I was in the midst of a great learning environment and the lessons were coming fast. A high point of my internship was about to happen. This involved the second group of inmates I alluded to earlier. They too, were housed separately from the main population.

As I previously mentioned, there was a large newer structure within the major central area of the prison called "The Adjustment Center." I was informed that the reason for its name was that when it was built a few years previously, it had been intended as a treatment center for the more recalcitrant inmates. It contained a group therapy room, art therapy room, and other facilities for therapy. These were never staffed or utilized. Upon completion of the building it had, however, become the prison within a prison, for custody. Within were the infamous "holes," a row of cells where inmates spent time stripped naked with only a specially made blanket, lying on a concrete bunk, a hole in the middle of the floor for their body waste, a slot at the bottom of the door where a food tray could be shoved through, and a recessed light high in the ceiling controlled from outside by the guards. Food for these inmates consisted of what was called RD, standing for "restricted diet." I was assured that this was prepared by a dietician and contained all the daily requirements of vitamins and minerals. Nevertheless, in appearance it resembled canned dog food. We did not tour this building. My training supervisor said that no one but custody staff was permitted in that building, and therefore none of the psychiatric staff had even been allowed in the building since it became operational.

One day I returned from the psych holding cells in the hospital to my supervisor's office to report on an inmate that had been on my rotation to evaluate. After we discussed my evaluation of the man, my supervisor told me about a new admission to the Psych unit. It was an eighteen-year-old from a Youth Authority Facility who had instigated a bat-swinging riot wherein several inmates and guards had been seriously injured. Under special arrangements he had been transferred from the facility to San Quentin's Adjustment Center. During the two weeks he had been there, he had created such a constant disruption that the Associate Warden of Custody had requested he be sent over to the Psych ward for observation, evaluation, and recommendations as to how to deal with this young troublemaker. He had been on the Psych unit for two days and had refused to talk to the chief psychiatrist or any psych staff. So far, my supervisor reported, it was a total standoff. "However," he continued, "if you want to make the effort next time you go up to the unit, you can have a go at it. But unless you have the time or interest, don't bother. It probably is a wasted effort." Of course, being an intern I couldn't pass up the challenge, so

31

when I went up the next day to talk to my assigned patient, I made a point to see the youth who wouldn't talk.

The guard keyed-open the cell door so that I could enter the small six by eight cell. The youth was sitting on his made-up bunk away from the door. I greeted him and sat down on the end of the bunk just inside the relocked door. I identified myself and tried to explain why I was there. I received nothing but a contemptuous glance as he turned to gaze at the opposite wall. I made a couple more futile attempts at engaging him in conversation to no avail and was ready to acknowledge my defeat. As I rose to call the guard to unkey the cell door, I impulsively commented, "You are fighting quite a battle, aren't you?"

A voice caught me by surprise. "What do you mean by that?" he asked. I sat back down and explained to him that I got the impression that he was fighting the whole world, that he felt he had no one to trust, that everyone was an enemy. This was the start of an hour-long conversation, at the end of which he agreed that, if I came back to see him the next day, he would take some tests for me and we could talk some more.

I reported this to my supervisor who expressed amazement. He encouraged me to take over the case and see if the young man would indeed cooperate in the testing. I did return the next day and this time spent some two hours during which I administered some psychological tests and we talked together. Over the next few days he completed a whole battery of tests and we were getting along very well. I had submitted a written report to my supervisor concerning the analysis of the tests I had administered to the boy from CYA.

The day after I submitted my report, my supervisor came in telling me what an impression I had made on the officers of the Psych unit and all the psychiatric staff. He told me that word had gotten back to the warden's office and the

Associate Warden of Custody had telephoned the chief psychiatrist with a request. The request was that when the inmate was returned to the Adjustment Center, I be assigned to come to the Adjustment Center every day to meet with the Youth Authority ward. The chief psychiatrist had agreed. My supervisor looked at me and said, "Do you realize that you are going to be the first clinical staff person allowed in the place?" I had no idea what to expect.

The next day I received a copy of a memorandum by the Associate Warden to the Adjustment Center staff informing them of my coming, what I was doing there, and instructing them to give me full cooperation. Among the psychiatric staff at the prison, I was a department celebrity. As for me, wariness and excitement were doing battle in my guts again.

The following Monday I made my first trek to the Adjustment Center. The young fellow I had seen on the psychiatric unit had been transferred back to the Center over the weekend. I had found no evidence of any severe mental disorder in my testing. He was of average intelligence and there was no evidence of any neurological dysfunction. There were indications of strong emotional conflict, impulsiveness, sense of alienation, suspiciousness, denial, over-reaction and other maladaptive traits. Background summary was that he was raised by his mother who worked to support herself and the boy. He began running around with the wrong crowd at age ten, was getting into trouble in school, dropped out of school in the tenth grade at the same time he began to run into problems with authority. He quickly graduated from juvenile halls to the Youth Authority with burglaries and car thefts.

I stepped upon the single step at the entrance to the Adjustment Center and pushed the door buzzer. A uniformed guard peered out through the barred window in the steel door and then unlocked the door. "Are you the psychologist?" he asked. I told him I was and he let me in. He turned and spoke to a man coming across the polished floor of the large open room. "Sarge, this is the psychologist from the Psych Department we were told to expect." He introduced me to the sergeant who was very friendly and courteous. He commented that they were glad I was here, that they needed all the help they could get with that boy. "He hasn't been a problem since he was brought back from the psych unit, but we don't know how long that will last." There were various comments by both the officer and the sergeant about what a problem he had been before. The sergeant in turn introduced me to the administrator of the Adjustment Center who took me on a tour of the facility. On the second floor I was shown what the cells looked like and introduced to the officer there. An inmate from a nearby cell called out, "Who are you and what do you do around here?" The sergeant stepped forward and replied, "He's not here to see you so that's all you need to know."

The administrator then turned to me and said, "I'll take you to the room we have set up for you to talk to Billy." Billy was the young man that I was going to see every working day for the next seven months. We met in a large room with cabinets and counters around most of the walls. In the center were two long heavy tables. The room looked typical of rooms you see in many residential facilities where patients are taught arts and crafts. But this one was empty of furnishings except for two chairs that had been placed on opposite sides of one of the long tables.

"This is where you'll meet with Billy each time. I'll leave you here and have an officer bring him down from the third floor. When you're through, just kick the door a couple of times and an officer will come and let you out. Good luck with Billy."

The sergeant and administrator left the room and I sat

down to await Billy's arrival, wondering if he would still talk with me now that he was back here. About five minutes later the door opened and Billy walked in. The door locked behind him. To my relief he seemed genuinely glad to see me. He asked if it was true that I would be seeing him five days a week. I told him it was and asked how he felt about that. He replied, "Great. At least it will get me out of that fucking cell for a while." Gee, I thought to myself, maybe I am serving some purpose here.

So our sessions began. Over the weeks I listened closely as Billy shared his life, his perspectives, his philosophies on several things, and later on some personal aspects of his past. He became more and more comfortable with me as the days and weeks passed. There never seemed to be a lack of something to talk about, and some facet of Billy to learn about. Once he commented in a tone of embarrassed self-awareness, "I guess you think I talk a lot. I usually don't talk to anyone, but you are the first person I've ever had to listen to me."

As the weeks went by, Billy's behavior was exemplary. Frequently, when I arrived on the unit I would be asked for advice on how they (the officers) should react to Billy in various situations. I received countless comments about what a great job I was doing with Billy. Somehow all this made me very uncomfortable. I already knew that any serious change did not go this smooth and easily. I suggested to the officers that they treat Billy like they always had, to be cautious, that he might relapse back to his old behaviors. The truth was that I was very pleased with the progress Billy had made, but somehow I was apprehensive that it was all too simple. Finally the day came that proved all my apprehensions true.

It was almost six weeks since I had begun my daily visits to the Adjustment Center. I was sitting in the big room on one side of the long table, awaiting Billy's arrival, as usual.

The door opened and Billy strode in and I got up to greet him. I was puzzled by his greeting, "Well, Doc, today's the day!"

"What do you mean?" I asked.

"I'm sorry, Doc, but I just can't stand this good time anymore. Don't ask me why. I don't want it to reflect on you and what you've tried to do to help me. It is just something I have to do." Billy didn't appear agitated. His statements were calm and matter-of-fact. I did ask why repeatedly, but he was adamant. I spent almost two hours that day with Billy, but the most I could get out of him was that he didn't know why, but he had to do it, and repeated expressions of concern that he hoped it wouldn't negate my work with him to the officers. Finally, I had to acknowledge that whatever "it" was that Billy intended to do was so compelling that it was beyond yielding to reason.

We stood up, shook hands, and he gave me one final apology. He walked over to the steel door, kicked it twice. Almost immediately the guard keyed the door open and Billy went up the stairs toward the third floor. I went over to the door and spoke to the officer, telling him that he might want to give the third floor officer some help with Billy. The guard called up the stairwell to the officer above—"Need any help up there?"

"No, I can handle it," came the reply.

I went on down to the first floor. The sergeant was sitting in his office. I went in to warn him of possible trouble from Billy. My exact words to him were "Billy insists that today is the day he is going to blow it."

The sergeant's reply was, "Don't worry, we can handle anything Billy has up his sleeve." I left the Adjustment Center feeling uncomfortable about how casually they had reacted to my warning.

The next day I returned to the Adjustment Center at my

36

regular time. I pushed the buzzer and the door was keyed open as usual. But once inside, the atmosphere was different. The sergeant came walking to meet me, a cold stern look on his face. "I don't think it would be a violation of your professional ethics to let us know when an inmate is going to be violent. I have my hand in a cast," he continued, holding it forth so I could see, "and an officer off duty with an injured shoulder, thanks to Billy. You hadn't even cleared the door yesterday when Billy started a rampage by tearing the bulletin board inside the entrance to the third floor off the wall and throwing things around. It would have been nice if we had been warned."

I saw the guard that had keyed the door for Billy after our session the previous day, and motioned him to come over to where the sergeant and I were standing. I asked the guard if he recalled my saying that the guard upstairs might need help with Billy. He affirmed that I did. I then turned back to the sergeant and said, "I came into your office and told you that I thought Billy was going to blow it. I worked as night charge on a violent ward for over a year and when someone said that a patient might blow it, we went on alert."

The sergeant stared at me, a look of surprise coming over his face, "My God, you did, Doc. My apologies. You did warn us! I really apologize." I accepted his apology and asked if I could still talk with Billy. He told me I could, but that I would have to see him in the "Hole." This resulted in the strangest circumstance under which I have ever conducted any therapy session.

I was taken upstairs to a small door, which was unlocked for me. I peered into a long pipe tunnel, a very narrow passageway. Alternately, pipe valves protruded so that you had to step sideways to pass. I was instructed to go down the tunnel until I reached a small metal cover with the number 9 on it. I was to slide the metal back, which would reveal a small hole in the concrete wall the size of a half dollar. I was to talk to Billy through that hole.

I passed down the narrow passage until I found the number 9. I slid the metal covering aside, called Billy's name into the hole and the black darkness beyond. Suddenly a voice came back, "Doc? Is that you?" with a note of incredulity.

"Yeah, Billy, it's me," I answered.

"Wow, Doc, I never thought I would ever see you again. You know, after I screwed up I didn't think you would want anything to do with me!" His tone of voice made it clear that he was caught off guard by my presence and was struggling now with his reaction.

I measured my response carefully. "Of course I'm here. This is our regular time and obviously you and I still have a lot of work to do." Billy expressed concern that he was going to be in the Hole for a while. I assured him that while it was a little awkward, we would make the best of it. We continued the sessions through the hole in the wall for several days. Then Billy was released from the Hole and we returned to our regular sessions in the big room on the second floor. I am happy to say that this was the last occasion that Billy reverted back to his old disruptive acting out.

I was to see more of the Adjustment Center. The Senior Psychiatrist approached me with an idea. He wanted to know if I would be interested in being co-therapist with him in conducting a therapy group in the Adjustment Center. This depended, of course, on his obtaining clearance from the Associate Warden of Custody. He further suggested that we each keep notes of the sessions and write a small paper on our observations in about five months. Permission was granted and we were given a list of names of men who volunteered to be in the therapy group. We were allowed ten men to participate. The group was to be conducted once a week

38

in another large room next to the one in which Billy and I had our sessions. This one was plain, without cabinets. We were provided with padded metal chairs. On one wall a covered wire came along the ceiling and down the wall to a small round button. A large red circle about ten inches in diameter was painted around the button, with stenciled letters "in case of emergency, push button." This became the target of humorous comments by men in the therapy group.

After the usual period of time taken to get to know each other, the group sessions became very productive. Both my co-therapist and I were pleasantly surprised at the seriousness of these men in talking about their lives. At the end of five months Dr. Murphy and I wrote a paper about our experience. We agreed that the time span was short and since we had selected volunteers, few conclusions would be drawn except that it was possible to conduct productive group therapy with such men in a high security setting.

By that time my internship was drawing to a close. I had continued seeing Billy daily over the months and felt very good about our work together. Our last session had been like a parting of good friends. I had seen practically all the prison, the sounds of steel doors slamming, the noise of dominoes slapping the tops of the tables in the main yard, the occasional echoing yells in the cellblocks, and the stories of a number of the inmates. As I mentioned before, I heard voices from movies of the 1940s and 1950s. Men who at some time when they were growing up identified with characters in movies. But these were grown men—or were they? I met guards who seem to have a good degree of understanding of the men they watched, others who were just doing a colorless job, and a few that took pleasures in their power over other men. Routine was the key word in prison.

In the custody force there was the paramilitary hierarchy of command. The communication between guards and inmates was minimal, as previously mentioned. Yes, I heard the rumors of occasional brutality by guards against an inmate, but these rumors seemed to be only what went on in the back room of the Captain's Shack. A young blond man in his early twenties, that I had seen briefly for evaluation, was rumored later to have received some disciplinary action in the notorious back room. Years later I would encounter him again in a medical facility with a skull flap as a result of some back room discipline he had received there. Other than this, I never encountered anyone that verified any mistreatment during the era of prison life. The most vicious acts I knew about in prison were those of the inmates against each other. These were hardened men who neither asked nor gave any mercy to anyone they did not consider one of them. Even the Disciplinary Committee during my internship at San Quentin had someone from the Psych department sit with them. I recall on one of my occasions to sit with this committee, a twenty-year-old of American Indian descent was brought before the committee and found guilty of some infraction. The Chairman (Captain of Custody), after a brief poll of the other two members, pronounced a sentence of 30 days in the Hole. The inmate sneered, "I can do that standing on my head."

The Captain then replied with 60 days in the Hole. The young inmate laughed. I pulled his file open and began to look through it. The social history prepared for his court trial contained the following: The young man had a sister two years younger than he. Both parents were alcoholics. According to the report, from the time the boy was age eight to approximately ten it was the parents' Friday or Saturday night's entertainment to go to a local bar and drink until closing time. Then they would go home to the two sleeping children, awaken them and take turns beating them for alleged misbehaviors during the week, until one or the other

40

parent passed out drunk. I looked at the young man, standing sneeringly before the committee, and wondered if indeed there was any punishment that the committee could mete out that this man would not see as a challenge to his ability to endure.

I learned a lot during those nine months. However, I felt that there were still so many more questions to which I could not find answers. Not the least of these had to do with why men become criminals and were they somewhat "made bad"? If the latter was true, how, when, and by whom? I had encountered some whom I felt I had understood the how, when, and who of their past that had left them with distorted reasoning, seething emotions, a deep sense of alienation that to them made their crimes against others justified. Fewer, like Billy, I was able to help to have the courage to confront themselves, to get beyond the anger and hate, to see their responsibility to shape their lives, to become the kinds of person they themselves could respect. This confrontation entailed giving up their defensive facades of seeing others as the cause of everything that happened to them and to see the role of authority separate from punishment and control. The most difficult step was helping them to see their parents as people rather than just their parents, and to help them understand the influence they had during developmental years. I was to discover over future years that this was not only the most difficult talk, but at times it was the most dangerous task. I will supply some examples in future chapters.

Yes, I now had my Master of Science Degree and was ready to move on to my doctorate. Strangely, I would miss the morning walk down the road past the high walls of the prison, seeing the sunlight sparkly on the waters of the bay. There was one more task I was invited to perform. I received an invitation to attend the California Youth Authority Parole

Board hearing on Billy. That was to be my last visit to San Quentin.

I did attend the hearing in the same room where I had sat with the Adult Parole Authority panels. The Board members introduced themselves to me when I was ushered into the room. They expressed their appreciation that my internship was completed and that I had come back for this hearing at their invitation. They asked me what, if any, condition of parole I would recommend if they decided to give Billy a parole. I gave them three conditions I hoped would keep him from regressing to past bad influences. They thanked me and indicated that I move to a chair at one end of the table.

Billy entered the room following the pushing of the summons button by a board member. Billy was halfway to the single chair facing the board members seated in chairs along the other side when he spotted me. He looked startled and then broke into a big grin. I nodded at him and smiled back. The hearing began. His record was read aloud by one member. His disciplinary record was recounted. Then Billy was asked why he felt the board should give him a parole.

"Because I'm a different person than the one you just read about, thanks to him," nodding his head and looking in my direction. He began to tell them about how he felt differently about a lot of things, and gave a few examples. He talked about changes in his thinking and that he wanted to go to school when he got out. Billy was very convincing in the way he presented himself. I felt warm inside.

Then the Chairman of the board gathered up the small pieces of paper from each member. "Thanks to this man here," nodding in my direction, "and the good work you have done on yourself," looking intently at Billy, "we have decided to give you a parole . . . with three conditions." He enumerated each of the conditions I had suggested. "I hope we never see you again!"

"You won't!" chirped Billy, as he rose from the chair and came over to me. He clasped my hand in both of his and said, "Thank you, thank you for coming and being here for me." As he went out the door, he paused and half turned to me and said, "I'll make you proud of me." The feelings I felt at that moment I am sure played a big part in my returning a few years later to work in the California prison system. The board members all shook my hand and thanked me once again, and wished me well on my future education. But nothing registered so deeply as Billy's parting comments to me.

So I left San Quentin by the bay, and pondered about my experiences there. I reminisced about some of the lessons I had gathered. I had decided that no matter how heinous the crime, I should not pass personal judgment on the perpetrator. If I did so, I effectively slammed the door to understanding. I was reassured that understanding a person was not excusing or minimizing his behavior. I had learned graphically that humans are all products of their past, like a flowing stream. No crime "just happened," as many inmates would claim. Some had their roots many years before. I learned that some people can make amazing changes. But I had learned not to be overly optimistic as change was beyond the capacity of some. Most of all, I learned that people had more in common, that most differences we place emphasis upon are superficial compared to the similarities. Most of all I learned that there, for the grace of God, or luck of birth, go I.

Three

Transitional Experiences and Thoughts about Punishment

My internship as a psychologist at San Quentin had been a new and exciting adventure, and it left me with some very profound lessons to ponder. It had whetted my appetite for more knowledge as I went off to the University of Oregon for a doctorate degree. My undergraduate studies at UC Berkeley had been largely in experimental psychology, with strong emphasis on scientific methodology. My Master of Science degree from San Francisco State College had balanced this with an emphasis on clinical methods of treatment.

My time at San Quentin had given me some definite clues as to how some men had been shaped and molded over time to commit their crimes. I had also learned a great deal about punishment and the complexity of its effectiveness or ineffectiveness. I had studied the reward and punishment paradigms of behavioral studies, but these did not explain the behaviors of the men I had encountered in the prison. I had come to suspect other factors from the extra credit research project I had done with Dr. Underwood.

Unlike rats in mazes, we humans attach meanings to our experiences, and these meanings often give other dimensions to simple rewards and punishments. Prisons have always been perceived as punishment by society, the taking away of freedom, and providing stark living conditions, and

44

tightly regimented routines. These penalties for committing serious violations against society at large, termed "felonies," was supposed to alter such behaviors by the individual and others who might be thinking about committing a crime. But Mr. Duffy, from his discussions with men about to be executed for their crimes, did not lend credence to this belief. This was not a new doubt. In one of my courses in criminology, this concept of punishment as a deterrent had been brought into question before, in England. Pickpocketing at public gatherings had become such a problem at that time it was decided to make pickpocketing a hanging offense. To further its believed deterrent effect, it was decided to make such hangings public. However, pickpocketers worked among the crowds gathered to watch the hanging of arrested pickpocketers to such an extent that the authorities had to stop the public hangings.

Listening to the men I had talked to, and conversations I had overheard, the deterrent effect of punishment was placed into very serious doubt in my mind in regards to inhibiting criminal behaviors. Some talked about their crimes with great pride, about their daring and cleverness, always blaming getting caught and being sent to prison as "just one of those things that happens now and then," or a crime partner's bumbling, or even on the victim for not behaving like they were supposed to do.

Excitement was a frequent factor, I discovered, that often intimated early criminal involvement. Indeed, Sigmund Freud had observed that breaking into homes and burglaries were possibly sublimations for sexual excitement in young males. I had on several occasions listened to a young prison inmate relate how he got started in crime, talk about how at age 12, 13, or 14, out of curiosity about what was inside a house he had passed, would return and ascertain that there was no one at home. Then, he would break into the house. The excitement of the forbidden made a deep impression and furthered such activities. Soon the young burglar would seek more excitement by entering occupied houses. In a few cases, the excitement evolved into slipping into a house and taking something out of the room wherein the family was focused on something such as watching television. Was this excitement factor the same as that which leads many people to take risks performing highly risky activities, even death-defying ones?

Material gain played little or no role for these excitement junkies since the items they took were of little use or value to them, and some were even discarded quickly. This may at first seem strange, but one only has to observe the patrons of a gambling casino, risking their money, the atmosphere of excitement that keeps them coming back for more, in spite of whether they win or lose. Risk taking and excitement are some of the human traits that can lead us to the rewards of challenge and discovery, or to injury or ruin. We have all read about adventurers who have suffered terribly in their endeavors, but insist on doing it again. Maybe it has to do with the meaning they attach to what most of us would consider punishment. Can punishment itself become an exciting challenge? Is it possible that some male youths can come to see the mark of manhood as not fearing risk, but how much punishment you can take and "hold your mud" and still come back for more, and how you can suppress all soft feelings as evidence of "weakness"? It seems that for some of these men, punishment was the ultimate challenge.

The old behaviorists had cautioned that "punishment" wasn't the same for everybody. Punishment to some might actually be a reward. Could it be that being sent to prison, rather than being a punishment or a deterrent, could actually be a reward for some? I had heard some men in prison flatly state, "Doc, I'm institutionalized." Later, I was to learn that the earlier a youngster began to commit crimes, the likelier he was to return to prison as an adult and repeat offender.

I learned another prison term, "State raised." This was usually used to refer to an inmate who first did something which resulted in being housed in juvenile hall for a period of time, frequently about the age of twelve or younger. By the age of fifteen he had been sent to a Youth Authority facility for a couple of years. By age nineteen or twenty he had experienced his first prison term. Men in their forties and fifties would often comment that the longest time they had ever remained out of prison was a matter of months. Others would figure that the total time they had spent outside of State facilities since adolescence was less than a total of five years. To many of these men, leaving the prison on parole was just a vacation. More than once I heard an inmate shouting at his prison buddies as he was being escorted to the prison gate, "Hey guys, don't let them take my cell, save it for me until I get back!"

Prison as a deterrent, the death penalty as a deterrent, punishment as a deterrent, deprivation as a deterrent (remember the American Indian youth who laughed at 60 days in the Hole), I now had serious doubts. Relating all this to myself, it was an expected discovery. As a child I had felt the sting of a switch, and on three occasions in my life, the blows of my father's belt. Even the threat of this had been an effective deterrence. What made the difference?

Another haunting question with which I departed San Quentin concerned Billy's compulsion to provoke his guards to punish him after he had been doing so well for several weeks. He and I had never resolved that question. It seemed to remain a mystery for him also. The incredulous tone in his voice the first time I opened the little peephole in the back of the dark "hole" cell, "Doc, is that you? I didn't think I would ever see you again!" went over and over in my mind. I could feel that something very important lay behind that whole event. But the answer was to come much later.

I had always been curious about people. As mentioned previously, soon after I graduated from high school I had become the youngest theater manager in the state. It was a small town theater and several incidents that occurred had amazed me and piqued my curiosity. During one evening's show, an usherette informed me that several patrons had complained about being hit with spit wads. She had watched closely, patrolled her aisles, but hadn't found the culprit. I decided to find who was guilty. I walked briskly down one aisle and through some velvet drapes that covered an emergency exit and access to backstage. After passing through the drapes I turned and peered through the small crack between the drapes. The reflection from the movie screen lit up the audience like a floodlight. I didn't have long to wait. On the aisle seat a third of the way up the auditorium a youth half-rose in his seat with his back to me. I could see that he was slowly taking careful aim with something. It turned out to be a small slingshot made from a paper clip and a rubber band. Before he could let go his missile I had my hand under his elbow, instructing him to come out to the lobby. Two days later he returned and apologized for his behavior. He asked if there were any job openings that he might be able to do. I had none immediately. Since he returned repeatedly asking for a job, I eventually added him to the cleanup crew. He hung around the theater from after school to closing time after the second showing each evening. Even though he had only short working hours, he seemed to enjoy helping with anything that needed to be done.

Occasionally a woman would telephone and ask if he was there. When I offered to call him to the phone, she would identify herself as his mother and explain that she just wanted to know where he was since she had not seen him for two or three days. She thanked me and hung up. This was so foreign to the attitude of my parents, and the parents of my friends growing up, that I was at a loss to understand.

There was another thing that I frequently observed. The theater was flanked by a bar on one side and a restaurant on the other. On weekends I would sometimes observe parents purchase tickets to the afternoon matinee for their children, send the children into the theater while they went next door to the bar. After the matinee was over, the parents and the children went to the restaurant. When the first evening show began, the children were again given tickets and sent into the theater while the parents returned to the bar. I was getting my exposure to the big world and the fact that all children were not raised alike. I did not realize it then, but those incidents were only the tip of a very big iceberg.

Well, off to the University of Oregon. Now learning was in high gear and concentrated. Prisons were far from my mind, except that I would occasionally receive a letter from the chief psychiatrist at "Q" or the senior psychiatrist asking me to contact them when I finished my doctorate, and saying that they wanted to hire me. I was flattered by these requests, but the challenge of the doctoral program at that time was all-engrossing. Two years of coursework, a practicum, two foreign language exams, another year internship, and then the big dissertation, and major and minor comprehensive exams, and I would officially have my doctorate. I was addressed as "Doc" at San Quentin, but that was because most inmates addressed guards as "Mister," or "Boss," and all hospital staff as "Doc."

But my life seemed marked. During my second internship with the Veteran's Administration, I became involved in a hostage situation brought about by a veteran at the outpatient clinic. Unbeknownst to us on the fourth floor of the downtown office building where the VA outpatient clinic was

49

located, this man had gone into the cafeteria in the basement of the building and with a gun in one hand and a knife in the other, taken seven people hostage. The VA receptionist informed my training supervisor and myself that the police had called and wanted all available VA psychologists to come down to the cafeteria at once. My supervisor and I got on the elevator and headed down. The elevator stopped unexpectedly at the first floor instead of the basement. When the door to the elevator opened a uniformed officer greeted us and asked us to follow him to where the police captain was, outside the building. As we exited the building we were surprised to see that the police had barricades around the building, blocking off streets on two sides, behind which there had gathered a crowd of people. As we approached, the Captain was directing several officers not to allow anyone through the barricades. He turned to us and thanked us for coming down. He explained that the man and his hostages were behind a barricade of overturned tables in the far corner of the cafeteria. He had the elevator stopped at the first floor so that the sound of the doors opening and closing would not spook the man, They had not been able to obtain any information from him other than he had some connection to the Veterans' Administration, probably a patient.

We followed the Captain down the car ramp into a parking area next to the cafeteria into the building's basement. There were four or five officers at the doors to the cafeteria, which stood open. On the way down the ramp, the Captain informed us that he had a sharpshooter crawling through the ventilating duct to an air screen just opposite where the man was located. He suggested that we carefully step inside the open doors and stop there, identify ourselves to the man, and see if we could find out who he was and what he wanted. My supervisor and I stepped into the open doorway and stopped. A man's head peered up over the top of a row of overturned tables. "Don't come any further!" he yelled. "Who are you?" My supervisor identified both of us as VA psychologists. "Good!" the man shouted back. "I want my disability level re-evaluated. It was dropped down."

"I need to know your name," my supervisor countered. He called back his name. "I'll stay here," my supervisor said to me. "You go back upstairs and see if you can locate his file and bring it down."

I backed out of the doorway and walked quickly to the elevator. Up in the files in the outpatient offices I located the man's file and started back down the elevator. On the way I read the file and discovered that he was under treatment by our consultant psychiatrist who was not there that day. I noted that he had a mother and a sister living in the city. When I returned to my supervisor and the Captain, I relayed the information. The Captain asked me for the addresses of the mother and the sister. He instructed one of his officers to take a patrol unit and see if he could locate them and bring them here.

As we waited, the man in the cafeteria kept calling out his complaints about the reduction in his disability payments. I heard a faint sound in the wall of the ventilator duct on the garage side of the cafeteria walls. The man asked what was going on. The Captain stepped forward and told the man that he had sent a car to bring his mother down here. He told him to stay calm. A police sergeant stepped into the doorway with both hands raised over his head. He assured the man that he had no weapons on him. He asked the man if he would accept him in place of the people he was holding behind the tables. The man refused. The offer was renewed, with attempts to persuade the man to release at least one of the hostages in exchange for the sergeant.

After what seemed an interminable length of time, a police patrol car slowly drove down the ramp into the parking area. The Captain rushed over and opened the rear door of the car. Two women emerged, one obviously older than the other one. The Captain asked the older woman if she would be willing to speak to her son. She agreed and the Captain escorted her to the doorway of the cafeteria.

"Mom? What are you doing here?"

"I came to see what in the world you think you are doing!" she exclaimed. She listened to his reply and then scolded him further for being so foolish. Finally, he asked to speak with my supervisor.

"Will you promise me that the VA will reconsider my disability level?" he asked.

"You have my word on it," came the reply.

"OK, that's it!" The man stood up with the gun and knife raised high. The Sergeant and Captain swiftly moved forward and instructed the man to stand where he was and not to move. The men and women whom he had held hostage slowly rose up from behind the overturned tables. The Captain and the Sergeant took the weapons from the man's hands. My supervisor turned to me and said, "That was certainly an easy promise to make!"

By this time officers were escorting the hostages to chairs. One of them was the cook, and he immediately offered them coffee to drink. The hostage taker was escorted to the patrol unit and placed inside. Another patrol unit was brought in and the two women got into it. At a signal from the Captain, the patrol cars activated their red lights and sirens and sped up the ramp and out of the building. Suddenly a mob of people came rushing down the auto ramp towards us. Flash cameras started going off. I stepped towards the elevator, but was cut off by a number of people pushing microphones at me while pummeling me with questions. I was able to get them away from me by telling them that I had not spoken to the man, my supervisor had talked to him. I then escaped to the elevator. I can honestly say that the most frightening part of the whole experience was that encounter with the press.

Now I had the experience of actually observing a crime underway. The hostages seemed to vary in their reactions to the ordeal. Some appeared relieved to the point of tears after their release. Still others seemed relieved, but calm. Most agreed that they didn't harbor any personal animosity for the man who held them hostage, but were fearful of what he might do in his emotional state of mind. I have no doubt that the two-hour ordeal of having their lives put in jeopardy left some residual feeling for each of them to cope with over time. While this book is mostly about the perpetrators of crimes, we must also keep in mind the impact they have upon their victims.

The episode was followed by a request from a newspaper reporter, a week or two later, for an interview. He was going to do an article on the death penalty. He was a friend of my supervisor and had been told by him that I had interned at San Quentin at the time of some executions there. Once again, this forced me to give some serious thought to my opinions about the subject, and the reasons behind why I was not in favor of this type of solution. As years passed and I learned more about factors leading to crimes in general and murder in particular, as well as how our legal system performs, I was to become even more opposed.

The bulk of my work at the VA Hospital and outpatient clinic gave me valuable knowledge about differences in the ways humans react to traumatic experiences, such as wars. Most veterans seem to recover gradually as they merged back into civilian life. From the reactions to sudden noises, the nightmares that recur over and over for a time and the bouts of tenseness and irritability. But others seemed marred for life, unable to settle down and cope with even the smallest demands, terrorized into depending on wives, parents, and the VA. Months of weekly psychotherapy could sometimes show improvements. I recall one man I had worked with for several months seemed to be making slow but steady progress. Towards the last of my work at the VA outpatient clinic, I was so pleased with the progress that I made a very premature and grievous error in timing. I made a comment to him that he was doing so well that we could look forward to the day when he wouldn't need therapy any more, and could go back to work. My mistake was made most obvious at his next appointment. When I met him in the waiting room, I noticed he was looking very sad. Three steps into my office, he fainted. I was able to catch him and ease him down onto the couch. When he regained consciousness he convinced me that he had a long way to go and as a result of my unwise remark, therapy was set back considerably. I have little doubt that my replacement at the clinic continued working with him, and probably the replacement to the replacement. The differences in how individuals deal with trauma was contrasted for me also at the VA Hospital.

One day at the hospital I received a telephone call from the Neurology Unit requesting that I see one of their patients. They wanted me to assess his ability to cope with his severe injury. He was a veteran who had seen active duty in war, and had returned to civilian life to become a successful building contractor. He had climbed up on some high scaffolding to inspect some work his men had done on a building when he fell, severing his spinal cord, resulting in the loss of the use of both arms and legs. I agreed to evaluate him and Neurology said they would send him to my office immediately. While awaiting his arrival, I began to think of the horror of such a loss, and doubt that I could adapt to such a loss if it had happened to me. I began to wonder what I could say to a man in his condition when my office door opened and two hospital orderlies wheeled him in on a gurney. He lifted his head up from the pillow, looked at me and said, "It ain't that bad, Doc!" He was reassuring me!

I saw him regularly for a while, visiting him weekly on the Neurology unit. I will never forget the day I went to see him on the unit, and he motioned with his head for me to lean closer so he could whisper something to me.

"You see that young man in that bed over there to your left? They brought him in yesterday. He is real down because he lost the use of his legs due to an accident. But you'll see, I'll have him laughing in a couple of days!" I have never forgotten this man's indomitable spirit! None of us want to have our coping skills put to the test that some of our fellow humans have had to face!

Oh, yes, I did get back to criminal offenders. My dissertation was based upon psychological reactions of juvenile offenders to areas of emotional sensitivity or conflict. I did pilot studies at three juvenile halls prior to the larger study in a state youth facility. I indeed found differences in reaction to a set of photos I projected on the screen, asking each boy to tell a story about the picture, what went on before, during and after the scene depicted. The photographs had been posed by the students in the University drama department and taken by the department's photographer, thus the necessity of the pilot studies to determine if the photos pulled the themes intended.

Each boy was hooked up to measure breathing rate, galvanic skin response, and heart rate. My dissertation entitled, "A Study of the Role of Arousal and Conflict in the Differentiation of Sub-Types of Delinquents" was very complicated, and my review committee commented, was really three dissertations. Since this is not intended as an academic report to you the reader, and by this time, dated in value, it is mentioned to illustrate that the past influence of my prison internship continued onward.

I was drawing to the close of my doctoral dissertation and was getting inquiries as to when I might be available to accept a position as Staff Psychologist with the California Department of Corrections. Since I was approaching completion of my degree, I indicated that I would be available in three months.

My coping skills were then put to a minor test. In an intradepartmental upheaval, four professors quit the university, and three of them were on my doctoral dissertation committee. I was advised to go ahead and accept my job position and then come back when new faculty was in place, and see if I could get them to serve on my committee, a sticky situation since they would not have been the ones to have approved the original study. Since I had been told that my research had been intricate enough for three dissertations, I decided to take the chance. I accepted the position at a prison facility after being further enticed by a two-step higher starting raise in salary, and with advance agreement that I would be allowed to take unpaid leave to finish my degree.

Oh, the plans we make! And how they go awry! After I completed my doctoral degree, I planned to work in corrections for two or three years, then apply for an academic position somewhere. After the harrowing experience with my dissertation, I was in no hurry to involve myself with academia for a while.

Thus, on February first, I began my position as staff psychologist in a unique institution at that time, a treatment facility for the medical and psychiatric treatment of adult male felon offenders, the first facility of its kind in the world. This institution would become my focus, not for two or three years, but for many years to come, as I will try to share with you the rise and fall of this very unusual facility.

Four
A New Beginning, A New Era

In the decades following the Second World War, there seems to have been a general social reaction to the war years in which mankind was forced to confront human behavior at its worst. Atrocities and destruction had been a steady diet throughout the years of war. So in the decade that followed, it seemed that the social climate was one that sought to re-affirm the positive in human potential. Prior to World War II, the history of penology had focused on simple confinement and punishment. Prisons were largely out of sight, out of mind, except for occasional movie dramatization or prison scandals that came to the attention of the news media. Road gangs, rock piles, jute mills, prison farms, and license plate shops offered the only constructive activity for prison inmates. Prison wardens ruled with absolute power as long as escapades, riots, or scandals did not come to public attention. They determined what qualified as humanitarian treatment of the prisoners, and a bond of secrecy protected the keepers from public awareness of any excesses. The concept of many was that criminal offenders were born bad, encountering few scientific challenges that had any impact on the way criminal offenders were viewed or treated.

Nonetheless, the general sense of relief and optimism that appeared to permeate American society after the big war began to influence numerous social programs. Education flourished as former servicemen flooded colleges under their GI benefits. In generations before the war, most of our population rarely entered or completed their high school education. Everything seemed up for improvement. Even prisons began to change to some degree. In California, the State Legislature passed laws directed at creating a special treatment facility within the California Department of Corrections. The law specified that the treatment facility was to be located in the northern part of the state, and that "the primary purpose of the Medical Facility shall be the receiving, segregation, confinement, treatment, and care of males under the custody of the Department of Corrections, or any agency thereof . . .", going on to specify mental and physical problems including the mentally ill and others, "not limited to psychopaths and sex offenders . . ." (Chapter, Sections 6100, 6102, of Deering's California Penal Code, 192 and prior).

The construction of that facility, the California Medical Facility, was not completed until 1955. Prior to that the treatment facility was housed temporarily in an old U.S. Navy disciplinary barracks in Terminal Island in Southern California. When the California Medical Facility officially opened, it gradually became recognized as the first institution of its kind in the world. Over the next two decades the programs there would expand, evolve, and change as treatment needs and knowledge accrued. It was built on what was termed the "telephone pole" design, that is, long broad central corridors off of which three-storied housing wings opened. This design allowed for further easy expansion. The facility became a unique and grand experiment in the treatment of adult male felons. Prior to this, even some members of the treatment professions considered that "character disorders," represented by the label of "psychopaths," were untreatable. As knowledge expanded, the label

58

of "psychopath" became known as the "garbage can" diagnosis. That is, if one could not come up with a clear understanding of why a person committed a crime, simply apply that label. Even the treatment of psychotics had for the most part consisted of medication and confinement in a mental facility.

But there was something else unique about this new facility. While it was a prison type facility, the administrator in charge was not a warden. Rather, he was called a Superintendent and was a medical doctor. While the Superintendent answered directly to the Director of the CDC during this era, each prison facility still had considerable autonomy. I have never forgotten my first occasion to go to the central office of the CDC. It was located in one corner of the first floor of the smallest State office building in the capital of the state. Besides the Director of Corrections, there were a total of twenty-seven employees. The main function at the time was to set policies and resolve any issues between CDC institutions.

While I was completing my doctoral work at the University of Oregon, one of my former mentors, the one with whom I had set up the group therapy experiment at San Quentin, had become chief of Psychiatric Services at the California Medical Facility. He wrote to me describing this new facility and the programs that were evolving. So, enticed by his descriptions, and the financial offers I received, I ended up joining the staff there in 1966. I was assigned as a Staff Psychologist to a newly completed wing at the far end of that long corridor. The three-story unit was an entirely separate program from the rest of the facility, and was called "The Intensive Treatment Center" (ITC). It had been conceived as an effort to move patients out of the existing acute psychiatric wings back into the mainstream of prison life, or, in a few cases, parole. This was another attempt to treat post-psychotic inmates.

The unit was self-sufficient from the rest of the facility in that it contained its own medical, psychiatric, nursing, teaching, recreational, and custody staff. Another difference was that the correctional officers working these psychiatric units had volunteered for these areas.

Another unusual feature of the California Medical Facility was that all correctional counselors there had Master's Degrees in either social work or counseling psychology. This was in sharp contrast to the regular prisons where the so-called counselors were promoted from officer ranks, and only counseled inmates regarding institutional matters and parole requirements. As a result, the counselors at the Medical Facility were ranked a higher level, and received higher salary, due to the added degree requirements.

Each of the two housing floors on the ITC unit had its own staff and community programs, including school, recreation, treatment, and community meetings. Each inmate coming into the unit was evaluated by staff and provided an individual prescription program. There was close coordination and working together of all unit staff, so that all staff knew where each inmate was in his program. I was responsible for individual and group therapy on my assigned floor.

It was here that I would spend a large portion of the next two years, sharing with the staff many exhilarating experiences, as well as the satisfaction of being part of a close-knit team. The program included a daily community meeting attended by all inmates and staff of the unit. The chairman of the meeting was an inmate elected by the resident inmates. Any problems on the unit or new changes were open for discussion and resolution. Ideas and proposals were aired in these meetings. One example of this was a proposal by inmates about the possible use of two small rooms on the third floor. These small rooms had been staff offices, but they were being used for excess storage. The proposal involved a suggestion that there should be some way of rewarding inmates who programmed well. Since everyone lived in dormitories, it was pointed out that time to oneself was something that everyone missed. Thus the idea was developed into reality by the staff. The two rooms were each furnished with a cot, a radio with record player, and a selection of records, books and magazines donated by staff. Awarded program points could be exchanged for hours in one of these rooms located directly across the hall from the custody staff office, thus ensuring no disturbance from other inmates. Since the initial idea had come from the inmates, it became a very popular reward system for them.

In contrast, there were six disciplinary cells walled off from the rest of the floor. I had to enter this area each day to check on the mental status of inmates temporarily housed in these narrow individual cells. Some of these inmates were returned to the acute psychiatric wing next to the ITC unit. It was towards the last months of my assignment to ITC that I experienced one of the rare frightening moments of my career in prison work, which also earned me the dubious nickname among inmates of "Dr. Mad."

The incident involved one of the inmates that I had been working with in psychotherapy. I had graduated him from individual therapy to one of my therapy groups. He was a very large, muscular man, who had obviously spent considerable time working out with weights. As I recall, his childhood had been one of chaos and neglect. Typically, he had grown up "on the streets," as they say, and ended up in the "State raised" pattern of juvenile halls and youth facilities. Now in his early thirties, he was into his second prison term. In individual work he and I had explored all of this, and "Big Bob," as the inmates called him, had resolved that he wanted to break this pattern, and learn to live like "squares," a term inmates used to refer to a typical citizen. Big Bob had adjusted well in the therapy group.

On this particular day, I had introduced a new inmate into the group. It became apparent that he was feeling threatened by this new experience of group therapy, even though I had tried to prepare him for how a group functioned. After a few questions by other inmates in the group, he reacted with a verbal tirade aimed at me, accusing me of being just another part of "the system" aimed at "brainwashing" inmates. Suddenly Big Bob rose from his seat and left the room. He didn't return during the rest of the group session. Meanwhile the other members of the therapy group helped the new member by assuring him that he could say what he wanted in the group without being punished, and that they had found the therapy group helpful to them. Because of this assurance, the group session ended on a positive note, and I received a tentative apology from the new member. But I was concerned about Big Bob's sudden, unexplained departure.

Big Bob was housed in the large thirteen-man dormitory at the end of the long central corridor on the third floor. I knew that all the inmates were locked in their dormitories for mid-day count, and awaiting release for lunch. I indicated to the custody officer that I would like to enter the large dorm to talk to one of the inmates. He complied, locking the door behind me, and returning to his office at the other end of the corridor. As I stood just inside the dorm, several of the inmates greeted me. Big Bob was seated on his steel cot with his back to the door, hunched over with his head in his hands. Suddenly he became aware of my presence, shouting "Stay away from me, I don't want to talk to you!" as he sprang up and grabbed the edge of the heavy steel bed upon which he had been sitting. The bed spun in the air, coming down with a crash upside down in the same place.

I had stopped in my tracks in the center of the dorm. All the inmates had jumped up from their beds and were standing with their backs to the wall. Unfortunately, there was a large pushbroom leaning against a wall directly in front of Big Bob. He grabbed the broom. I didn't move, but stood frozen to the spot, repeating in as calm a voice as I could muster, "I'm not here to hurt you. I was concerned with how you were feeling" etc. . . . I don't really remember what all I said, just my determination to appear and sound calm while Big Bob proceeded to smash out several small wire glass panes in the large steel-framed window facing the corridor. He suddenly dropped the broom, walked over to his overturned bed, and collapsed in his former position. Slowly I walked over and sat down on the overturned bed beside him. I continued to reassure him as I placed my hand on his shoulder. By this time he was sobbing.

As I continued to speak to him, out of the corner of my eye I saw the officer walk up to the door to the dorm. He obviously had heard the noise and came to investigate. With a startled expression on his face as he saw the broken panes and the overturned bed, he started to unlock the door. I motioned him to back away with my other hand, feeling now confident that things were under control. The other inmates were returning to their beds, except for those nearest to where I sat with Big Bob. They gave us respectful distance as I continued to converse with Big Bob.

The occurrence in the group had triggered deep conflicting and confusing emotions in Big Bob. Over the past months he had begun to idealize both me and our relationship. When the new inmate in the group began his verbal tirade against me, the anger he expressed tapped into deep-seated emotional fears over which Big Bob had begun to develop tenuous control. All these emotions surfacing so quickly left him confused and terrified about his feelings towards me and all authority. The job was helping Big Bob and others work through some of these same feelings once again, and pinpointing their sources in their childhoods that were very much alive within.

While this was not a new or original discovery, since the early writings of Freud and the subsequent decades of study had clearly established this process, but it had not been widely applied to criminal offenders. Most of us who were fortunate enough to have had relationships with parents and other caring adults who modeled appropriate behaviors for us, tend to take for granted that most others had the same advantages. None of the men I worked with on that unit had had the emotional support to develop much of anything but superficial defensive facades. I was again learning more about what lay behind these facades.

About my acquired nickname of "Dr. Mad," as usual stories became embellished by eyewitnesses. To most inmates Big Bob was a large, muscular, intimidating-appearing individual. The story was told that I stood up against Big Bob as he was wielding a big push broom, as calm and cool as a cucumber. Thus, I must be "Dr. Mad." This time it was my facade of outward calm, learned from previous work as a night charge of a violent ward in a mental hospital, that had helped me in this critical event. At least I had earned a "rep" among some of the inmates that in their culture held some degree of admiration and respect.

The work on this unique unit was satisfying to the staff to the degree that one could see improvement in the mental condition of the vast majority of the inmates, a few even to the point that they were able to parole directly from the program into free society. However, with this exception, most were transferred back to general prison populations when they showed sufficient capacity to cope. In keeping with its name, the Intensive Treatment Center was indeed the most intensive treatment program at the facility.

While the California Medical Facility displayed the largest effort at trying to rehabilitate inmates at that time, other small programs had developed in some of the other prison facilities. There was the effort at San Quentin prison I described during my internship there. In numerous other prisons, as well as parole units throughout the state programs were created by correctional counselors, some correctional officers, and parole unit staffs. These included small therapeutic communities with structured peer counseling. This was a time of trying various approaches to reforming inmates based upon different ideas and observations by different levels of professional experience.

Still the positive approach did not include the majority of those in the prison systems. Many inmates refused to participate in any of these programs. There were still excesses within prison and cover-ups of abuse. I occasionally became aware of some of these via the prison "grapevine," that is, word of mouth from some guards and inmates. Prisons still remained secretive institutions with very rare outside scrutiny.

After two years I was beginning to feel the need to follow my original plan to work in corrections for two years, and then seek out an academic position somewhere, or set up a private practice. Once again, fate seemed to anticipate me and stepped in. I had not been aware that the California Department of Corrections had begun to set up a wide range of data-collecting systems and research. One day I received an invitation from the Central Office in Sacramento to accept the position of Supervisor of Clinical Research Unit of the newly created Research Division. Since I had an extensive background in research, and an ongoing interest, I accepted the position immediately. I did ask that my new title be changed from Senior Research Analyst to Senior Psychologist in order to maintain my professional identity as a licensed psychologist. I was now responsible for sitting on a panel of medical and mental health professionals to approve or reject all types of research deemed to be clinical in nature. I was also given the task of supervisor of a data collection unit that collected vast amounts of data, processed the data, analyzed and stored it. To do this, I was given an assistant research analyst, who in turn supervised the crew of twelve selected inmates. These selected inmates were trained to operate the data processing equipment after it had been coded by the assistant research analyst. The analyst turned out to be one of my fellow classmates in my graduate classes at San Francisco State University. He was very knowledgeable and skilled, a fellow student, Charles Jew, with whom I had become good friends.

The new position placed me in a situation where I would over the years, be able to observe directly not only the broader workings of the correctional systems, but later on, the politicizing of crime and punishment. When I first met the Director of CDC, I was most impressed by his openness, and his instructions to me to "tell us if we are doing something we shouldn't, if there is something we can do better, or if there is something we should be doing." Mr. Procunier had worked as a correctional officer, and had moved up through the ranks via performance reports, civil service exams, and interviews over the years to become the Director of CDC. Therefore he knew the operation of prisons from the ground up. From my own experience he asked very direct and pertinent questions. His openness to new ideas and new information encouraged those under him to try new things, and even be critical of some of their long-held ideas. I found this to be stimulating and full of opportunity. To be sure there was a lot of nuts and bolts learning for me to do about the overall prison systems and programs being tried in prisons of other states, as well as California's.

Although my position was now a Central Office position, the clinical Research and Data Collection unit was set up at the Medical Facility due to the space needed, and the inmate crew trained to operate the processing equipment. The equipment at that time included cardpunch machines, card sorters, collators, the modern methods of that time. When a new superintendent took over the Medical Facility, he arranged for me and my secretary to be moved into a suite of offices directly across the hall from his office. The new superintendent explained that he wanted my office near his so that if he needed any information he would not have far to go. One thing I quickly learned from him was that when I was asked to attend his staff meetings, I should come prepared to provide any data or information I had relevant to the agenda. He did not like any items left unresolved due to lack of needed information. He had been a former doctor in charge of medical services on a U.S. Navy hospital ship in WWII, and he liked to run a tight ship!

I met each month with the director and his staff. By this time Central Offices had moved from its little corner of the small State office building to two floors of one of the twin tower office buildings newly constructed by the State, more space, more employees, more sense of importance. Now there was another research unit whose function was to look at parole operations, and programs for possible improvements in reducing recidivism. In the course of my duties, I looked at programs in mental hospitals, prison, and Youth Authority facilities throughout the State of California.

One of the Youth Authority facilities was heavily involved in a large scale research and treatment program aimed at matching personnel and their methods to particular inmates styles of interpersonal interaction. This program was through a large financial research grant, and also involved other out-of-state juvenile facilities. The findings of this study had generated considerable promise. I spent time visiting the State youth facilities and looking into these programs. However, the basic concepts and the programs were aimed specifically at very youthful offenders, and did not translate well into use with adults.

While all these programs were producing very promising results, it was obvious that there was no one type to fit all inmates. Too often we tend, as humans, to treat everyone the same, ignoring important differences. Other times we over-emphasize differences and ignore commonalities. Why were efforts to change criminal offenders into law-abiding citizens successful with some, but not others? Why did some inmates become motivated to involve themselves in constructive programs while others refused? Why did some, who spent years coming and going in and out of jails and prisons, finally become motivated to make efforts to change? Obviously if we could obtain more answers to these and other questions, we could focus our efforts more efficiently on those who might benefit. Like other social problems in our society such as poverty, the solutions are not simple or absolute.

As we know, punishment has a wide appeal in the shaping of human behavior. Most of us can recall as children, when we were told not to do something and we did it anyway, our parents responded with some form of punishment. The worse the offense the greater the punishment, and most of us learned not to repeat the offending behavior. Thus there is a tendency to extend and project this early lesson onto those who offend against our laws and rules of behavior. However, the complexities and differences of human experiences, and what meanings a child attaches to events in their lives, can lead to varied outcomes in their later life.

With the help of my very capable assistant research analyst and colleague, we were able to complete a number of research projects and publications illuminating important factors that helped create and maintain these aliens from our society. The data system we maintained at that time provided a rich source of potential information on factors which contributed to criminal offenders and subsequent success and failures to rehabilitate them. The information was very broad and detailed, including such items as birth order, education level, age of inmate when parents separated or divorced, whether other family members were ever incarcerated, etc. It was a treasure trove for use in ongoing and future research. For this research I established liaisons with graduate programs at several colleges and universities.

As a result of these liaisons I became involved in part-time teaching. I also established professional intern programs at the Medical Facility, and encouraged some graduate students to use data collected by the research unit in their theses and dissertations for their advanced degrees. In turn, I was able to achieve another one of my personal goals—to teach college courses, rising to the level of Adjunct Associate professor. My own learning continued and in the next chapter I will introduce you to several aliens who taught me important lessons about how they became alienated from our society.

Five

Some Illuminating Examples of True Aliens

During the era of hope and efforts to change the lives of some of the men in prison, there were some very rewarding results as well as disappointments. The examples I describe in this chapter were not exceptions in regards to their tumultuous lives or the pain and sorrow they caused others with their crimes. These five men varied in their struggle to make changes in their lives. Two of them were unable to probe deeply into their emotional drives, continuing to rely on external guidance from the few authority figures in whom they came to trust. In contrast, the other three were deeply dissatisfied at who they had become and were eager to confront factors, often painful, that had influenced the paths their lives had taken. This resulted in decisions about self-determination, that is, taking responsibility for becoming the kind of individuals that they determined they wanted to become. The degree to which these men had become violent, dangerous individuals, alienated from the mainstream of our free society, would leave many to believe that they were hopelessly unsalvageable. I must confess that during my initial encounters with these men that I, too, had my moments of doubt, as you will see.

To be sure, staff wondered if some of the treatment efforts made during this era were perhaps "corrective re-parenting." I recall a brief interchange between two inmates in one of my therapy group sessions. One inmate in the group casually asked me if I had any children. Before I could respond, another member of the group piped up, "Are you kidding? He has twelve right here in this room." This began a very lively group discussion. As mentioned before, therapy staff commented often that many of their inmate cases reacted to them as idealized parents. This is a point that I will repeatedly emphasize. These men were some of the "walking wounded" from their individual wars with what they perceived to be an alien, hostile world.

Father's Vicious Guard Dog: The Story of Joey

When I first met Joey, he didn't appear to be the kind of person one would expect after reading his record. He wasn't tall or large of build. He was direct in what and how he spoke. This particularly included the reason he gave for why he wanted to talk to a therapist. His father had died a few months prior to my first meeting with Joey, and since then he had experienced a lot of confusing thoughts and feelings about his father that he had never had before, and didn't understand. There was one point, however, that he was able to state most clearly and emphatically. While he wanted to talk about and understand his feelings about his father, he was fearful that if anyone else made any comment about his feelings, or more important, about his father, he was not sure he could control himself and not hurt them. Then came one of the most succinct and clear statements of a treatment goal I have ever heard. "Doc, I don't want to hurt nobody ever again!"

The sincerity of this goal statement was reinforced over the following two years that I worked with Joey. When departing after either a therapy session or casual conversation in a corridor, Joey would never say "goodbye," or "so long," or any of the standard departures. Rather his departing statement to me was always, "Don't hurt nobody, Doc." We both knew well the meaning of this departing remark and that for Joey it was not a goal to be achieved easily.

Joey was the eldest of four siblings born of Mexican-American parents. He was the only son. The family existed on marginal income, the father employed as general laborer, the mother occasionally working as a domestic. Joey's memories of childhood were mostly memories of juvenile halls. He always seemed to get into fights and end up being kicked out of school or hauled off to juvenile hall. His teenage years were more of the same, only more serious, with graduation into the Youth Authority system for such offenses as assault and battery, and assault with bodily injury. Even in prison he had numerous disciplinaries for fighting with other inmates. In spite of his very unpromising background, Joey exhibited a capacity for understanding concepts far beyond what one would expect from one with such limited education and negative social exposure. Also surprising was that Joey rather quickly built a strong trust in me. It was made very clear on many occasions that I was able to say things to Joey that would have provoked a vicious verbal and possibly physical attack upon anyone else saying something similar. Even so, I was often very careful of what and how I said some things to him. This was not so much out of a fear of attack from Joey, but an effort to avoid provoking emotional defenses that would prevent his hearing and considering what I was saying.

As weeks went by, my confidence in my influence upon Joey grew. This resulted in my making a decision about which I have subsequently had doubts, and even some guilty feelings. After a few months of individual therapy sessions, I decided to assign Joey to one of my therapy groups. Yes, this decision was in part based upon time pressures. Individual therapy was a luxury that had to be dispensed sparingly due to the constant influx of others with legitimate treatment needs, and was not smiled upon by the prison administration.

I prepared Joey for his entry into the group I had selected. It was an ongoing group made up of men with extensive histories of violence, but many of whom had developed considerable insights and had become both knowledgeable and supportive of the therapy process. I wasn't anticipating the reaction I received from the group members, two of whom came to me after the first time I told them of the new member who would be joining the group. "We have a good group here, Doc." "You sure you want to put this guy in our group?" "I don't think he can handle this group, Doc."

These were just a few examples of comments I received from other inmates who rarely make any comments or statements to staff members outside of group therapy about another inmate. If you may recall, negative comments to staff about another inmate is termed by some inmates as "dry snitching." Thus, I knew that the members of the group were expressing some very deep concerns. I tried to respond to their concerns as honestly as I could, and told them that I had elected to place Joey in this particular group because I had very strong confidence in them. Nonetheless, there were occasions over the following months that I felt I had jeopardized the therapy progress of some other inmates in the group in order to help Joey.

For a while, the group did allow Joey to just "sit in" with no efforts to draw him out. However, Joey himself began to participate after warning the group, as he had me, to make no comments about his father. Mostly Joey talked about his fighting, and how other family members, including his mother and sisters, were afraid of him, as were all his relatives. As he talked more and more about how his family members feared him, he would come to the point of tears. The group would listen quietly without comments or questions. Finally, an image of Joey's father began to emerge before the group and it was evident that this group of men with their own violent histories were sensing the depth of Joey's conflict. It was also evident to them that he had formed a strong positive transference towards me. Whenever possible, Joey would sit next to me in the group. I noted that at times the group members arriving first would leave one of the chairs next to where I sat down vacant. Joey would invariably take that vacant chair.

There was one occasion towards the end of Joey's first year that I was made clearly aware of the extent of that transference, and was very thankful that he was seated within reach. That incident involved my attempt to help a young American-Indian man with a history of violent episodes against others to become a part of this particular group. The group had sensed his "tenderness," and after initially introducing themselves to him and telling him why each of them were in the group, they allowed him to sit quietly for a couple of sessions. During the fourth session some questions were directed toward the young man who initially seemed comfortable responding. However, as the session progressed, he seemed to become more tense, until finally I asked him if he was feeling uncomfortable at the group's questions. I had worded my question to hopefully sound encouraging, and to allow him to let the group know if he was not ready to go further at that time. Unfortunately, he interpreted my question as an attack. He accused me of instigating the group to try to find some weakness in him and he stood up and took a step towards me in a menacing manner. I kept my voice calm and even as I assured him that that was not either my or the group's intent, and that if he felt too uncomfortable he did not have to respond to any questions and was free to leave the room.

In the middle of this attempt to discharge the tension, I became acutely aware of Joey seated next to me. I heard him mutter under his breath as he shifted his position, "He's going to attack the doc!" His arms were on the arms of the chair in preparation to spring out of the chair. I tried to not be obvious but I'm sure everyone saw me place my hand on Joey's arm and I left it there, pressing down on his arm. My confidence that I could on my own diffuse the situation of the young Indian man facing me was severely threatened by Joey's intent.

After my comments and comments by two other group members who assured the young man that he would be wise to just leave for now, the man turned and left the room. I could feel the muscles in Joey's arm relax and my own heartbeat return to normal. Out of my many years of work in prison settings, this was the second of three times I can honestly say I felt raw fear. I knew that if Joey left that chair there would be blood flowing. By this time, I knew Joey's story.

Joey's earliest childhood memory went back to when he was about two or three years old. He knew it was sometime after he had learned to walk. He remembered his father picking him up one day and carrying him out to the back steps leading out of the house. His father stood him on the ground and seated himself on the steps facing Joey. All of a sudden the father slapped Joey on the side of the face, knocking him to the ground. The father reached down and stood Joey back on his feet. The father waved his clenched fists back and forth before the crying child's face, shouting, "Fight! Fight!"

Suddenly the father repeated the whole episode, knocking Joey to the ground, picking him up and yelling at him to fight. Joey was not sure how many times this was repeated before, through the tears, he waved his small fists in front of him, whereupon his father clasped him in his arms, gave him a big hug, saying "That's my son!"

Joey did recall that this episode was repeated again a few days later. The second time Joey was only knocked down once. He sensed that he should wave his fists back and forth at his father when his father said, "Fight! Fight!" The result was that again his father picked him up, gave him a big hug and carried him back into the house.

This was the beginning of Joey's training to become his father's vicious attacking animal. As Joey grew older, the father used him to intimidate other members of the family, and eventually others outside the family. By the time Joey was ten years old, the father was taking him to a local tavern with him. The boy was allowed to sit on a stool next to his father while his father drank. Joey soon learned what was coming. As his father began to get drunk, came the inevitable challenge to another patron of the bar. "I'll bet my son can whip your boy any time." Sometimes his father would back the challenge with a money bet. As Joey grew into a seasoned adolescent, the challenges grew bolder. Joey would sometimes find himself pitted against others three or four years his senior and larger in size, in the alley back of a bar. But Joey confessed he learned a secret. He would black out his mind and go for blood. That way he felt nothing until he was pulled off the other person and the fight was over.

Joey's negative feelings about his father came out when Joey admitted that he sometimes dreaded going home after he was released from juvenile hall or the Youth Authority. He knew no one was glad to see him except his father. He recalled one time he arrived home and his father, after greeting him, started telling him about a man at the tavern who had hit him and taken some money from him while Joey was gone. When his father suggested they go to the tavern, Joey knew what was going to happen.

Joey's records revealed that the longest single time span that Joey was not locked up after the age of twelve was one five-month period. The rest were matters of weeks, two or three months at most. Joey finally told the group that he felt safer when he was locked up.

Perhaps the most dramatic point in Joey's therapy came, not in individual or the regular group therapy, but in a large extended community group meeting. A young female intern and myself conducted a large community group on the housing wing where most of the men in our caseloads were housed. This community group meeting held once a month in the TV room, was aimed at giving the men a chance to work out any issues or grievance they might have or to talk about anything they felt they wanted to discuss. One of the correctional officers on the unit and a correctional sergeant would usually attend these meetings. It was at one of these community group meetings that Joey began to talk about something that unnamed inmates did that made him angry.

Somewhere in the discussion Joey began to talk about his father. The emotion that began to enter Joey's voice evidently grabbed everybody's attention. Other than Joey's voice the room had become so quiet that you could have heard the proverbial pin drop. I was feeling a high level of emotional tension building in the room, and I looked around the room to see how intensely everyone was fixed on Joey. The intern seated at the far end of the room was staring at Joey with both hands clasped over her mouth. Joey continued for several minutes longer, then suddenly broke off and got up and left the room.

The meeting ended quickly. No one seemed to have any more to say. As the others left the room, the intern came over to me and asked me how long Joey had been in my caseload. I told her about two years. She stated immediately that she had never sat through anything that emotional before. I told her that I had noticed her sitting with both hands over her mouth. She looked at me and said, "I did that to keep from screaming out, 'Let your son go!' " She told me that she did not think of herself as being much of a believer in spirituality, but that she had a strong feeling that Joey's father was present and that Joey was fighting to be free of him. While I perhaps did not feel the spiritual presence of Joey's father to the degree that she did, I had felt as others obviously had the emotional chains that Joey was struggling to break. Other members of the therapy group were aware also and sessions after that took on more interaction directly between Joey and individual members.

From there on the tension level that had previously seemed to accompany Joey dissipated. A simple statement made by Joey in the group seemed to sum it all up. In a soft voice he said to me and the group, "I think I finally buried my father." Joey eventually paroled out and I received my final admonition from him, along with a hug. "Don't hurt nobody, Doc." I never saw Joey again.

Again, a couple of years later, I heard through the grapevine that he had married. In the area of working in prisons, the adage that no news is good news most often holds true. When the former life pattern that brought the person to these places of confinement are finally broken, you seldom see them again. I continued working in the system for many years and never heard any more about Joey. I hope he achieved his goal and never has hurt anyone again.

Perhaps a poem Joey wrote a short time before he was released tells it all:

From boy to man, two in one,
My body, his mind—was it wrong?
Remade for him to live over again,
Is this so impossible to do,
To become a second chance tool?
Yes, I loved him with all my heart and soul,
Even if my manhood he unknowingly stole.
I fought hard to satisfy his lie,
Until the day that he died.
And in doing this I became a shell
But you unknown lady have opened
A new door that I long to know.
So I fight to be one man, my own.
Is this wrong to fight for freedom,
To be at least, just me?

Another Billy the Kid

I first encountered Billy while I was attending college and working afternoons and evenings as a ward technician (later termed a psychiatric technician) at a mental hospital. One of my duties was to escort more able patients from my assigned ward to the weekly dance held in the institution's large auditorium. Billy was always at these events, and a focus of attention. He was a very handsome child of about twelve when I first saw him with black curly hair, fair complexion and deep blue eyes. He was often the focus of attention from the female ward technicians due to his striking good looks, and they often engaged him in social conversation. When he went out on the dance floor, it was often one of them showing him some dance steps or insisting he dance with a female patient.

That was the extent of my initial knowledge of Billy, until he was in his mid-twenties. At the Medical Facility he was assigned to my caseload. When I read his file in preparation for our first session, I suspected that he might be the little boy at the mental hospital years before. This was verified at our meeting. Billy's file revealed some of the terrible ways our society had in the past dealt with unwanted, troublesome children. The file revealed how Billy came to be in the mental hospital.

His parents separated and evidently divorced not long after Billy was born. At the age of five Billy was made a ward of the court as a result of a petition that the child was out of control and the mother was unable to care for him. His father could not be located. From the records it appears that the judge was somewhat at a loss of what to do with the child, and in an effort of misinformed benevolence consigned him to the State hospital where he would receive good care and "could go hiking and ride horses." Reading this, I shook my head at the naiveté of the judge. Indeed, the hospital was located in remarkably beautiful surroundings, but the patients were confined to the wards and fenced yards. There were no horses for them to ride.

The further justification for housing Billy at the hospital was another part of a dark past history of our mental health system. There was a popular theory at the time that troublesome children who became criminal adults suffered from a deficit in their brain, particularly in some area of the brain believed responsible for the development of a conscience. These bad humans were termed "constitutional psychopathic inferiors." They were not insane or intellectually retarded, but believed to have brains that were constitutionally inferior to the task of developing adequate moral controls. To be committed to the hospital, Billy had to be given a diagnosis and at the age of five years, this was Billy's ticket of admission for the next twelve years of his life.

Due to its tenuous scientific basis, the label fortunately was not long in vogue. Nonetheless, it gained sufficient appeal that some politicians believing it to be an opportunity to reduce crime, passed a law that such persons should be sterilized in order to prohibit passing on their inferior genes. The idea that criminal and delinquent behaviors were symptoms of bad inherited traits has been around for a long time. Less than a century before, Lombroso in 1876 had described the accompanying physical traits of stocky build, narrow-set eyes, and low forehead to be of such inheritance. Even recently studies occasionally appear that purport to discover genetic predisposition to certain types of crime. But none of these findings have yet found any acceptance in the scientific community. However, this did not save Billy, who was sterilized prior to his release from the State hospital as were others so diagnosed with this infamous label.

In our early sessions, Billy filled me in on some of his memorable experiences that he had growing up in the mental hospital. The hospital had two wards built on a hillside overlooking the rest of the hospital buildings. One was devoted to delinquent males under the age of sixteen, some carrying the same label as Billy. The other was the segregation or violent ward of the hospital. Billy related two nightmare type experiences that contributed to understanding some of Billy's later behaviors.

Tragically both were instigated by a ward technician, whose name I knew. I worked as night charge of the violent ward next door during a later year of employment at the hospital, while getting my first degree at college. One experience involved a technician, who, when assigned to supervise the residents in the ward's recreation yard, would make Billy stand with his back to the concrete wall of the building. The technician would then practice his pitching accuracy by throwing a softball very hard and seeing how close he could come to Billy each time. Billy described the terror he felt, standing as still as possible, closing his eyes as the ball sometimes struck the wall with a loud smack next to his head or body.

The other experience was equally nightmarish to Billy. Billy claimed that it was instigated by the same ward technician. There was an older, larger man from one of the other wards who was assigned along with three others to kitchen duty on Billy's ward. This man had repeatedly asked Billy to become sexually involved with him. The more Billy refused, the more aggressive the man became, threatening to rape Billy if he caught him alone. This was overheard by a ward technician who ordered the man to stay away from Billy and do the work he was assigned to do. Word was passed to other technicians to keep a watch on the man.

One day the technician who enjoyed using Billy as a handball backstop was supervising the kitchen crew. He allowed the older patient to harass Billy about sex. Later the technician announced that he was going elsewhere for a while and locked the kitchen door behind him, leaving Billy alone with the older patient. Billy claimed he saw the technician wink at the older patient when he announced his departure. Billy became tearful again as he described being hit, choked, and raped by the older patient.

By the time I met with Billy at the Medical Facility, he was experiencing his third incarceration as an adult. This time was for armed robbery with prior burglaries. He had grown into a very handsome man by now. Because of my knowledge of where he had spent his young life, he established a rapport with me very quickly. He confided in me about all aspects of his life, including the fact that he was homosexual. However, he denied that anyone else in this institution knew, because he feared consequences like the rape in the mental hospital. After almost a year in the treatment program, Billy got into some trouble and was sent to disciplinary confinement. Periodically I would receive letter from him assuring me that he was going to renew his efforts to change his life around. Reminiscent of that young inmate years earlier in San Quentin's Adjustment Center, I did go to the solitary lockup to see Billy. Here is Billy's letter that inspired me to visit him there:

Dear Dr. Mattocks:

Just these few lines to let you know that I have been doing a lot of thinking, and since you cannot come to me and talk, because you're very busy, so anyway I thought I would come to you through pony express (smile).

I have been doing an awful lot of thinking about now and the future. Anyway first I want to let you know I have been getting an awful lot in therapy. I've learned a lot about self-control and believe it or not I've just about figured why I keep coming back. Most of all I found someone I can talk to more freely than any person in all my years in jails, and I think this is one of the biggest problems. I've always wanted to find someone that I could tell my problems and feelings to. Before I never felt I could trust anyone. I guess I was afraid of being laughed at or told to get out of here. Anyway now that I have gained all this I want to start working on getting out and staying out. I feel that I don't belong in jail. I realize I have enough smarts and fit as far as no disease or anything else wrong, except maybe a little stupidity and immature, trying to be what everyone else wants me to be instead of myself.

Well, I thought I would let you know I'm not wasting my time in isolation. I guess I'm on that positive kick and I hope I stay on it. This (disciplinary infraction) I got was a bad thing for my record, but I didn't just sit in here and sulk. I used it for my advantage. I want you to know I'm getting confused a lot too, but I guess it will work out. I want you to know I sure appreciate all you have done for me and I will do my best to not let you down and myself too.

Thank you,

William
February 2, 1967

After his release from his disciplinary confinement, I again saw him on a regular basis in therapy. Not too long after this he was given a parole. I would receive letters from him telling me how he was doing. He had developed a friendship with a police sergeant which he had met via his parole agent. He would go to this police sergeant occasionally for advice on what he should do. Eventually, he wrote and told me that he had met a young man and they were living together. Billy completed his parole and moved to Seattle, Washington. Now and then I would get a letter from him telling me how he was doing at his job as a janitor in a convalescent home. Then came the sad news that he had become ill and was diagnosed with HIV. Subsequent letters he wrote from an apartment he was living in provided by a hospice organization. In these letters he would talk about the views from his window, and seemed to maintain a positive attitude.

Then came a letter from the organization that was providing for Billy's care. It stated that Billy was approaching the terminal stage in his illness. Their organization sought to fulfill last wishes for patients who were approaching this stage. Billy had requested to be allowed to visit me at my home.

I was home alone at that time and gave it serious thought. I could not find it in my heart to refuse his request. If I was agreeable, the letter said, they would pay for a round-trip flight for Billy. Two weeks later I greeted Billy at the airport. He was in a wheelchair and his once handsome features looked old and gaunt. We had a quiet three-day visit. Billy seemed at peace.

Two months later I received a letter informing me of his death. The letter was accompanied by a large colored portrait of Billy, which the sender stated Billy had told them he wanted me to have. To the end, Billy faced whatever life sent his way. I never heard from him any words of self-pity. He simply made the decision that his freedom was up to him, and he didn't belong in jails or prisons. He had learned to trust others and himself.

Diamond in the Rough: The Story of John L.

His whole appearance was as though he didn't see anyone present, while at the same time issuing a challenge to one and all. And he was built for it. While only average height, John was husky, little fat, all muscle. His narrow cold grey eyes peered out from under his dark sandy hair. When he talked, his shoulders moved in such a way that one could easily imagine that he had a chip on his shoulder and was daring anyone to knock it off. Indeed, one therapy session I asked John to leave the room and come back in. I instructed the group to pretend they had never seen him before, and to tell John what impression they received from his body language. It was amazing how consistent the feedback, and even more surprising was that John seemed unaware of the impression he made on others before this. As I came to know him better, I realized that this challenging demeanor had been a part of him since childhood and he didn't realize it was so obvious.

John had grown up without a father. In fact, he could

not even remember what his father looked like. Early childhood was mostly a blur. He had contracted polio at about age five and his clearest memories were of the early part of his school-age years. He described these as miserable, due to the fact that polio had left him with a limp, one leg a little shorter than the other. He was teased a lot by other children and not allowed to play in any running games with them. However, at age ten or eleven this all changed suddenly.

John remembers that one day during recess at school, he had tried to join some boys playing baseball. This resulted in a particularly harsh round of teasing and pushing by the larger boys, and John fled the playground in tears. He didn't go back into the school, but ran crying to his home a few blocks away. His mother was home from work when he arrived. John, telling the story, is at once defensive of his mother's seeming lack of compassion that day. He points out that she was working hard to support him and herself, was tired from work, and now at her wit's end as to what to do with a crying kid! What she did was to bawl him out for letting kids continue to tease him. "Wasn't there a stick or baseball bat or something you could use on them?"

She continued telling him he was going to have to stand up for himself and then ordered him to return to the school ground. John did as his mother instructed. He went back to the playground, and when one of the boys started to tease him again, John grabbed a baseball bat and chased the boy. John doesn't recall whether he hit anyone that day, but after that, attack became his best defense. As he matured physically, nature lent a hand. He outgrew the limp and developed a muscular build, and he never let a challenge go unanswered after that momentous year.

As one can easily guess, the solution to one problem contributed to the rise of others. Getting sent home from school for fighting became the least of these. John gravitated towards and won respect from the rough kids now. Daring behavior led him into delinquent behavior. He began to hone his fighting skills in youth facilities. By the time he reached his early twenties, he had experienced his first prison stint. Making it clear that he "wasn't going to take any shit off nobody," he was quickly moved into hard-core status in one of the tough prisons in the state.

Underneath this rough exterior there lurked a desire for acceptance and recognition by individuals other than tough guys. He observed some guys playing a game called chess. It was more challenging than the domino games played by most of his peers in prison. With characteristic determination he began to teach himself the game, learning from others and from everything he could get to read about the game. After a time he began to make another reputation for himself to the extent that he was consistently winning at chess. His reputation even came to the attention of the warden of the prison where he was housed at the time.

Some time later John read in a newspaper that a syndicated columnist on chess plays had issued a challenge to his readers to a game of chess by mail. As one could guess, John quickly responded to the challenge. Sadly, the columnist elected to use John's letter to make disparaging remarks in his column, to the effect that a prison inmate had the audacity to think he could be a worthwhile challenger to someone as good at chess as he, the columnist. This somehow came to the attention of the prison warden who had observed John play chess. I read a copy of the letter the warden wrote to the chess expert in John's record. The warden very effectively told the "expert" that if he didn't want to accept the challenge from an inmate, that was one thing, but that this inmate had considerable skill and did not deserve the denigrating comments made in the column. The warden hinted that he believed that John could beat the columnist at chess if the columnist had the nerve to play him. There were no further words from the columnist.

But this episode seemed to bring about another turning point in John's life. Prison officials arranged for him to be transferred to the treatment facility where I encountered John. It was evident that behind his piercing grey eyes there was a potential for change. This was borne out over the time he was at the facility insofar as he didn't get into any more trouble.

One must admit, however, that by this time John had established a sufficient reputation which preceded him through the prison grapevine, that no one seemed to want to cross him in any way. Other inmates showed him respect. This respect continued on even after John broke one of the prison taboos. John fell in love for the first time.

Allen was a very youthful, boyish-looking young man, about three years younger than John. I had seen them together a number of times in the corridors, going out to the exercise yard or to the dining halls. It was several months after I had first noticed John and Allen together that John asked to see me privately. John had introduced me to Allen in the corridor a few weeks before. In my office, John got to the point in his usual direct manner. "Doc, I'm in love. What can I say, it's with another guy."

I was not caught unawares. Since I sat on the screening committee which made program assignments on all inmates, I had had occasion to see Allen's file and knew that he was listed as an admitted homosexual. We talked about what this meant to him. John admitted that he didn't understand it all either, but that he just felt different about Allen than he had about anyone else. He confessed that he had had a few encounters with homosexuals in the youth facilities and a couple of times in prison. But those had been purely sexual encounters and he had not had any particular feelings about the person. We talked about loneliness, feelings of wanting to give and receive affection, and sexual feelings, how they often become all bound up together. We talked about how his friends reacted and whether it would cause him problems with the other inmates. He summed the latter up by saying as long as they respected him, he respected them, and there shouldn't be any problem. Indeed there were none. John seemed more relaxed, less challenging now.

I noted that John did not treat Allen as a subservient as was usual with other "cons" who took on a "kid" or lover. It was common that a convict who formed a liaison with a homosexual would provide protection from other convicts and treats from the prison canteen in return for exclusive sexual favors, and servient chores such as cleaning their cell, laundry, and various tasks. It was understood that when the convict was with his peers the homosexual partner was to keep a distance, not to try to be involved in the conversation of men and to do whatever his "old man" told him to do.

As previously noted, in the social heirarchy of prison, there was a distinction to be made between the prison-wise "convict" and the less experienced or less prison-wise "inmate." John seemed secure enough in his prison reputation that he did not show much concern for those distinctions, and treated Allen more as a friend and equal.

But the old need for challenge and recognition by those John saw as "refined" people also pushed John into another arena. The prison treatment facility allowed a number of volunteer citizens from the community to come into the prison and sponsor various types of clubs that might encourage more constructive social behaviors in the inmates. Among these groups was the local bridge club. With the same fervor that he had applied himself to learning chess, John now applied to learning bridge. It was not long before John began to proudly report his successes, progressing up through "the tables" in the bridge tournaments. I also began to hear from others about what a good bridge player John had become, and that he was considered a key member of the bridge club. John himself seemed particularly pleased about how well he got along with the free people who came in for the club meetings and games. I began to realize that this acceptance by people in the club, schoolteachers, the mayor of the city, storeowners, housewives, actually meant more to John than the winning of the bridge playoffs. He talked to me more about these people than about winning the games. This was a happy time for John.

There was, however, an ominous note for John's future that came to my attention. One day when John came into the group therapy room he accidentally kicked a "butt can" across the room—a gallon-size can with water in it for those who smoke to deposit their cigarette butts. Startled, John exclaimed, "Where did that come from?"

Another inmate in the room replied, "John, you do that a lot. We keep telling you need to make an appointment to get your eyes checked." After the group was over I motioned John over to me. Upon my questioning him he told me that he couldn't see things close around him, particularly immediately in front of his path. I made a medical referral for John to have his vision checked. The report was not good. John was showing some deterioration of optic nerves. There was a possibility that the deterioration might be progressive. Only future periodic tests could determine that. John's reaction was another stoic, "whatever will happen, will happen," and commented on it no further. I did witness a couple of subsequent occasions of John stumbling or tripping over something immediately in front of him, but he passed it off as clumsiness and not paying attention to where he was going. No further mention was made of it. As far as therapy group was concerned, John did pay attention, which was attested to by his direct but insightful comments in the group.

The day eventually came that John was released from prison. Upon his departure he stated, "I'll be in touch." I never noticed Allen pair up with anyone else, and he usually appeared sad when I saw him in the corridors, and finally he, too, was released on parole. I soon began to receive letters from John. He had become a merchantman with a shipping company sailing out of the San Pedro harbor area. Occasionally I would receive letters from ports of call throughout the Pacific. On one occasion, he was involved in a fight in a Japanese port, but wasn't injured and only had to pay a fine. From his letters I gathered that much of his sightseeing while in foreign ports involved ladies he encountered there.

John's letters altogether seemed positive. He enjoyed his work as an engineer aboard ship. I gathered that much of his job consisted of keeping the ship's engines running smoothly and that time in port usually was only as long as it took to offload and onload cargo.

I was more than a little surprised one day when I received a telephone call at my home from John. His ship was docked in port only an hour's drive away. He wanted me to meet him at a landmark nearby. He wanted to take me to dinner at a restaurant of my choice. At first I was hesitant, but the pleading tone in his voice quickly overcame and I agreed to meet with him. It was an interesting evening, to say the least.

John greeted me warmly and, for him, with much enthusiasm. Since we were in the area of San Francisco's famed Fisherman's Wharf, I suggested we pick a restaurant there. John was most insistent that I pick a nice restaurant, not just any restaurant, that he wanted to treat me to a "real" dinner. I chose a restaurant that I knew served excellent food, was above average in sophistication, and I calculated not too crowded that early in the evening. It seemed to meet John's expectation, so we entered the restaurant. John plunged ahead of me, mumbling something about picking out a good table. The maitre d' approached with a quizzical look on his face, looking at me standing in the foyer and then at John wandering among the tables. I quickly asked the maitre d' for a table for two near the windows, and he asked me to follow him. I caught John's eye and motioned him to follow. Again, John seemed impressed both by the maître d's formality and the table by the windows, the view seemingly going unnoticed earlier in his excitement.

When the waiter brought the wine list and menu, John asked my advice and urged me to pick a bottle of good wine. Not believing that John knew how expensive a tab in such a restaurant could be, I selected very conservatively. When the waiter returned, John happily addressed him as "mate." The dinner was very good and John seemed in total enjoyment playing the role of host. After dinner when the tab arrived, John leaned forward and quietly asked what size tip was customary in a place like this. I told him and he immediately reached in his pocket and counted out the amount I had suggested. Without a moment's hesitation he motioned for the waiter. When the waiter came to the table, John grabbed his hand and shoved the tip into it, exclaiming, "Good job, mate! Keep up the good work and they might make you chief engineer some day!"

It was evident that the waiter was caught off guard and didn't know how to respond. I quickly laughed to relieve the awkwardness and commented, "What, aren't there any demands for chief engineers here?" The waiter relaxed into a smile and thanked us both and make a quick retreat. While John paid the tab, I quietly slipped a bill to the maitre d' who was watching with a somewhat quizzical look on his face. I smiled, and followed John out the door.

I was aware that John had left a rather unique impression, and that the waiter and the maitre d' were no doubt trying to figure out the connection between us.

The evening was pleasant and I showed John some of the local sights. We talked about his travels and he then popped his second request. John wanted me to come aboard his ship and see his quarters which he extolled as real comfort! However, as he informed me that visitors were not allowed, so I would have to tell the watchman at the gate this story that John had concocted, I grew wary and finally declined over John's insistence, and evident disappointment. We sat in my car near the ship and talked for a while. Then John announced that he had to be aboard ship by a certain time as they locked the gate, and then he wouldn't be able to get to the ship. We said our farewells and I thanked John for a wonderful, memorable evening.

Months passed before I again saw John. I received occasional letters, but fewer from foreign ports. It seemed that John was working ships that sailed from Los Angeles to Seattle more. Once again I received a telephone call from John at my home. This time he informed me that he had just gotten out of the hospital in time to get back to his ship. Again, he was in San Francisco and wanted to see me. This time he wanted to take the bus to my town and have me meet him at the bus depot. When I picked him up he had a dark woolen cap that was pulled down over his ears, and a dark pea coat. Upon arrival at my house I was totally unprepared for John's unveiling. I had commented at the depot about some discoloration under John's eye, which he passed off as the result of the fight he had mentioned on the telephone. But when he removed the woolen cap, his whole head was heavily wrapped in a gauze bandage. He also told me that he had lots of bandages around his chest due to a couple of fractured ribs. The story emerged.

His ship had docked in San Pedro. He had a date one evening with this girl he knew. He was going to take her to dinner and was going to pick her up at seven after she got home and freshened up. He stopped in a bar on the way to kill some time before going to her house. When he entered the bar there were only three or four people there. He sat at the bar, slowly sipping his drink. After a while he noticed that the other patrons all seemed to finish their drinks and leave about the same time. However, the bartender said nothing. In a matter of minutes men in leather jackets and pants began arriving. John continued sitting at the bar sipping his drink.

After a while one of the new arrivals came over to John and in an "in your face" manner asked John if he was a cop. John replied in the negative, with an additional comment to the effect of "what the fuck business is it of yours who I am?" The fight was on and the bartender ordered them to take it outside. Six of them joined the first one. John followed his old pattern, and proceeded to pound on whoever came within range. Apparently the bartender felt that things were getting out of hand and came outside with a shotgun and ordered the men to back off John.

How John arrived at the hospital emergency I don't recall, but as he finished his story, and I eyed his heavily bandaged head, I became concerned that he might also have left the hospital prior to a doctor's release. He assured me he hadn't, but admitted the doctor told him to take it easy and he was going to have to stay on his ship and do no physical work for a couple of weeks. We had dinner and a pleasant visit. I drove him back to the ship and that was sadly the last time I saw John.

I received one or two letters after that, but they were

shorter and less frequent until they stopped. Then one day I received a letter from John's mother. She was writing to tell me that John had been found dead in a hotel room by the police. The police had ruled it as death by cardiac arrest. She related that John had become more and more despondent the past year due to failing eyesight. He was no longer able to go to sea. A few days before his death he had visited her and had commented to her, "I wish I could talk to Doc." In the letter, she told me that John often spoke to her about me in high regard. She stated that she wrote because she wanted to thank me for all I had done for her son. I must confess I was unaware of what exactly I had done for John, but then one doesn't always know what may have reflected a little light into this diamond in the rough.

Who Am I? What Am I?: The Story of Greg

Greg shared with me his earliest recollection. His older sisters seemed to enjoy dressing him, the then youngest child in the family, in their outgrown clothes. If mother was feeling good, after a few drinks to start her day, she would allow the girls to use some of her make-up in their play with Greg. In this particular memory, Greg was feeling depressed and disappointed. His father, as he often did, had taken Greg's older brother somewhere fishing, but did not take Greg along. To Greg it seemed like a particularly long day. The girls continued to entertain themselves by taking turns putting some of their clothes on him with various make-up. Mother seemed more and more amused as she prepared herself another drink. Occasionally she interrupted the activity by ordering one of the girls to pick up some things, or to wash the dishes. Finally, they heard father returning with Greg's older brother. Mother pulled Greg up from the chair

95

where his older sisters had placed him, and told him to stand next to her. As father entered, she lurched forward a step as she announced to father, "This is your other son," pushing Greg towards his father dressed in his sisters' clothing replete with make-up on his face. Greg could sense the tension, but was not old enough to understand the reason. He could not recall how old he was at the time of this event, only that it was prior to his beginning school. All he knew was that about a year or two after this, father left and didn't return. Greg commented to me that through his early years he felt more like a play toy than a person.

As he grew older, he also became part of the work force who kept the house and cared for younger half-siblings when mother was otherwise "disabled." Father's departure began a series of mother's boyfriends, stepfathers, and more children. The final score was husbands five, children nine.

Later Greg shared another memory with me, one of terror and pain. Mother had gone out one evening, Greg had placed the younger children in their beds, and was in bed himself when he heard a knock at the front door. He got up and went to see who it was. It was one of mother's boyfriends who had been there a few times before when mother was home. The man pushed his way in and engaged Greg in conversation, showing evidence that he had probably enjoyed more than the bottle of beer he held in his hand. He began making comments to Greg, who was in his underwear, about what smooth legs he had. The man began pushing himself against the boy, touching and grabbing him with his free hand. Efforts to get away from the man by Greg only resulted in more aggressive and rougher handling by the man who forced Greg towards a bed visible through an open door.

In the process the man hit Greg in the mouth with the beer bottle, whether by accident or deliberately Greg doesn't know. He noticed that his mouth was bleeding, and two of his teeth were loose. The pain in his mouth was quickly replaced by the terrible pain of the sexual assault the man committed as he pushed the boy face down on the bed. After a while the nightmare eased somewhat as the man released Greg and abruptly left the house. Greg managed to get back into his bed. Through the dark hours the physical pain subsided, but he was missing two of his upper front teeth. At long last he heard the front door open and his mother's voice. She had someone with her, and from what he could hear, he knew she had been drinking heavily. He stayed in his bed.

The next day Greg remained in bed, telling the younger siblings he didn't feel good. They occupied themselves getting ready for school, and were soon gone. The house was quiet. Finally Greg got up, dressed, and went to the kitchen where he too fixed himself some cereal and milk. Mother was still sleeping and he knew well not to disturb her sleep under such circumstances. Mother did get up from her sleep shortly before the other children came home. She wasn't feeling well and seemed preoccupied.

Greg does not recall whether his mother asked why he was home and not in school. He does recall that his mother did not notice his swollen lip and missing teeth until the others came home from school and brought it to her attention. He made up a story about having fallen. He was terrified about what mother's boyfriend might do the next time he came to visit mother. Fortunately, that boyfriend never returned, but Greg's fear continued until mother married another man. It was a heavy secret to carry at age thirteen.

By the time he was sixteen, Greg had made another discovery. He learned that when he joined Mother in having a few drinks, things seemed much more pleasant and fun. By age eighteen he was lying about his age and sneaking into bars. He didn't have to buy his drinks too often. He discovered that his youth and effeminate gestures drew interest from some men, who then bought him drinks and then took him to their apartments so he could "sleep it off." He quickly discovered that was not all they wanted. At twenty, he was in the big city and the "gay bars" became his haunts. He worked at odd jobs and prostituted to support a small apartment. A few men who encountered this good-looking young man sensed that all was not well, and offered him help with his alcoholism. But Greg plunged further into his self-destruction until he could no longer face his circumstances.

Following a drunken argument with his mother over the telephone one evening, Greg made a botched attempt to commit suicide by setting fire to his apartment. Fortunately, he survived unhurt, and damage was restricted to his apartment. With no place to live and a possible arson charge pending, Greg decided on a change of scene, and took a bus to California and another large city. More gay bars, more getting picked up by men, and then a fateful evening.

It began with the usual scenario. Greg was standing outside a bar. A man approached him and asked Greg to join him for a drink inside. The man bought a few drinks for the two of them. Finally, the man suggested that they have a final drink and then go to his place. Greg agreed. As the final drinks arrived, the man reached into his pockets, fumbled with something, and then placed his hand over Greg's drink, commenting, "There, that will make you feel better." They finished their drinks and left the bar to go to the man's apartment. Greg was beginning to feel very strange, but attributed it to the drinks he had consumed. The weird feelings continued and Greg began to have some strange sensations.

After arrival in the man's apartment, things began as

expected. They both were soon naked. But by this point, Greg's strange sensations began to expand into some bizarre images. He recalls that at one point he saw his mother pushing or pulling him and yelling something at him. He recalls seeing a broom leaning against the wall, grabbed it and struck the image in front of him over the head, breaking off the handle of the broom.

Greg woke up in jail with no recall of how he got there. To this day he has no recall of what happened. According to the police report, neighbors called police, reporting sounds of a terrible fight in a neighboring apartment. When police arrived and gained entry to the apartment, they found the nude victim lying on the floor, dead. He had been beaten, and the jagged end of a broken broom handle was protruding from his rectum. Greg was staggering around the apartment, mumbling, and apparently trying to put on his clothes. It was clear to the D.A., the appointed defense attorney, and the court that this was a clear case of a homosexual tryst gone sour under influence of alcohol, in brief, murder. Greg was off to a life in prison.

The circumstances under which I first met Greg in prison were unusual. A psychologist on my staff, to whom I had assigned an intern to supervise, had expressed interest in forming a therapy group for effeminate homosexuals housed in a segregated unit at the facility. Such attempts had been made previously and had been unsuccessful. I explained this to them. Nonetheless, they wanted to try a volunteer group with that population. Since it was voluntary, the attendance quickly declined as before, when the members discovered it was not a gossip group and they were not to be allowed to bring their "boyfriends" to the group. However, one member of the group continued to attend regularly, and, I was told, he seemed very earnest about therapy. Thus when the group was disbanded, I was asked if I would

99

take this person into individual therapy. On this basis of their recommendation, I agreed to do so. However, upon my first meeting with Greg I was seized with second thoughts. He appeared as much a woman as prison denims would permit, with prison-made make-up on and hair in a very distinctive female style, and almost theatrical female gestures.

Nonetheless, as I talked with Greg it became obvious that he had many questions about himself, and was motivated to understand how a shy boy grew up and ended up in prison for murder. Yes, Greg stated that he had a "husband," a seasoned older convict who acted as his protector from other inmates in return for sexual favors. It quickly became apparent that Greg was seriously lacking in both self-confidence and self-esteem.

That became the first target of treatment. He began participating in the educational program also. As we traced his childhood and adolescence and he recounted some of his early emotionally laden events, I noted some collateral changes beginning to take place in Greg and his demeanor. He had quit wearing make-up, and his haircut was more conventional. One day he began the therapy session by informing me that he and his "husband" had broken up. A few weeks later he began growing a mustache and beard. The feminine gestures were also diminishing. All this time Greg continued to piece together the events and the meanings he attached to them in therapy. The deep hurt and sadness about his father's lack of interest in him, the lack of attention he received except when his sisters dressed him up like a girl for his mother's amusement, his ultimate surrender to a "if you can't beat 'em, join 'em" attitude, which thinly veiled the deep resentment lying underneath an otherwise passive, compliant exterior.

In short, the flighty butterfly slowly evolved into a

sturdy caterpillar of self-determination. Before me now stood a handsome man with mustache and trimmed beard. Eventually therapy came to an end and he was transferred to another prison, his status as an effeminate homosexual also having ended. After he left to another prison, I received regular letters from him keeping me informed about his life and activities in which he became active. He joined organizations such as Alcoholics Anonymous and a religious group. He was very proud of his prison job assignment and the compliments prison staff made about his work.

Over time Greg informed me about a woman he had met through one of the volunteer organizations that sponsored activities for inmates at the prison. They began to correspond, and eventually she came to visit him regularly. They fell in love and I received letters that could only come from a man in love. After a year they were married in a simple church ceremony in the prison. They were soon scheduled for a conjugal visit, a privilege at that time for all married inmates who had clean disciplinary records.

Not long after that "honeymoon" came about, I received one of the most beautiful letters I have ever read. Greg was ecstatic and the words spoke of the beautiful angel, his wife, who had joined him in his fulfillment as a man and as a husband, and the faith they shared with each other. The past was now history, almost.

After two years of wedded bliss, a not uncommon event occurred. After Greg once again received denial of parole, the reality began to confront his "angel." Even though Greg had been sentenced under an indeterminate sentence of ten years to life, and had participated in all recommended programs, been evaluated by all staff including a mental health evaluation and was deemed eligible for parole, times had changed. Politics had formed a new way politicians could win votes, by declaring war on crime. Governors changed and it became a reality that there was diminishing possibility Greg would ever be paroled under the new political climate. It was a bitterly sad moment for Greg and his wife I am sure, as he received notice from her that he would be getting divorce papers. She assured him of her affection, but could not handle the thoughts that she would never be able to share a normal life with him. Greg wrote me sad letters, but always reassured me that he would never cease to grow personally or in his faith. His strength became more and more evident in his cards and letters.

As time passed I began to receive beautiful handmade cards with letters inside. The cards began as a new hobby for Greg, created by meticulous cutouts of flowers, birds and animals, greenery and various other objects skillfully and artistically arranged into very beautiful collages. In the letters he talked to me about his philosophical ideas, views of life and people. He talked about his family and how he was establishing new adult relationships with his brothers and sisters, and even his mother. He shared many things about members of his family so that I began to feel I almost knew them. He shared his sadness and memories of his older brother, and his deep disappointment about one younger brother who continued to refuse any contacts with him.

The years continued to pass, and Greg took pride in helping other inmates mend their lives. He became a man to be admired for his heart. But I detected in those letters that there was still a deep underlying struggle for acceptance. He had over the years, as noted, re-established relationships with his family. Then came the sudden death of his mother. The strong emotional chains of childhood resurfaced and the final stage of resolution began. In letters he has kept me abreast of his struggle, along with his siblings, to resolve all the emotional conflicts resulting from childhoods with an alcoholic who later, in their adult years, redeemed herself and became the mother they wished for as children.

As for Greg, he has become stronger in his religious faith, and an influential member of his Alcoholics Anonymous group. Most important to him is his family, a number of whom visit him when they can. He now has twenty-seven years straight in prison. Each time he goes before the parole board, they recite his crime and make mention of the fact that he has programmed well in prison, and received strong recommendations for parole in his clinical evaluations. Each of these evaluations point out that at the time of the crime, the symptoms described fit those of someone under the influence of a hallucinogenic substance, probably placed in Greg's drink by the victim. Notwithstanding the law under which Greg was sentenced specified that he would be eligible for parole after ten years if he was evaluated as rehabilitated, governors seeking to prove their tough stance against crime ignore all of this for political purposes.

I should note here that a subsequent law also specifies that parolees must parole to the county in which they committed their crimes. Many committed their crimes in counties in which they did not live or have any ties. One of the strongest factors that contribute to a man not returning to crime or failing parole was found to be family support. Members of Greg's family have made repeated requests that Greg live with them when paroled, so that they could give him support in gaining employment. But the parole authority insists that Greg bring to them at each hearing parole plans for release to the large city where he had been less than two weeks prior to his crime, where he knows no one and would have no place to live. Greg still manages to maintain a strong positive attitude and mild hope after all these years.

Heaven to Hell: The Story of Steven

As I begin writing this I am gazing at a photograph of five smiling children sitting in front of a decorated Christmas tree, all in pajamas and robes. Behind them are wrapped presents, and their faces are lit up in the anticipation of children who still believe in Santa Claus. Steven is the one on the left, obviously the oldest, with a big grin. There are two more boys and two girls, all between the ages of eight and three. As I looked at this photo I began to feel a sense of profound sadness descend on me. The oldest boy is serving life in prison now. The second, I was informed, was killed in a drunk driving accident at age nineteen, the little blond boy with the missing front teeth later became involved in drugs. The first little girl also graduated to drugs, disastrous rela-tionships much like the five marriages her mother went through, and the angelic-looking little girl on the right of the photo became a "Moonie" and other members of the family have never heard from her since. How did such happy little children in this photograph grow up to become adults lost in their own hells? This is Steven's story, the eldest of the group.

My first contact with Steven occurred as I was leaving the Medical Facility one day. He was one of the inmate workers assigned to clerk the inmate crafts shop just off the facility's large lobby. He called to me as I crossed the lobby to leave the building, and asked if he could speak with me. He said that another inmate whom I had seen in my caseload had recommended me as someone who could be trusted. He wanted to know how he could get into therapy with me. I took down his name and housing number, and informed him that I would send him an appointment card. This was the beginning of one of the most dramatic and clarifying cases of my career. It began very inauspiciously.

In our early sessions, Steven asked most of the questions with me responding mostly with hypothetical answers. It was obvious that he was cautiously sounding me out, and that even though he had taken the initiative to get into therapy, he hadn't yet decided how much he could trust me. So our sessions began slowly, with Steven starting to talk about his adolescent drug abuse and how it had led to his crimes. I learned that Steven had also married a young divorcee, who visited him regularly. She already had four children, and now she and Steven had two daughters and a son following their marriage.

Finally, it was evident that Steven was trying to confront the horrors of his crimes. It was very difficult, since they were crimes that no rational person would have committed, brutal and senseless. He spoke of the surge of power he experienced during the commission of the two murders. At the. time he was the quasi-leader, of a group of four guys and two women who had moved to the Los Angeles area. They worked odd jobs just long enough to get food and drug money, living as transients out of a car, and at other times in small apartments. Now in the Los Angeles area they found themselves in a desperate situation, no money for drugs. The last of their money had been used to rent an apartment. This was the impetus for the first crime, the robbery of a service station. One of the young men and the young women remained in a small apartment while Steven and the two others males went looking for some quick money.

After selecting their target to rob, one of the guys remained in the car as Steven and his other cohort, a huge hulk of a teenager, approached the young service station attendant. Steven was armed with a knife, while the hulking young seventeen-year-old cohort armed himself with a hatchet. After they forced the service station attendant to give them the money from the cash register, they forced him into one of the restrooms so they could effect their getaway. However, once they were all in the restroom, the two robbers realized that they had nothing with which to tie up the attendant. Steven exchanged glances over the shoulder of the young victim with his crime partner who loomed behind the hapless attendant. Steven raised his hand with his thumb pointing down. The hatchet came down hard, ending the young service station attendant's life. It was at this moment, Steven later reported, that he felt this great surge of power.

The two culprits quickly returned to the awaiting car with the ill-gotten money and were off to find a connection to purchase more drugs. Once purchased, they returned to the apartment with a couple of new-found female acquaintances. There followed a scene typical of the drug world, a party of drugs and sex.

A couple of days later the original five were back on the freeway, once again on a drug-hazed trip, looking for a place to eat. Steven was driving as a California Highway Patrol car came up behind them with its red lights flashing. Momentarily the passengers in the car were trying to decide what to do about the drugs they had with them as Steven pulled over and stopped. The officer came up to the window of their vehicle and explained that he had pulled them over due to a broken tail light, and wanted to check for other items in the car that might need to be repaired for safety. However, almost immediately the officer received an emergency call. He told Steven to get the tail light fixed and then returned to his patrol car and sped away in response to the emergency call.

Relieved, but shaken, Steven and the group in the car decided they had better get off of the freeway at the next off ramp. The car's gas gauge was low as they rolled into a service station. They parked the car next to the off ramp. They exited the car and stood discussing their problem, again about money. During the discussion, Steven noticed a woman stopped a few feet away at the stoplight of the nearby off ramp.

"Wait for me here," he ordered his companions, and bolted towards the woman's car, pulled open her car door and jumped in beside her. The woman's body would later be found lying in an orchard, murdered.

A few drug binges later, Steven and his small group were arrested. They were connected to the crimes they committed. Steven was twenty years old, and would spend two years in a mental hospital for the criminally insane. Initially he was strapped down to a bed due to his violent outbursts. One can only imagine the turbulence in his drug-twisted brain during those two years. Following his being found competent to stand trial, he returned to court and was found guilty of his crimes. He was given two seven-to-life sentences with possibility of parole after fourteen years, if rehabilitated.

After telling me all the terrible details of his offense, Steven asked me if I wanted to continue therapy with him. I assured him that our task was not over and, as painful as it was for him to confront himself, it was important for us to continue.

He soon began to share his memories about his childhood. One could say that childhood for Steven, not long after the photograph I described earlier, took a turn for the worse for him and his siblings. I asked Steven for his earliest memory. It was a memory of being dressed up in a little sailor suit to accompany his mother to greet his father when his ship docked in port. Father was a naval captain and was away at sea long periods of time. Thus, Steven did not remember much about his natural father, or the divorce, as he was too young. He had a later impression that his parents had divorced because his father discovered that mother entertained other men in his absence.

Soon after, a new stepfather entered the home, and the

hell for Steven began. Eventually the slightest infraction of rules dictated by this scripture quoting man brought incomprehensible punishment and held up as a warning to the younger siblings. Life became a routine of fear; screams accompanied the daily discipline with belts, sticks and ropes. But even more dreaded was the closet where Steven, and occasionally one of his siblings, would spend hours standing with arms extended above, the rope binding the wrists passed over the clothes rod in a darkened closet.

Steven recalled one occasion he was ordered to mow the lawn, when he came home from school. He was about nine years old at the time and he and a little school buddy dawdled along the way home after school. When they reached Steven's home, the stepfather came out of the house yelling at Steven for being late. The little friend of Steven's was frightened by the tirade and started to leave. The stepfather ordered him back, saying that the boy needed to watch what happens to little boys who don't do as they were told. Then the stepfather proceeded to quote scripture as he beat Steven brutally in front of his friend.

The little friend ran and Steven was dragged into the house for the remainder of his punishment, which resulted in sufficient injury that Steven was subsequently taken to the hospital. He does not recall what his parents told the hospital staff about the cause of his injury. In those days, parental explanations were usually accepted, and interventions were rare. Sometime later during his life with this stepfather, Steven was again taken to the hospital with swollen testicles after being kicked by the stepfather.

However, it was not long after this that a discovery about the stepfather resulted in relief for Steven and his siblings. The stepfather was involved in sales, and was often gone for two or three days on business. Steven doesn't know how it happened, but it was discovered that the so-called business trips involved visits to another wife and children. The step-father was convicted of bigamy and sent to prison.

For the next two years, Steven's mother would go to the prison to visit the stepfather. Steven and his siblings stayed in the car during these visits, refusing to go into the prison to visit. Finally came the fateful day when mother returned to the car and announced, "Your father is going to be paroled next month, and I have decided to take him back."

A shock went through Steven. Terrible memories flashed into his mind. As his mother started the car, Steven opened the car door, jumped out, and ran. He continued running until he could no longer hear his mother yelling at him. He found his way to a highway. Just shy of fifteen, Steven hitchhiked his way to San Francisco to become a "street kid." There he soon joined the other runaways and learned about drugs and living on the streets of a large city.

Even prior to this, Steven had already begun preparation for his violent future. He had on occasion been sent to juvenile hall for shoplifting and other minor infractions. Initially, he found short sojourns in juvenile hall a relief from the home environment, but these escapades eventually resulted in a stint in the California Youth Authority. These were places where his resentment towards authority grew, and he learned new ways to deal with his fears. There he also saw how the bigger boys preyed on smaller ones. He learned that if one did not retaliate, the bullies would come back again and again. When a larger boy began to harass him, Steven realized he had to be smart and make a plan.

One day when Steven was in the chow line, a larger boy shoved Steven back and cut into the line in front of him. Steven came up behind his tormentor and hit him hard with his metal food tray. When the bigger boy fell to the floor, Steven continued hitting him until a staff person pulled him away. In Steven's own words, "I got my first taste of blood and

109

power that day. Suddenly I was to be feared and with that fear came respect. Because respect is earned through violence and a willingness to do whatever it takes to get revenge." Later, the stint in the California Youth Authority further reinforced this lesson.

During our early sessions, Steven was usually very direct in his responses to my questions, but showed little emotion, except when speaking about his crimes. Then there was a sadness that came over him. Nonetheless, he continued to be very much in control of his feelings. Then one day Steven came in and began to talk about a visit he had with his wife two days previously. The visit had been dominated by a discussion between them about the discipline of the children, a topic that had triggered a strong emotional response from Steven. They had a heated argument, and as she departed the visiting room, Steven told her that if she didn't discipline the children the way he wanted her to do, he was going to divorce her. "Don't you agree with me, Doc?" he asked.

I quietly replied, "No, Steven, I don't."

A strange expression came over his face. I sensed anger of such intensity that I felt strong apprehension. The room was silent for what seemed like an awful long time. I observed his hands, which clasped the arms of his chair turn white-knuckled. As I would later describe my feeling at the time to colleagues, I felt as if the paint on the wall behind me was peeling off the wall, leaving only my silhouette. Finally, I heard Steven speak with clenched jaws, "I think I'd better go now."

I replied as calmly as I could that he knew he was free to do so if he wished. He arose from his chair and walked slowly out of my office without a word. I wondered at the time if I would see or hear from him about further therapy sessions. I was somewhat surprised a few days later when I received a request from him to continue his scheduled therapy sessions.

At the next meeting, as Steven sat down, he began to relate his experience of our last session. He explained that he did not like anyone disagreeing with him, that he saw it as a challenge that had to be met with violence out of a fear that they might strike first. He further explained that he realized as he sat there that I was not physically threatening him, and he was confused, trying to figure out what he should do. After he left my office he went straight out to the prison yard and walked around the track that went around the perimeter of the big exercise area. Some of his inmate friends came out to talk with him. They said they had seen him from the cellblock window that faced the yard, and sensed that something was wrong. When they approached Steven, he shouted at them to get away and leave him alone. They wisely withdrew. For three hours he continued to walk the track until the prison guards closed the yard for the evening mealtime. During that time he walked the track, he gradually gained control over his anger. The next few days he thought about why he had become so angry, what provoked it. He told me he had some ideas he wanted to discuss with me.

We did discuss his thoughts, ideas and feelings. But there was a dramatic difference in the man sitting in front of me. He spoke more freely, and with evident emotion in his face and in his voice. At moments during our sessions now, there were some tears, expressions of some anger, even joy at new discoveries about himself. Not hard to understand now, but the serendipity of my disagreement with Steven had cracked the dam that held back emotions compressed and buried from childhood. The catalyst was the topic, discipline of children. At that moment Steven acknowledged that he somehow felt that I was like his stepfather, and while walking the track had struggled with thoughts about whether or not I was or was not like his stepfather. It was as if we had lanced an emotional boil of anger and hatred. It began with the stepfather who terrified and brutalized him as a child, and then his mother who did not protect him from this monster, but who announced later that she intended to bring him back into their lives when he paroled. He expressed his anger at the police who talked to his parents at the hospital and accepted what they said and did nothing. He talked about how he began to get into trouble and the terrible experiences in juvenile hall and later in a California Youth Authority facility.

He did get his high school diploma, but on paper only. The facility's school wanted to get rid of him due to his angry outbursts. He told me that when he entered prison as a young adult, he was tested as having a sixth grade reading and writing level. He expressed that he felt rejected and abandoned, and became angry at a whole society who became his enemy and rejected by him in turn. Over the years, any emotions other than anger, he learned, were a sign of weakness and he had adopted control as his creed. He vowed that he was never going to be a victim again, but would control those around him through strength and fear.

With the confrontation of his anger and the source, putting it all in perspective, Steven could now allow himself to experience his other emotions in a new light. Over subsequent sessions with Steven, the person that began to emerge was so different that it began to amaze me in so far as his capacity for self-analysis. This included his analysis and understanding of the terrible crimes he had committed. As a result, he wrote a very profound letter to the community in which the crimes had been committed. In the letter he apologized to the families of his victims and to the community at large for the horror and fear he had caused, along with the sorrow and loss. The letter was so well composed and sensitive that I realized there was a remarkable intelligence emerging that had long been imprisoned behind his former hate.

A few months later, Steven, who had entered prison with only a sixth grade reading and writing ability, expressed interest in taking some college courses, but was wondering if he had the ability. I assigned an intern to give him some aptitude tests as well as a structured, highly valid test of intelligence level. I went over the results carefully as they were staggering.

Steven tested at the highest level of any inmate, I or any member of the staff had ever tested. He scored in the genius level of intellectual ability. This gave some degree of understanding about why I had not observed any of the sequelae that is usually encountered in someone who had been in a mental hospital for two years as a result of severe withdrawal from illicit drugs and associated cognitive distortions. Steven had not exhibited relapse into any symptoms that characterized his mental hospital stay since his entry into prison. This partially explained his great ability to deal with very abstract concepts in treatment. Steven did begin to take college courses and in time he obtained a four-year college degree by extension in prison. He has also learned several skills in prison, through work assignments and vocational training.

There is one other episode that occurred that revealed the depth of change in Steven that needs to be told. This was several months after psychotherapy with Steven had been terminated. Once again I received a written request from Steven to meet with me. He stated in the request that he had something very important to discuss with me.

Two months prior, there had been a rare occurrence at the California Medical Facility, a fatal stabbing of an older inmate in the institution. The investigation by the correctional staff had some strong suspects, but no proof against any of them. As usual, inmates claimed they had not seen anything. In our meeting, Steven informed me that he had witnessed the stabbing of the victim by three other inmates. He was walking past the cell of the victim, heading to his own cell, when he heard a commotion and saw through the window in the cell door the victim being stabbed. Apparently, during a brief unlock when the guard automatically unlocked all cells in the block, the three inmates had charged in on the victim, beat him and stabbed him, and got out of the cell prior to the relock. Steven had gone on to his own cell, and according to the inmate code, saw, heard or spoke nothing.

"It was an older inmate. He didn't deserve to die like that," Steven told me, with obvious sadness. "Before I would have given it no thought, but it really bothers me now. From our talks in therapy I look at things different. You taught me about social responsibility. I took from society. Now I feel that if I am the kind of person I think I am now, it is my duty to give something back, to do the responsible thing. I have decided after a lot of thought to give the names of the culprits to the Security and Investigation Unit. I wanted to tell you first."

I was initially thrown for a loss by Steven's revelation, and didn't know what to say. Both Steven and I knew the import of what he was about to do. At the moment I felt an intense fear for his welfare. But I reminded myself that it was not my decision. Steven's reasons contained strong elements of atonement, as well as the desire to prove to himself that he had changed from the antisocial animal he had once been, and that he had the strength to stand up for his new moral beliefs. Nonetheless, I cautioned him that other interpretations could and would be made, some that could be very negative. My big concern was that he was about to place himself in great jeopardy and I was unsure what protection the

114

administration could provide. Steven knew well enough that he would be labeled a "snitch" by fellow inmates, which in prison society is virtually a death sentence. It would make him the target of every young tough who wanted to "make his bones," that is, prove to other inmates he had what it takes, and thus gain their respect. Other inmates would "shine him on," act like he didn't exist, or show their disrespect in any manner they dared.

There was no possibility of anonymity, since Steven would be required to testify to what he witnessed in a court of law. Nonetheless, Steven had made his decision and after leaving my presence, did go to the Search and Investigation squad and report what he witnessed. Later, the head of the S and I squad shared with me his admiration of how Steven handled himself through the whole ordeal, but also shared my concerns about Steven's future. He assured me that he was going to do everything in his power to keep Steven safe. To my knowledge, he kept his word.

Over the ensuing years, Steven reported to me that only on one occasion did he have to violate his personal anti-violence code. While he was working out with weights one day, a young inmate walked up and pushed him aside. Steven recognized that this was a challenge and the young inmate's friends were closely watching. Steven turned and faced the young man and hit him, knocking him to the ground. He then looked directly at each of the inmate's friends. The young man got up and quickly left with his friends. The young inmate was later paroled, but sadly returned to prison in a short time. Steven has stuck to his risky decision and has survived, partially thanks to being housed in less violent units in prisons and given very important job assignments that have kept him away from the general population a lot. His work supervisors have been very impressed by his skills and have allowed him to do some very sensitive tasks.

In chapters to come I will refer to the five cases I have described herein. There are significant commonalities among these men that characterize the prison population in general. These common factors, together with the knowledge of important aspects of child development, have the potential to lead us into better prevention, and a realistic reduction of social aliens who require incarceration. I will repeat several times that the goal herein is not to excuse any criminal behaviors, but to try to understand the factors that led to those behaviors. Hopefully, the knowledge obtained will help us develop preventative programs and effective treatment measures to reduce the number of initial incarcerations as well as the reoffenders.

Six

Early Alienating Factors— The Path to Prison

Prediction of who will eventually commit a crime has not been successful overall. One general pattern has been accepted by many over time and seems to have a significant degree of validity from the standpoint of hindsight. However, as a predictor, there is little utility other than providing a source of increasing concern as it unfolds.

It begins with extensive bedwetting beyond the years of the establishment of normal controls, wherein there is no evidence of physical problems. The belief is that this occurs as the result of childhood emotional problems. The second alarm is repeated fire setting, which, it is theorized, exhibits a strong need for excitement. A third alarm factor is cruelty to animals, theorized to be evidence of decreased empathy and increased need to exercise power. These childhood behavioral acts are followed by actual antisocial behaviors that result in stints in juvenile halls, followed by increasing criminal acts that send the teenager to Youth Authority facilities. Prison comes into this pattern in late teens or early twenties. Prison inmates refer to these juvenile facilities as "gladiator schools" or "prep schools for prison."

To be sure, early signs of emotional and other adjustment problems followed by delinquent and criminal behavior are strong warnings of future crimes, and follows an old adage that the best predictor of future behavior is past behavior. The major problem here is recognition of the beginning factors. Many parents have no knowledge of child development and write off some early behaviors as normal, which often indicate actual problems that need special attention. In the case of a great number of children who grow up to become criminals, such behaviors are either ignored or seen as justification for extreme punishment. Sometimes parents unwittingly teach a child to become a criminal. But let us look at some examples.

Remember little Joey and his very early training program by his father? As a small child he was taught to fight by his father, even before he could comprehend why. Initially he feared his father, but quickly learned how he could appease him. Small children normally try to become like their models (usually parents) and can be observed to mimic their behaviors. This process is called *identification,* wherein the child strives to become like the parent or other significant adult in their lives. This process is enhanced by a second process termed *idealization.*

The naiveté of childhood perceives the parent as all-powerful, further encouraging the child to mimic the parent. The strength of this early training that expanded throughout his childhood and adolescence was so strong that Joey became unable to establish an identity separate from his father. His poem clearly illustrated this melded identity. His struggle to become his own person was only possible after his father's death. Only then could he begin to confront the fact that he did not want to continue as his father's vicious defender, and become aware of his own needs and wants.

The importance of fathers in their contributions to setting the foundation for who the child eventually becomes is too often not recognized and neglected. One's identity begins with the early processes of identification, and idealization, and mimicking of someone who gives guidance, protection, and attention. Children have a strong need for attention and approval. This is where they obtain validation of their worth, and further reinforcement of "proper" behaviors. Due to these needs, a child is very emotionally sensitive to the feeling tones of the parents and their interactions with each other.

The early childhood of Greg is an excellent example of how a child's needs can lead to a distorted identity when parents fail to become aware of what they are contributing (or not contributing) to the child's developing identity. Due to the friction between the parents, the family became divided. The father and older son bonded together to become one unit of the family. Mother, Greg's sisters, and Greg formed the other family unit. Greg gained attention and approval from his mother and sisters by allowing himself to be dressed and made up to look like them. This was probably an expression of anger at the father by his mother as clearly evidenced by the remark Greg recalled her making when the father and the oldest son returned from the outing together.

Even after the parents divorced, the father continued to take Greg's older brother to spend weekends and summer vacations, but not Greg. Strong feelings of rejection by his father and mother's continuing to reinforce Greg's emerging feminine behavior was all that got him any sense of worth. Again, we should not forget a symbolic aspect that one often encounters in such identification processes. That is, the seeking of attention, approval, and protection by an older male via sexual activities. It has been speculated that some male sexual liaisons are unconscious acting out of needs for male approval not received in childhood.

Billy provides an even more chaotic example of identity confusion. The divorce of his parents and abandonment by

119

them placed him at risk for confusion and distortion. Billy is a more extreme example in some ways. The early emotional acting out that often occurs in children who lose their parents and find themselves in the hands of strangers was misinterpreted at that time as evidence of a mental problem requiring hospitalization. So as a youngster, Billy ended up under the impersonal care of changing faces among a ward full of others suffering from various emotional and mental problems. Institutional staff became his substitute parents.

In the mental hospital, jails, and eventually prison, he won attention from others by either getting into trouble or by occasionally attaching himself to an authority figure with whom he established some level of trust. His life later remained chaotic, with patterns of behavior reflecting his developmental years.

He seemed constantly on the move and supported himself by occasional jobs. Later he told me about the only long-term relationship he had with a very passive, dependent young homosexual. Continuity was not a part of Billy's life except that he determined not to return to prison. His self-identification, for the most part, was as confused and fluid as his childhood. Stability was something he had not had and thus his lifestyle reflected a very fragmented identity as an adult. This is a very common pattern among repetitive criminal offenders. To many who had very chaotic childhoods that prevented any stable bonding with a parent figure, prisons became a refuge. In other words, the free society became a threat to them. Since they have never learned self-control, they seek out external control. I have had a number of such inmates admit that they feel a sense of relief when they get back to prison. Some have told me that they have fears and nightmares when out of prison. In prison they feel safe. The guards are checking on them, they are told when and what to do. It is common to hear them remark about how good it is to get back into their "routine." Their identity is that of a "good inmate" among other attributes they have picked up over time from fellow offenders.

This paradoxical relationship of resentment towards all authority and seeking out the external controls and highly structured environment of prison has been commented on by professionals working with non-criminal individuals. When individuals are dependent upon someone else due to physical conditions, financial circumstances, or other factors for years, it is not uncommon that they develop an underlying resentment of their dependency, unconsciously projecting that resentment onto the person upon whom they have been dependent. Thus, in the prison population, this factor serves to further enhance this paradoxical resentment/dependency factor among repeat career criminals.

John is another example of a firmly set identification. He learned as a child that he was going to have to deal with teasing from other boys. Therefore, he clearly identified himself as one who would respond to any challenge with physical force. Growing up he had few cultural opportunities to develop positive social skills. Rather, he, like many others, honed his fighting skills in youth facilities and ultimately prison. John was bright. His involvement in both the Chess Club and the Bridge Club evidenced his ability to pick up complex skills. Here again was the element of challenge, but in a socially acceptable way. He won tournaments in both clubs, and it was evident that he much enjoyed his contacts with the outside club members. This seemed to help him later in his effort to avoid criminal behaviors. Nonetheless, he remained involved in his work and social life after prison and accepted all challenges. He liked his forays dealing with what he termed "classier people," but was acutely aware that he didn't fit in. From the concerns that he expressed to me about the slow deterioration of his vision, I feel that it awakened those early childhood memories and fears that he might not be able to meet the challenge any more.

Finally, there is the case of Steven. Most readers will probably think that his childhood was a rare exception. Not so as I encountered so many men in prison that suffered extremely cruel punishment growing up as children. In these cases, frustrations, resentments, anger, rejection, and outright sadism were disguised and justified under the word "punishment" by the parental figure. Compensations for underlying inadequacies on the part of the parent figure often were assuaged by exercising extreme power and methods of control over the defenseless child, as well as other family members. All of these motivations ignored or distorted any beneficial impact on the child and instead passed on to the child anger, resentment, and rejection towards all authority figures. Again, the impact on the child's identity often took the form of what professionals term "identification with the aggressor." In lay terms, this can be described as "When I get big enough, I will be the boss."

While I have described Steven's nightmare childhood, I received many years later a letter from Steven telling me that his younger brother recently contacted him and revealed that he was having some emotional problems which emanated from childhood memories. This had inspired Steven to write a description of a typical incident in their childhood, capturing it as closely as possible from the perspective of their child view. I share it with you, the reader.

"The Closet," by Steven

There are a great many things to be discovered while locked in a closet—a slice of juicy orange wrapped in a napkin, stowed in a forgotten shoe by a panic-stricken sister, its sweet nectar biting at open wounds, yet somehow cradling the soul just moments later; last night's blood caked in a crevice, a corner; dangling pants legs and swimming shirt-sleeves which whisper like toys but shout with pain when touched; the wondrous relief to muscle and bone when stretched to meet the cool comfort of a hardwood floor. You'd be surprised at the lies told in dark confines.

In the beginning, it takes too much energy to search for either salvation or joy. Time is measured while shifting from one cheek to another, the relief an amazing gift. It's more difficult not to move your neck or arms or draw a breath or taste the salt on your lips, or wonder at the bruise just above your eye, afraid of the truth. Have you never been terrified that the door will slide open?

He was such a great guy in the beginning!

Abandoned by Dad long ago, this new Dad changed the world. He had a good job, there was plenty of food on the table, finally, and he made Mama laugh. She had stopped doing that. This new Dad, well, they laughed and giggled about secret things when the door to their bedroom was closed. My brothers and sisters and I thought it very unfair that we weren't allowed to share in all the fun.

He's coming! Two loud, screaming steps from his room to the carpeted hallway, a turn of the knob, a pang grabs at my chest, the door slides, rips open.

"Are you sure you know what you did wrong, boy?"

"Yes sir!" A panicked reply falls from my lips. "I'm very very sure!"

"Don't test my patience, boy," he says, smiling, the tone quickly followed by a boot to my naked leg. "You just stay in there a while longer and see if you can come up with something better."

Something better?

Desperation is surely discovered in dark places. Panic

holds your hand. He'll be back, and I must have the right answer.

While waiting, pains need to be hidden, so other marvelous distractions fill the void: spiders and bugs and mice and other such crawly things. In the beginning I could feel them plotting against me. In time, we began to speak to each other—they want to live as well, you know. Dark nights used to be filled with voices and scares and monsters and little else, but no more. I now know every inch of my haven: eight of my legs long, three and a half wide, taller than I can imagine. A small hole, peaked in one corner, where my crawly friends come and go at will. Hanging things that tickle my skin. Shoes where Kathy and Michael and Terry hide tasty treats. Rolled-up socks that make perfect pillows. A small cat's-eye marble to roll against the wall, quietly. Robyn sometimes inches her way, so bravely, into the darkness to hold me at night. She's the youngest. I discovered fear for her. Terry, the sullen one, drinking in messages of hate, blows me a kiss when the monster isn't looking.

He was such a great guy in the beginning!

We'd all jump into the '59 DeSoto and head for places unknown, the beach our favorite. Sand in the toes. Water that hugs your skin and makes you feel a part of something bigger in the same instant. We'd bury him in the sand, laughing. I should have left him there. Five children as happy as larks. The future a mystery, a curse. The beach, the Grand Canyon, Irvin Park, mystical journeys like *Father Knows Best*. He bought us sleeping bags and water guns and lots of candy.

The door quietly slides open. I didn't hear him coming, socks on his feet. His power rips me into the air. He slams me into the back of the bedroom door. Rope eats at my underarms as he twists it and me to fit his needs. My toes scream, beg to reach the wooden Coke-bottle box that prevents me from hanging like a chunk of meat. His huge body jams against my little penis, it hurts so much. Still today.

"I just don't think you understand, boy," the rasp in his voice makes everything clear. "Now you just sit here" (sit here?) "and think about your sins. The only way you'll understand God's will is to think about your sins."

He was such a great guy in the beginning!

One time he found me and my brothers playing in the front yard just as the Good Humor man drove by with his truck filled with ice cream goodies. It was like being sixteen and watching a car full of pretty girls waving and smiling as if you were the only boy on earth. His six foot five frame flew past us as if on wings. He turned in mid-flight and said, "You boys just going to sit there?" We launched into his arms. Ice cream sandwiches, my favorite.

Michael is crying on the other side of the door. The devil has gone to work on his car, his parting remarks clear. "You have to understand, boy. This is for your own good."

"Michael," I whisper, "it's going to be okay." His tears reach through the door to embrace, clutch me.

"But he's hurting you again," his trembling voice still cries inside me. Got to be brave. What is brave? I'm twelve, but he's nine.

"He'll leave in the morning for work, Michael. You can come back and get me then." I try my best to sound calm, but I can hear, feel him bouncing his tiny forehead off the door. "Please, Michael, he'll come back." Little feet rush away. There's no sound so pleasing, so painful. Alone!

It's funny, but when you're hanging from the top of a door, ropes burning every place they touch, feet barely able to reach the raft below, the closer doesn't send cold shivers. ". . . for your own good." A familiar retort. "God has sent me to straighten you out, boy," the most troubling.

In the first nine years of life God loved all of His chil-

125

dren. Church was filled with caring, warm people who hugged all the time. I pretended not to like it, but, well, you know. Whatever happened to that God? And why is this one trying so hard to hurt me? I hate this God. Those other people lied—God doesn't answer your prayers. No one does.

Thoughts of the first time the police came to investigate the screams came to my head. "You just sit here, son, and tell me everything," the smiling policeman said. I did. The closet, hangings, ice-cube baths, whipping, punches, ropes, bruises teachers can't or don't want to see, the time he made us eat Number 2 because Terry, then five, had pooped his pants (you'd mess yours too if someone the size of a truck smacked you across your face). The pains suffered when I tried to stop him. I told the smiling policeman everything, everything. I even cried.

I stood in the doorway of our house and watched them drive away. His massive hands clutched my shoulders, the pain forcing me ever closer to the ground. They turned the corner, out of sight, out of mind. I was hurled across the room. The front door slammed shut, it's ring a permanent part of my soul.

"He's only a boy!" my mother cried. He knocked her to the floor. I stood to face him, help her, the action barely a movement, when darkness fell. Last thoughts screamed through the pain—why did they leave? I told them everything. I even cried.

Small children learn very quickly, you know. The seeds of a conspiracy began to grow within me—Him, God, the smiling policemen, the teachers who did nothing, the mother who never left him. The screams continued, the smiling policemen came again and again. I told them nothing. I never cried. My mother continued to laugh with him behind the bedroom door, at me, I bet. Her touch slowly meant nothing as if lost on retreating winds.

He was such a great guy in the beginning!

Terry fell into a bed of roses, once, he came like Superman. His giant feet made fast work of sticky bushes. Terry was free of thorns quicker than a flash. The tenderness of this man assaulted the senses. Terry's pain meant something to him, that day. Standing in the hot summer sun, I watched what was supposed to be, wondering why the bruise on my left thigh wouldn't heal so I could go back to school. I wondered if he'd hold me like that if I . . .

"You thinking about your sins, boy?" His maddening voice pushed beneath my thoughts. A hard bang on the door knocked the Coke box from my feet. I scream as my body drops into the air. He pushes his way in, settles me in place, and lies, "This hurts me far worse than it does you, Steven."

Time is like the last fifteen minutes of the school day when the feeling begins to slowly ebb from your arms and shoulders. How long as it been? An hour? Two? Three? I've got to get away. I know what he'll do to me, but anything is better than this.

I listen for his footsteps. The carpeted hallway betrays him, little squeaks. I kick the Coke box free, screams enter my throat, refuse to leave. I slam my heels into the door, he pushes it open, catching me suddenly. From side to side he twists and turns me violently. Dreams begin to shake out of my head. And somewhere between four or five or ten or twenty the moment I woke curled in a corner of my haven, I had this thought—I've got to kill this asshole.

Thoughts of death and violence where toys and bubble gum should be, are we born to kill? Am I all the things he says I am? Sinner? Worthless? I know where he keeps the gun. How do I shoot him? Where? How many times? I'm all the things he says I am.

He'll be coming back before he goes to work, I can't afford yet another trip to the hospital. Even heroin, recently discovered, failed to ease the dread. It worked so well in the beginning. The older boy who knew of my plight and felt the rage of his own father's insanity made me a promise.

"It'll make you sleep. It will help you not care. There won't be a single bad dream." His vacant eyes spoke the truth. He said the first fix might make me sick, I wish it had. By the third or fourth I could ram steel into my arms and fall to a safer place without help, regard.

He was such a great guy in the beginning!

I've got to get out of here. As quiet as someone gazing at the night sky, I dressed, painfully, listening real careful like, sliding the door open. He had rigged a bell to warn him of such "evil" but I wasn't stupid—I found a way to silence it long ago. The window was just as easy. I slid into the night, free, unafraid of the darkness.

I hopped the backyard fence like a wounded gazelle, making the railroad tracks in several excruciating leaps. It's hard to explain how free air injects power and hope into the body of the dead. Little whispers of something better become shouts as first feet, then yards and miles fall away. Even a sudden plunge or trip leading to agonizing reminders fail to temper the joy. I am gone. I am in control. I ran through orange groves, past Old Lady Martin's house, through the schoolyard, finally settling with wondrous relief in the drainage ditch at the old electric way station. Home. I could hide here forever.

Like a snowball rolled down a hillside, the plan to kill him grew. I was as ugly as he was to me. I imagined great floods of blood, his blood, streaming without pause or mercy from his dying remains. I saw him beg for compassion, ask for forgiveness, call upon his God for help. I dreamed of his pain and found great comfort, as my own wounds healed, in the thought that he would soon know my suffering.

Weeks went by, I stole to survive. Cold nights were

warmed with visions of revenge, justice, his pain. But, like finding nothing at the bottom of the cookie jar, he evaded my grief. In the days that followed my flight for life, my mother pretended to go insane with worry. The police were called, the bruises, the cuts, the fear and cries of desperate children finally made the authorities take notice. An investigation discovered blood in the closet, and ropes and belts and instruments of terror hanging like Norman Rockwell paintings from my bedroom door. Seasoned veterans were said to have cried at the truth revealed. I never believe that. And oh, by the way, he had another family some distance away. His other wife and other kids, never beaten, were shocked, disbelieving. I wasn't.

On one of my many treks home to feel the warmth of my brothers and sisters, I was lured into my mother's lying arms. So many "I'm sorry's" had little effect on a weakened heart. My arms couldn't hold her back. Something dies inside when your mother no longer matters. Try as hard as you can, her smell, once a call of serenity, is now like the stranger who steals a hug at the supermarket.

I testified at his trial. I gave them plenty of details, too. I looked him straight in the eyes unafraid, terrified. I just knew that he'd get sent away for life. The judge found him guilty, bigamy, two years in prison. He had spent three filling my heart with hate. No mention made of closets, ropes, beatings, humiliations, lost dreams, or children crying themselves to sleep. No mention made of a little boy banging his head on the back of a bedroom door, or little girls scared for their brother's life, or a sullen child blowing kisses into the night. For me, the etched impressions of formal proceedings leading to nothing ripped at the last fiber in the back of every child's head that just knows, instinctually, that every adult is a savior. Feeling betrayed has a funny way of crystallizing seeds planted many beatings ago.

Two months later my mother drove me in the '59 DeSoto to what turned out to be the parking lot of the prison where he was being held. We seemed the only car there on an early Saturday morning. I could smell him.

"Honey," the betrayer's voice began. "I know you won't understand, but I've decided to help John turn his life around and let him come home."

You know exactly how I felt, don't you? Can you hear my little heart beginning to race? Can you see the stare of dread as I search my mother's eyes for the joke this obviously has to be? Disconnected from the moment, you know what that feels like, don't you? "I know you don't want to come in," she continued. I only half heard "So I'll be back in a little while. Everything will be okay, Steven. He's changed." Liar!

I've got to get out of here. Her figure disappears ever so slowly, fading like so many dreams, out of sight, out of mind. Her purse rests under the seat, I grab it, take what I need. The heat through the window assaults me. Blue and gold upholstery turns hot to the touch. Visions of tortured nights and Kathy and Michael and Terry and Robyn rush to the surface.

My hands begin to tingle. I reach under the cuff of my pant leg and fumble for the makings that will drive the pending disaster away: a little piece of China White, my sister's baby spoon, a cold Zippo lighter, and a rig as sharp as my fears. A few minutes later, warmth enters my body as steel melts into my arm. Nothing matters. There's safety in warm places.

Little beads of sweat sting my eyes. Memories of the closet scream at me, muted but still there. I've got to get out of here. He'll never, no one will ever hurt me again. I open the car door, felt my bottom, somehow still sore, slip from the seat as my legs and feet begged the ground for attention. I looked across the steaming asphalt, nothing in sight. My enemies were everywhere, it doesn't matter which direction I take.

One step follows another. I begin to run. There's that freedom again. One look back, a '59 DeSoto fades quickly, quietly. No one will ever hurt me again!

He was such a great guy in the beginning!

I doubt that many who read Steven's story can fail to recognize the source of Steven's intense anger, his rejection of authority and general mistrust. Not untypically, all these underlying identity sources are enhanced by the dangerous street drugs used to escape from the realities of their lives. The lack of trust prevents the sharing of any underlying feelings, or needs, fears such as "weakness," another commonly shared feature in the criminal culture.

Self-identity is common to all humans. It is expressed in our strong beliefs and behaviors, and occasionally expressed in thought or words, as "I'm the kind of person who . . ." or, "I'm not the kind of person who . . ." It is our own internal belief of who we are, our capabilities, our attitudes towards others, our personal values. Trust determines how much of this identity we share with any other human. Severe distortions, that mis-shape and alienate one from the larger social culture in which one is born and raised are labeled as personality or character disorders by clinical professionals.

There is another element commonly found among many criminal offenders—poor impulse control. Again, all of us humans are born impulsive. Normally, we learn throughout our childhood and adolescence to control our impulses, learn connections between our behavior and its consequences, learn that others have feelings that we need to consider, and other social adaptive skills that allow us to function with minimal friction with others.

In contrast, many criminal offenders operate on raw

impulse. They want something, they take it with little empathy for others or with shallow rationalizations that their victims have insurance to cover their loss, or are rich enough to replace it. Projecting blame onto the victim has been mentioned before. That is, it becomes the victim's fault because they didn't follow some self-serving script that the perpetrator later uses to justify his behavior. With this lack of empathy and respect of others and their property, there is a much deeper lack of self-respect, which they deny to themselves, and indulge in compensatory behaviors. This involved hypersensitivity to anything they interpret as disrespect from anyone else towards them. The need for power and control over others is another compensation for underlying fears and self-doubts.

The general public reacts with incredulousness to the impulsive lack of planning type offenses committed by some criminals, and the rationales they offer. As I said before, their thinking often makes one think that they consider the rest of society as deaf, dumb and blind. But again, we need to remember that the developmental process in these cases began early in life and was reinforced by similar peers and authority figures in juvenile and adult facilities.

I have often heard comments by people that all children who had traumatic childhoods do not end up as criminals, and some who had good childhoods do. Yes, these cases do exist. As to the former, they were lucky to later become exposed to positive adult role models such as foster parents, relatives who took them into their homes, and other sources of guidance that allowed them to adapt to society at large. It would be of value to have more studies of these exceptions.

As to those with more normal childhoods, I have had some of those in my own caseloads in the past. There was one young inmate that appeared to meet this criterion. He was raised in an intact family with a younger sister. He was never abused or neglected. After the birth of his younger sibling, the mother was pretty focused on caring for her daughter. The father could well be described as a "pillar of the community." He was a successful businessman and was involved in community activities. Nonetheless, the son began to get involved in petty thefts and vandalism which escalated to his first felony offense for which he was sent to prison. Again, I met the parents in the visiting room at their son's request. It was evident that they were very concerned about their son. I was hard pressed to understand how the son had become involved in crime. As our therapy sessions progressed, the young man began to reveal some unusual clues. He described how each time he was arrested as a juvenile, his father would be called to the police station to pick him up. When the father arrived to pick him up, the father would castigate him in front of the officers for his bad behavior, and express how disappointed he was that his son would do such things. However, after they left the police station and were driving home, the father's emotional tone changed along with the conversation between them. The father would ask details about what the boy did, showing evident excitement as the boy related how and what he did. I noted the expression on the young man's face as he recalled these incidents as if he was recalling happy memories. Finally, I made my interpretation of what he was telling me. I told him that I was aware that his father was a very fine example to the community and his family. But underneath he had a need for adventure and excitement that he never allowed himself. "When you got into trouble he experienced adventure and excitement through your escapades with the police. This sharing with your father gave you a sense of closeness and attention from your father." I paused for his reaction to what I had said. There was a quiet moment in which he looked down and cupped his head in his hands.

His response when he raised his head and looked at me surprised me. It came in form of a plea, "I know you are right, but please, please don't tell my Dad, he couldn't handle it!"

He then explained that he had begun getting attention by playing the class clown in school in late childhood. By high school he had become more daring, drawing not only attention from police and other strangers, but most important, his sharing these adventures with his father made the bond between them stronger.

In the chapters to follow I will share with you other examples of the impacts of adults on children that carry over into adult behavior. It should be noted, as in the example above, that the intent of the parent does not always get interpreted by the child as the parent believes or intends. An example of this was that of a young rapist assigned to my caseload. He had been convicted of two separate rapes in which he had used excessive, violent force. During our initial sessions I was at a loss to understand the source of his need to overpower and exercise such forceful control over his female victims. He claimed that he had good parents who had never abused him, gave him good guidance, and sounded like good parents overall. One day he asked if I could come to the visiting room to meet his parents at their next regular visit. I agreed to do so and joined him and his parents at a table in the large visiting room of the facility. After introductions, the mother began to talk about the family. Within the next fifteen to twenty minutes I had the answer to my dilemma about his rapes.

The mother was a very dominating and controlling woman, and the father was a very passive and non-assertive man. Within the short time of the visit she made several denigrating remarks about her husband. He just smiled and generally said nothing. The son, however, interceded on behalf of his father each time, and was obviously upset by these remarks about his father.

In another case I saw, the inmate also came from a middle class family with high expectations of their two sons. In our sessions he recalled making a resolution to himself when he was about nine years old. He had overheard on several occasions his older brother, who was a teenager at the time, having arguments with the parents. My young inmate recalled that he vowed to himself that he would avoid such confrontations by doing everything right. To a large extent he was successful, developing much self-control. He was a good student and athlete in high school. He dated a neighbor girl and became closely involved with her family. In spite of his accomplishments, he did not socialize easily with other students. His girlfriend, however, was very socially adept and became his entrée into high school social activities. When her family took vacations they often invited the boy to join them. This happy picture began to change in the middle of the last year in high school.

It began when the boy had his first major disagreement with his father. The boy wanted to attend a Western college so he could maintain contact with his girlfriend. His father was insistent that the boy attend an Eastern Ivy League university. The second problem arose when the boy was hoping to obtain a football scholarship, and had asked his coach to write a letter of recommendation in his behalf. After two weeks wherein the busy coach had not yet written the requested recommendation, the boy reacted uncharacteristically. In a fit of anger and spite, he stole the coach's typewriter and hid it. Later he forged a couple of his SAT scores that he felt were too low for him to get into the college of his choice.

To make matters worse for the young man, the parents of his girlfriend had decided that the couple were getting too involved too young, and needed to focus more on their respective college careers. That summer they did not invite the boy to join them when they went on their vacation. They apparently utilized the vacation time to convince their daughter that she should focus on her college plans and date other boys for a while. After the family returned from vacation the young man noticed some changes in his girl-friend's attitude towards him. They had both selected the same college to attend. At the end of their first week on cam-pus, they had a confrontation. She told him that they should not see so much of each other and should date others. He claims he told her that if she did that he would quit the foot-ball team. But she did not relent and the argument contin-ued. He claimed that he had taken a gun from her father's extensive gun collection and given it to her their first day at college for protection on a strange campus. He further claimed that during the argument, she produced the gun he gave her from her purse, and that it accidentally discharged and killed her on the spot. He said he picked up the gun and ran, threw the gun into some water, then returned to his col-lege dorm.

Such cases as these I just described are rare exceptions. The vast majority of those who end up in prison, as stated, are products of abuse and neglect, "street raised" is a com-mon term many use to sum up their developmental years. A large number of criminal offenders are products of un-wanted or unplanned births, by parents who were products themselves of chaotic childhoods and unresolved emotional issues. Early attachments were too often short-lived, with frequent passage back and forth between biological parents, relatives, foster homes, group homes, thus fragmenting at best a child's early social learning, developing sense of iden-tity, and consistent learning. A typical example of this type of childhood and its impact is the following case example who I will call Larry.

Larry's father left the family when Larry was an infant. Mother, who was an alcoholic, rejected Larry, and he was first placed in a foster home at age two. He remained there until age nine when he was returned to his mother. The records reported that even after Larry was returned to his mother, she still was unpredictable with drinking episodes during which she beat Larry and her six other children, and would often embarrass them before their friends with disparaging remarks. He had difficulty in school due to learning problems that were not addressed. As an adolescent, he was arrested several times for offenses such as joyriding, petty theft, and burglary. At age fourteen, he began using alcohol and experimented some with drugs. He began exhibiting more severe signs of mental problems in his early twenties and was hospitalized on two occasions following suicide attempts, one by slashing his arms, and the other by attempting to hang himself. His offense of manslaughter involved a stabbing of another man. The victim, clad in undershorts, was stabbed several times. Larry, who police described as having slash wounds on one side and both forearms, together with scratches on the side of his neck and biceps, stated to them that "The man tried to rape me and I stabbed him." Examination by three psychiatrists after his arrest found that Larry was suffering from severe emotional problems and was functionally impaired. Two of them found him capable to stand trial, while one found that he was too impaired to cooperate in a rational manner in his defense.

The records indicated that Larry had attended a party prior to the incident, and was under the influence of alcohol and the drug PCP. The offense occurred in the victim's apartment at 4:00 A.M., and discovered after Larry panicked and set a fire in a wastebasket which ignited some drapes.

Prior to his assignment to my caseload, Larry was given a thorough evaluation, including a battery of psychological tests. His intelligence test indicated a borderline level of intellectual functioning. However, it also indicated normal potential and that the deficits were in keeping with people who suffered from attention disorder, with deficits in planning, organization, and sequencing materials due to inability to focus their attention. He was physically coordinated and possessed good social perception with some social skills. Other tests indicated that he had characteristics of what was sometimes referred to as a "burnt child syndrome." That is, while he sought approval and was sometimes very naive and trusting, when he formed an emotional attachment he became very fearful and suspicious, developing paranoid fantasies based on past abuse and betrayals.

When I began to work with Larry, these characteristics were very evident. He was given medication to help calm his racing thoughts so that he could better focus his attention. As I began working with Larry it became clear that he was capable of being insightful and perceptive when not under pressure from environmental or internal emotional stress. He became a very rewarding case to work with in treatment. It was evident that while he was initially very suspicious, he had a strong need to talk to someone about his fears and conflicts.

Larry enrolled in school. Initially he tested at the sixth grade level academically. He began to bring me his "Certificates of Achievement" as he completed class after class. He also brought me other things that revealed his insights into his internal conflicts and attachment needs. The first was a remarkable sketch he made picturing two overlapping faces. The lower face was agonizing and in flames and overlapped a more normal face, but with an expression also of distress. Twice he brought me pictures of a puppy. The first was a cut-out from a newspaper. The puppy had his nose and paws poking through a chain link fence, obviously looking winsomely at someone or something. The second one was a picture card of a puppy. Above the picture he had written his name with an arrow pointing down at the puppy pictured on the card. On the card was an imprinted question, "If I followed you home, would you keep me?"

I would say that treatment outcome with Larry represents at least a partial success. He was not able to achieve two of his major goals as a result of his learning disabilities and his severe emotional problems. He wanted very much to obtain his GED in school, and to be able to live on his own. Due to his panic reactions under stress, and organic impairments (it was later found out that he also suffered a brain injury as a youth when a hammer bounced off a tree stump and struck him in the head, knocking him unconscious), including his learning disabilities. I wrote a report that later qualified him to receive ongoing care upon his release from prison under SSI benefits. His last note remained one of hopes and doubts.

There are several lessons to be learned from Larry's case. First, studies done by clinical staff clearly found that incidents of learning disabilities and other brain defects occurred in a much higher proportion among the criminal population than that reported in the non-criminal population. While this was a survey rather than a controlled study, we were not sure if the differences were significant. However, since then numerous studies have shown that alcohol and drug abuse by mothers do increase the frequency of birth defects which results in various levels and types of brain dysfunction. Larry's mother was an alcoholic before and after his birth. The confusing factor here, possibly, is the later blow to his head. There was no information in his record or reported by Larry of any differences in his abilities before or after this event.

Secondly, his childhood of parental abandonment, foster homes and reunification with his alcoholic mother is one frequently encountered in the backgrounds of criminal offenders, and illustrated in some of the cases I previously cited. Research studies have long cited the damage from such changes in caregivers to a child's ability to identify and emotionally attach to another person. Larry's emotional neediness and deep mistrust of others, with deep fears of betrayal, is frequently found among criminal offenders who have not been able to effectively seal off all deeper emotions. The major difference between Larry and many others that end up in prisons is that the underlying unresolved emotions are not only fear, but anger.

Thirdly, the effort to confront and understand these underlying emotions is difficult and often threatening to the individual. Larry reacted to this threat with confusion and fear. Technically we say that such a person lacks sufficient ego-strength. In simple terms such a person lacks a sufficient sense of self-identity to question this adaptive facade. The struggle is again illustrated by the following description given to me by another inmate, who was struggling through his early weeks of psychotherapy. Although he was much stronger psychologically than Larry, the struggle to confront himself was still difficult as evident in what he stated to me. Inmate talking about feelings in prison is why he is reluctant to reveal any of his feelings to anyone.

"You know, the problem in here is that 'the man' is not really the enemy. We have to fight ourselves. You can't trust the 'blues'. If you show any feelings, it's taken as weakness by your own fellow inmates who will fuck over you. If the guards were really our enemy, we could ban together. We'd stay out of these places. Hell no, he represents food, shelter and all

140

that goes with it. Most of the time he don't mess with you unless you ask for it."

It is obvious that this man was better educated and more able to express himself than many inmates. The element of depression is not uncommon during this early stage of therapy and before. Depression is often described as anger turned inward, and it has been found that among murderers one often finds records of prior suicide attempts. This suggests that underlying anger can be alternatively turned outward or inward. Clinical staff became well aware of the dangers of tapping into that underlying anger, either to themselves (recall my experience of tapping into Steven's repressed anger), and to the inmate in terms of possibly triggering a suicide risk.

One more example of this struggle was expressed to me by another inmate in his attempt to evaluate himself. The man had the typical childhood and adolescence of criminal offenders I described earlier—at age three parents divorced, ward of the court at age thirteen, foster homes, and California Youth Authority. Narcotics and stormy marital situations characterized his non-institutional life.

The occasion of his writing a self-evaluation occurred during his second year of therapy with me and his approaching appearance before the Parole Board for parole consideration. He expressed concern about my forthcoming report to the Parole Board on his progress in the program. I suggested that he write out an evaluation of how he viewed his progress and readiness for parole. The following is the result of his attempt to evaluate himself. In his effort to be objective, he wrote it in the third person:

"I have never written about myself, or then maybe I have when I was writing poetry. I suppose I am to evaluate who I am and what gains I have made in psychotherapy. Who is Ron? Big question, but how should it be answered? It would be easy to say that he is a very scared person, and a very alone or lonely person. He has never had a very secure or a very good feeling of being secure since he was very young. His father was seldom there, in fact he doesn't even know his father really. He does remember being mistreated by him. In fact, a very severe beating was given him at the age of four or five. He remembers this well. He wonders if this may have any link to the beatings he gave to his stepchildren. Perhaps getting back at them the way his father did him. It could also have been the attention they were getting from the mother in which he felt he was entitled. That seems to be the way it's been all his life. Everything for Ronald, fuck everyone else. But why the molesting of a child? Can it be explained? There is no justification. His knowledge of what came down is shallow. He was high on heroin which was not uncommon for him.

"This early addiction to drugs or education to drugs started at about twelve or thirteen. He's tried everything from weed and pills to acid and stuff on heroin. To him there's no greater escape in the world than drugs. Maybe I should rephrase the above statement, for he has found other means to escape if he wishes, such as landing in prison. He never wanted to face reality, but during the past two years, one month and twenty-one days he finds reality is what you make of it."

At this point Ronald describes how he has observed other inmates and has talked mostly with older convicts, "Because they have most of the answers about life. In me they see themselves twenty or thirty years before, and when they look at me they shake their heads as if to say there I was and here I am now. I get sick for I don't want to be like them. I know that in order for me not to be I must change and change and change. I've started my progression and now I feel I know the way. I'm not saying my head is perfectly straight for no one is that straight in mind. I am saying I have made goals and I have and will stay away from heroin or any drug that will bend my mind. I value my freedom and will not, having earned it back, sell it for a bag of dope. I've done my share of existing out there and now I'm ready to live.

"Responsibility the key word, huh. He hated it, he hated it, he felt the world owed him a living. Why should he be responsible for anything but himself? Ronald was a child and remained one for fourteen years. So he felt he had no responsibility for anything. At fifteen he graduated from a child to an immature animal, taking what he wanted and giving nothing in return. At eighteen he became a full-grown piece of shit, hurting everyone especially the ones who cared, such as his family and his wife or wives. He didn't look at these women as women, but as objects to keep his arm or mind well fed.

"He now has since learned to respect women the way they should be, and also that they're not just something to use and throw away. I can now talk to a woman although at times I find it hard to think of what to say. When learning to talk on an adult level, it is quite a trip!

"Violence potential—at present time very very low. Not because of the controlled setting as stated once before, but because there is no longer a need for drugs which induced his violence. The man is tired of hurting people, both physically and mentally. Now he wants to help others, especially the kids in their early teens who are involved or getting involved with drugs. Drugs have ruined his life and he does not wish to see others ruin theirs.

"Goals—there are perhaps many. To maintain my freedom, to help others as I have been helped, to keep and maintain a job no matter if it be cleaning toilets in a service station or washing dishes. To get to know my son and daughter as well as my brother, mother and sister. For these are the people I will turn to if ever I feel down and out, along with Dr. Mattocks and different individuals of seventh steps. If given a date, I hope it to be a contingency basis, the contingency to keep in therapy till time of release."

I think most of those reading Ronald's self-evaluation could tell that he was not yet ready for parole and the free community. While he had begun to look at what he was doing to himself and those who cared about him in the past, he remained oblivious of the basis for his behaviors. He blamed it all on his drug abuse with no recognition of his underlying strong dependency needs and anger at those who did not, in his eyes, sufficiently take care of him. He still has a long way to go but there were encouraging flickers of awareness in his self-evaluation that indicate at some emotional level he knew this.

In these past chapters I have given you some of the things that were learned from extensive work with criminal offenders. I have included numerous examples of a spectrum of criminal offenders with whom I directly worked. I feel very fortunate to have been involved in research about different program efforts to rehabilitate criminal offenders. While the era was perhaps the golden era of rehabilitation, prisons were still very harsh places where extreme punishment was the prevailing tool. Other types of efforts were small, scattered, and lacking major support within the environment and the society at large. It would be most accurate to sum up all the programs at the time and since as too little, too late. Only a minority of the prison population was exposed to any rehabilitative effort and it was generally done in a hostile environment. Many inmates adapted to this hostile environment, once again a testimony to human adaptability. To these inmates, prison became another escape from an alien world where they had developed no self-control or means of adaptation.

Even during my extensive contacts with adult male offenders, I heard many stories about their adolescent experiences in California Youth Authority facilities. These facilities established patterns of behavioral codes that prepared their youthful charges for adaptation to future life in prisons, rather than learning how to adapt in free society. The primary goal that most of these youths had already learned from their chaotic childhoods was survival. Those who had not learned this before entering these facilities were terribly victimized. When the "counselors" were not around, a hierarchy was quickly established and maintained among the imprisoned boys. The bigger, older youths took over. Fights would break out as the more aggressive boys tried to establish control over others. The younger boys often became the followers who tried to ingratiate themselves with the older leaders. The small and weaker youths became the slaves and their constant humiliation served to keep others in line.

One young man in his twenties gave me a very vivid description of a nightmare memory that had a strong impact on his later life. It was shortly after the first time he entered a youth detention facility at the age of fourteen. The dormitories were divided by partitions that extended slightly more than the length of the beds from the walls of the dorm. There would be a partition, then four beds, then another partition, followed by four more beds, throughout the arrangement of the dorm. He recalls early one morning before wake-up call, that he was awakened by whispering noises. As it continued, he crawled to the foot of his metal cot and looked around the adjacent partition. What he saw was a large boy dressed in underwear and undershirt leading a smaller, naked boy. The small naked boy wore a ring on one finger through which passed a string by which the bigger youth led him from bed to bed, stopping when someone in one of the beds expressed interest in the naked boy. The small boy then serviced the interested youths in whatever sexual manner they desired, in return for canteen scrip given to the small boy's guide or "owner."

My inmate patient told me that he was so horrified by what he saw that he vowed to himself that nobody was ever going to treat him disrespectfully. He became a fighter, spending as much time as he could learning boxing. It was later, of course, that the defensive attitude became offensive and landed him in prison as an adult. Survival and demand for respect are words repeated like mantras by repeat criminal offenders. They develop an aggressive pattern of demanding respect in order to survive or feel secure.

Then what about the violent world of youth and adult prisons as deterrents against returning again and again to these places? As has been illustrated, the childhoods of the vast majority of criminal offenders were never guided toward mature thinking and emotional control. Reasoning ability remains at a pre-logic level. The survival fears and compensatory aggression remain their principal goals. The underlying anger alienates them from mainstream free society, while at the same time reacts like a weathervane dependent upon triggering factors of the moment, turning inward or outward. Having little self-control to protect themselves, they are prone to find some level of security in absolute external control. Security simply can become a matter of establishing a program "routine" while in prison, maintaining a fearless, aggressive facade, gathering a few "home boys" around you and avoiding "hot spots" within the prison where troubles tend to occur.

Periods of parole can become nothing more than breaks in routine or short vacations from restricted prison life. When outside society and its demands get too much, you simply "buy a ticket" back to prison. That is very simple—get caught using or possessing drugs, commit a burglary or maybe just shoplift, anything that violates the conditions of your parole. It is this life and world of aliens that separate from mainstream free society.

The illogical, simplistic reasoning of repeat criminal and first criminal offenders is very obvious when examined closely. The underlying anger that continually shapes their lives perhaps is not always obvious. But aren't these same factors present in all humans? When you and I hear about a horrendous crime, don't we respond with some thoughts about the revenge that should be perpetrated on the person who did such an awful thing? I confess that sometimes, especially when it involves a brutal crime against a child, I think about some methods used by our medieval ancestors.

Then there is the general tendency toward illogical reasoning which continues to be of great bounty for politicians. When a certain crime or type of crime gets widespread public attention, the cry for increased penalties drowns out all logic. In spite of examples of the ineffectiveness of punishment over the centuries, most in this country see it as a deterrent and avengement on those who disrespect the laws we live by. These ideas, if given too much consideration, might lead us into some very uncomfortable discoveries. So to avoid that, we just lock them (criminals) up and throw away the key, out of sight, out of mind. Let us see where that leads us, in the next chapter.

Seven

How the Winds Changed— Trends over Time

In the very early part of the Twentieth Century, the criminal justice systems in this country seemed to be of little or no concern to the general public. Aside from an occasional notorious crime, most crimes only came to the attention of locals where they occurred. Prisons were few, and consisted of dark, foreboding-looking structures, most often located in some relatively isolated place. Local jails were small, and, with few exceptions, used to house miscreants for short periods of time. To the average citizen, these symbols of crime occupied little thought or concern.

However, the "Roaring Twenties" filled with more forms of crimes, and new media tools such as radios, better photography, and motion pictures, as well as our changing society, crime was brought to the forefront of public attention. Prohibition laws, mobster organizations, and the rivalry between them began to dramatize crimes, and resulted in motion pictures portraying the escapades of tough-talking gangsters riding on the running boards of a speeding car, spraying rivals seated in restaurants or other public places with machine guns. While catching these public enemies and locking them up was the job of the law and justices, politicians began to campaign on how they were going to make it safer for the average citizen.

After reading some sensational news stories and watching some of the films of the day, it seemed like a good idea for average citizen to vote for those who made the best-sounding promises to eliminate the problem. Again, the problem subsided and it drifted back to the "out of sight, out of mind" attitude.

The only general reminder of criminals for most became the occasional sight of a group of men wearing striped suits and leg chains, working along a road or in a field guarded by armed uniformed men. Chain gangs, as they were called, served to offset some of the costs of prisons. In many cases, state prisons and federal prisons became small fiefdoms ruled over by the warden of the prison, and his second in command, the Captain of Custody. No one was concerned about how the warden ran his prison, so long as escapes by convicts were few and inconsequential to the public. Convicts deserved whatever they got, was the prevailing attitude.

Then another side of the picture of prisons began to emerge, and via media attention, grabbed public awareness. Events surfaced which brought attention to prison scandals, and what happened to some criminals in these secretive places. From Thomas Dewey's efforts to eliminate the continued depredations of "Murder, Incorporated," there began an expose of graft and corruption, and brutal excesses rife in prisons.

A criminology professor from whom I took some classes at UC Berkeley, Austin H. McCormack, described how he worked under Dewey in carrying out a surprise raid on Sing Sing prison, with a carefully selected group of law enforcement officers. Based on information about how some notorious gang leaders housed there were still operating via connections in and outside of Sing Sing, the raid had to be carefully and secretively planned.

He described the conditions they found there. Some cellblocks had been turned into sort of luxury suites with comfortable furnishings. Dinners were brought in for imprisoned mob leaders from expensive restaurants, girlfriends came and went freely along with other visitors. He further described the arrest of numerous prison officials, and the removal of furniture and appliances from these cellblock luxury suites.

But this represented only one extreme of the spectrum of prison corruption. Other prison exposé occurred over time. It was found that some wardens "rented out" prisoners to work for private farms and businesses, and pocketed the money. Cruel beatings of inmates, sometimes resulting in death, that were perpetrated by prison guards and covered up by superiors, began to come to light with the discovery of mysterious graves on prison property, marked the other extreme of prison scandals.

As mentioned in the early part of this book, the horrors exposed in German and Japanese prisons during and after World War II, together with the above discoveries of the scandals in our own prisons, sparked a new attitude and trend in how to treat inmates and reduce the crime rate. Rehabilitation became part of the new wave of thought about criminal offenders. Politicians got behind this new social theme, talking about reducing crime by reducing the gap between the "haves" and the "have nots," and "rehabilitating" delinquents and criminals, most of whom came from "have nots." Numerous social programs were inaugurated with high expectations. Adolescent facilities were labeled "homes" or "schools." Prisons became "correctional facilities."

As already noted, while many programs aimed at rehabilitating criminals were begun all over this country, California led the way with the establishment and construction of a unique facility, the first of its kind in the world, devoted to the specific purpose of treatment of criminals felt to have emotional and psychological problems that resulted in their criminal behavior. The State also introduced large extensive treatment programs in its youth facilities. Eventually, research was made an integral part of these new programs. Efforts were made to study the offender, set up programs, evaluate their effectiveness, and attempt to tease out the most effective elements of each rehabilitative effort.

These were certainly steps in a positive direction in penology, but were limited by many problems. There were decades during which punishment of criminal offenders as a means of "reforming" them was still a powerful force in our society and the penal system. Providing educational opportunities, vocational training, and treatment to criminal offenders was looked upon as "mollycoddling" or rewarding them for their crimes. For over a decade factors previously described at the California Medical Facility, and in some small units of prisons, were able to counteract the negatives. Educational and vocational training programs were carried out in all the California prisons. To avoid duplication, different prisons offered some unique vocational training programs such as the highly successful underwater welding program offered at one of the prisons in the southern part of the state. All the graduates of this program had job offers even prior to their parole releases.

At the apex of the move to attempt to rehabilitate inmates of the California Department of Corrections, those entering the system were received in one of the two reception centers, one at the Chino State Prison known as the "Southern Reception Center," and the other located at the California Medical Facility, known as the "Northern Reception Center." Here inmates underwent a sixty- to ninety-day evaluation, where they received extensive reviews of their offense histories together with vocational, education, and psychological testing. Determination as to which prison an inmate would be transferred was based upon level of security and program needs. This was referred to as "prescription programming." The level of each inmate's determination to make changes in their lives, and requests for certain programs, was taken into consideration. Violence-prone individuals, unmotivated to participate in any program, were sent to a prison which had higher levels of security, but still had programs available, if later the inmate decided to participate.

Another important contribution during this rehabilitation phase was the community volunteers mentioned earlier. Local citizen organizations and college groups gave participating inmates social interactions, providing hope and motivation to change. These contacts cultivated feelings of acceptance and mutual respect by members of society from which, in the past, they felt alienated and scorned.

Imagine for a moment how it might have impacted some of the inmates involved in these programs. From early childhood neglect and rejection, through scorn and abuse as delinquents by their childhood and adolescent peers, they lived into their adult years labeled as "scum," "sickos," "animals," and worse. Reading and hearing references to them as "low-lifes" who should never be allowed back into free society again, and even worse, that they deserved to suffer or be executed. Through the years, these criminal offenders had never experienced any positive interaction with anyone in our free society. Now, in these weekly volunteer groups, they were getting treated positively, and encouraged to develop their social as well as interests and skills.

Previous specific examples given in case histories and letters reflect similar reactions from inmates who became involved in psychotherapy. "You are the first person who ever listened to me." This was a frequent remark heard by the therapists. These first experiences of acceptance by "free people," the nicest term inmates used to refer to non-criminals, often opened up a window of hope. For some, this began more determined efforts to make changes in their lives with the goal to become a part of "free society." For many the term "free" involved a frightening and emotionally painful effort, as again illustrated in the case histories provided. That is, they had to free themselves of fears, anger, resentments, and hatred, that had alienated them throughout their lives. "Free people" who have gone through the process of resolving painful issues from their past understand. In my private practice, I witnessed some very emotional and corrective breakthroughs from the individual's past. Most of us were fortunate to have had positive childhoods and adolescent years free of traumatic events, guided by loving, nurturing parents. However, many of us were not so fortunate. Again the meaning we attach to experiences in life plays a vital role at times. None of us are comfortable with opening and probing old wounds. I emphasize all of this so that it can better be understood why efforts to treat and rehabilitate is not a simple all-or-none process.

As we have noted in this chapter, emotions and politics sometimes stop or distort the true advancement of knowledge. The era of hope that gave birth to the California Medical Facility, and other efforts to study and rehabilitate criminals, began to change, and once again reflect history. Even in the heyday of rehabilitation, the California Department of Corrections (CDC) received little public attention except when some security incident occurred at one of the "hard core" prisons. Budget for the Department was limited as it progressed through this era, as it was of little concern to legislature and politicos. Nonetheless, subtle changes over time began to become evident. I will try to describe some changes that I witnessed directly.

As the custodial staff that had aided in establishing the more positive and cooperative atmosphere at CMF retired, or moved on to positions at other facilities, they were replaced by officers who tended to have experience working within more typical prisons. It was notable that some resented the influence of non-custodial staff. Other problems were brought to my attention. Custody administrators including the Captain of Custody and his lieutenants asked to meet with me. They informed me that they were having an increasing problem, which included having to escort an average of three or four officers a month off the premises, and subsequently discharge them for misbehaviors including smuggling contraband into the facility, and improper behavior with the inmates. Additionally, a number of new officers just out of the training academy quit after only a few months at the facility. These men had come into the job thinking they were supposed to help inmates become rehabilitated, only to encounter negativity in the attitude of fellow officers towards them. Considering the time and expense of training new recruits in the academy, this represented a costly loss. These custody administrators told me that they had discussed the problem, and had decided to ask if I might know of some tests, or maybe could construct a screening test, that would indicate which new recruits might be unsuitable.

I was aware that some efforts along this line had been attempted by some police organizations elsewhere in the country, and told the custody administrators I would give it a try. I would put together a written test that would pick up such things as anti-social factors, job expectations, and the handling of power over others. I cautioned them that this would take time as I would want to test a large number of recruits, and do a one-year follow-up on their job performances. It was agreed, and over the next two months I came up with what I believed to be a suitable test.

Subsequently I gave the test to over two hundred new recruits and planned another testing of a second group of about two hundred more. However, before I could test the second group, I received a telephone call from a high-level correctional administrator in the CDC central office. He informed me that the correctional officers' union had contacted him, and demanded that my testing project be stopped, as they feared it might be mis-used. Under those orders I scrapped the project and informed those CMF custodial administrators of the reasons. They expressed surprise and disappointment.

I, too, was disappointed, because I felt that the psychological screening of individuals who would be in positions wherein they would be exercising extensive control over others was very important. While I had worked with many fine correctional staff, I had also witnessed the questionable behaviors of others, including the results of brutal beatings and humiliations. The code of silence among the inmate culture also held sway among the prison guards. There is no question that prison personnel often have very dangerous and threatening situations to confront. Sometimes without such situations the result is long hours of boring duty resulting in reduced alertness and observation. For some it enhances a need for excitement. Then there are the few who reveal their own anti-social personality traits by making extra money smuggling contraband such as illegal drugs into prison. Usually such incidents result in the quiet discharge of the offending guard. The general public attitude that criminals deserve what happens to them discourages further efforts to develop remedies for this problem.

The role of personality traits in both youthful inmates

and their guards were explored in the California Youth Authority with promising outcomes. With youthful offenders it was recognized that those officers with whom they had daily contact were influential role models, and thus enhanced rehabilitative efforts. I visited some Youth Authority facilities experimenting with this approach with the hopes that some of the findings might be applied to adult offenders. As noted in previous chapters, adult criminals are extremely immature in their emotional and psychological development.

The winds of change, following the era of attempts to rehabilitate and further study criminals, did not begin just in the criminal justice system. The seventies were the era of "love, peace and freedom," in our society. Demonstrations on college campuses and city streets became common. This also had its impact on research involving criminal offenders.

One of the programs at the medical facility that was highly popular among the inmates involved testing new medications, cosmetics, and other products for possible allergic reactions or other side effects. The applications were processed initially by a community organization, the Solano Institute for Medical and Psychiatric Research. This group would meet regularly at the California Medical Facility to present proposals that they had received for studies. As the supervisor of the research unit at CMF, I chaired these meetings. Each proposal was carefully reviewed for any possible risk to those inmates who volunteered to participate in each research study. To provide for special laboratory testing, the sponsoring company had to provide any lab equipment needed. After the completion of the study, that equipment became the property of the California Medical Facility. As a result, the medical laboratory at CMF became noted as the finest of any state institution.

This program became popular with inmates since they were paid for their participation according to any risks or discomfort while the project was under way. Participation was totally voluntary on the part of the inmates. Descriptions of the individual projects were posted on large bulletin boards together with a sign-up sheet. Each inmate's medical psychiatric records were reviewed by a medical staff panel, and thus the inmate was approved or disapproved accordingly. The sign-ups for these projects far exceeded the numbers needed, as inmates liked to earn the money to purchase items in the canteen, or save it for forthcoming parole needs.

Again, the social climate began to change. On one side arose the ultra-liberal freedom movements of the era which began to protest that inmates, due to their confinement, did not have freedom of choice to volunteer for these research studies. At the time I had formed a liaison with a major nearby university, and arranged to meet with faculty. The purpose was to inform them of the vast amount of accumulated testing data from the two reception centers as well as data collected by the research unit. This data could be utilized by graduate students at the university who were doing related doctoral studies and dissertations. Suddenly, the doors to the conference room burst open and a large noisy group of student demonstrators entered. There were some threatening confrontations between members of the medical facility staff present, and the students who accused them of forcing inmates to participate in harmful research. They even insisted that psychological tests were harmful to inmates.

On the other side, the conservative movement was busy closing mental hospitals in the state to save money, under the idea that mental patients could best be treated in the community rather than in large "warehouses" like state hospitals. Here again, both political sides found common ground and closure of state hospitals began. The patients returned to the community, but local governments had no money for expanded treatment and those mental patients became very visible on the streets.

Once, I recall walking a couple of blocks to a university where I had been asked to attend a meeting. On the first corner I encountered a disheveled man flailing his arms and shouting at passersby, who quickly hurried away. In the middle of the block I came upon another man pacing back and forth shaking his fist in the air, ranting at the brick wall of a building, seeming oblivious to his surroundings. Within the two blocks I observed six more poor, deranged and apparently homeless individuals. I had never previously seen such a scene except in intake units of mental hospitals. Slowly over time such persons began arriving in increasing numbers in jails and prisons.

As political appointments took over the administration of the California Department of Corrections, other counter-productive and politically driven changes occurred. In the earlier chapters on my orientation to CDC at San Quentin prison, I described the jute mill where clothing and linens were made by inmates for state institutions, and the beautiful office furniture made by inmates for use in state offices. Not only did these products offset prison costs, but many inmates gained pride in their work, and honed skills useful to them when later paroled. In addition to prison industries, mental hospitals utilized labor of mentally retarded patients to operate dairies, hog farms, and chicken farms. Some prison grounds were utilized to raise vegetable and fruit orchards, and a cannery at Folsom prison prepared and canned these products for institutional use. These projects offset costs to the prisons and rescued inmates and custodial patients from the horror of "dead time," those long hours of mind-deadening inactivity. I had over the years toured and personally witnessed the pride and pleasure expressed by the participants and their supervisors.

But again, the political winds changed. The California farm co-ops convinced legislators that for various ludicrous reasons the State should buy all these products from private sources. Soon after, other industries convinced the legislatures that the State should close down prison industries as they did not allow private industries to do competitive bidding for these products on the open market. I personally heard all the arguments put forth for shutting down these cost-saving operations, and was even assigned by the Director to a small committee to plan how to phase out the Folsom cannery. Subsequent political appointments were made to administrative positions in the California Department of Corrections. Many had no previous knowledge or experience of corrections, and later would even announce that they did not want to hear about the past, that they were going to move ahead.

One prime example of this was when a newly appointed Director of Corrections made a decision shortly after taking office, to tour the Texas prison system to see how their prisons operated. She returned enthusiastic about how the Texas prisons had inmates working, providing crops and other farming operations to feed the prison population. She announced to the CDC administrator that they were to make plans for a work incentive program, wherein inmates would receive time credits on their sentences for their labor. Of course, this involved passing a piece of legislation to allow the program, which easily happened.

It closely followed the wording contained in past legislation specifying activities that inmates could participate in for "good time," credits, except for omission of one, treatment. Later, when this law was implemented, some legislators protested, claiming that when they voted for the new work incentive law they had not noticed the omission of the word "treatment," and felt treatment should have been included. However, CDC administrators had what they thought they wanted, and so a series of somewhat comical events began.

During a large meeting at the California Medical Facility to outline the new work incentive policies, the new Director's representative described the reasons that they were going to copy the Texas system. I raised my hand and said, that in my capacity as Supervisor of Clinical Research, I kept up with what was happening in other states and prison programs. I then asked if they were aware that the Texas prison system, at this very point in time, had more lawsuits pending against it in federal courts than all other states combined. The response I received, "We aren't going to have that problem," made me aware that this administration was ignorant of the power of federal courts over prison systems of states, and this was strengthened by the monies provided by the federal government. Less than nine months later, CDC faced its first federal lawsuit against the administration, which was largely ignored for some time.

At CMF, the new administrators took over, stating that the institution was going to be just another prison. The Medical Superintendent was replaced by a "Warden." We were told by one of the new wardens and his deputy that "doctors ain't going to have nuttin' to say about nuttin'." Doctors were ordered to plan their schedules around inmate work schedules, and thus needed to plan to work evening and weekend hours. Inmate work was to be the focus and future weeks would focus on planning how to put inmates to work producing food. Appointed administrators and inmate work supervisors began meeting and planning. I was told about a suggestion that the large storage rooms under the wings of the institution were to be flooded to raise fish for consumption. It was quickly rejected when someone pointed out that all the electrical circuits for the facility ran through these basement spaces.

But some other suggestions were implemented. The raising of potatoes in large barrels was carried out without success. A turkey ranch aimed at raising turkeys for forthcoming Thanksgiving dinners for all the prisons fared slightly better. They were able to raise and kill enough turkeys for Thanksgiving for CMF, but not enough for any other prisons. However, this ran into still other problems. In preparing these turkeys for inmate consumption, they violated the rules of the State Health Department and were ordered to stop the program. In short, the lack of knowledge about the previous history of CDC by these new administrators proved costly. The new policies began to increase the problems of the department, especially at the California Medical Facility.

As mentioned, inmate working assignments took precedence over treatment, both medical and psychotherapeutic. Inmates were forced to change therapy groups and even therapists, factors that are strongly contraindicated by years of research. Even medical appointments were ignored by work supervisors. As predicted, more of those previously treated and housed in mental hospitals began to find their way into the prisons.

One of the new administrators, whose qualifications for his position, besides his political connections, was that he had once been a tank commander, announced that we were going to have to cease treating the "walking wounded," referring to the general treatment program, and focus on those more seriously disturbed. Orders were issued that inmates who had been in therapy the average length of time by the research unit, had to be dropped from therapy immediately.

As could be expected, the administration who knew all they needed to know, closed down the research unit. My office was moved, without previous warning, out of the Administration Building to the treatment wing at the far end of the facility. I was placed in charge of the general treatment program and instructed to follow the new policies of the administration.

These were very difficult times, but thanks to a very close-knit, capable professional staff and some cooperative custody personnel, we were able to maintain the major core of the treatment program.

But some incidents reflecting the general character of the new administration occurred. First, they had replaced the former superintendent initially with the former head of custody of the facility, telling him he would be the new warden, and to keep the treatment programs running. After passage of the work incentive law, in a large meeting called for all staff, a representative from the Director announced the new policies. The new warden who had worked very well with the treatment staff protested that this was not in keeping with what he had been told. The representative of the Director looked sternly at him and stated with emphatic voice, "You misunderstood."

Our new warden was transferred out of the California Medical Facility shortly afterwards. It became apparent to those at the facility that the administration had played a charade until the new work incentive law had passed the legislature. All the data collected by the research programs was subsequently destroyed.

But, remember the federal lawsuit they ignored, together with several more federal judges' orders also ignored by this new CDC dictatorship? Judgment day did arrive. The federal judge finally got the attention of this administration by issuing a number of orders concerning getting the

California Medical Facility licensed as a treatment facility, and threatened penalties if the department did not comply. Thankfully, the warden appointed to the facility at that time was a very intelligent man, and could see what was coming. He and I had established a good working relationship after I had told him, in private conversation, that I understood his situation. He well knew that if he did not follow policies of the present administration he would lose his job and any future in CDC. He thanked me and we worked together as much as possible. He would call me to his office to ask questions, and get my advice on various problems related to compliance with the federal orders.

Time passed, and not much changed. Finally, the federal judge decided to speed things up. He gave a time line for the CDC to come into full compliance with the federal orders. He stated that for every day the medical facility was not in compliance after the target date he set, the director of CDC and the warden of CMF would be fined ten thousand dollars per day, and the monies for the fines were to come out of their personal pockets, and not the taxpayers of the state.

Things began to happen at a rapid pace. By this time, however, I had retired from CDC and my friend, the warden at CMF, had been moved to become head of the Parole Division. Shortly thereafter I received an invitation from him to work part-time in the outpatient evaluation and treatment offices of two parole units.

Initially my semi-retired position was very rewarding in my ability to work closely with parole agents in helping parolees in their efforts to stay out of prisons. But over the past decade three governors of the state made political gains by following the "get tough on crime" political stance. Thus, once again, centralizing decisions at high-level administration, and ordering of the appointed Board of Prison Terms to limit the number of paroles given and to violate parolees on the slightest excuse began to have impact. So now those at the top of the bureaucratic ladder, who had no personal contact with the parolee, decided his or her fate. Let me provide you with an example from my own clinical caseload.

I had this young parolee in follow-up therapy. His offense was that he had sexually molested his underage niece at the direction of his older brother, the father of the young girl. This older brother had repeatedly sexually molested both his daughter and his young brother over several years. He too went to prison for this. The younger brother was borderline mentally retarded and very compliant. One can only imagine the hell he went through in prison. He was later paroled to live with his grandmother. The rules were very specific. The granddaughter (victim of his offense) was to telephone the grandmother whenever she planned to visit her, so that the parolee could leave the house while she was there. This is a standard restriction. Parolees cannot have contact with victims of their sexual offense. My mentally limited, but very compliant, parolee patient complied very religiously with this restriction. He also adapted exceptionally well to his condition by becoming an outstanding horticulturist, applying his talent in raising award-winning vegetables to enter in fairs. He often brought award ribbons to show me during our therapy sessions aimed primarily at monitoring his overall adjustment. Both his parole agent and I agreed that he was doing exceptionally well, given his mental limitations.

However, an incident arose that caused his return to prison. The grandmother left the house to do some grocery shopping. Since he had been working diligently in his garden, her grandson, the parolee, decided to take a shower while she was away. In the course of his shower, he heard the front door of the house burst open. He finished his shower

164

and wrapped a towel around himself and opened the door to discover his niece pacing back and forth in the front room. At that moment there was a knock on the door. It was the parole agent. He, upon observing the parolee there, demanded an explanation. The niece explained that she had had an argument with her boyfriend, and was very upset, and wanted to talk to her grandmother. In her emotional state she had forgotten to telephone first. The parolee explained that he was in the shower when he heard the front door and thought it was the grandmother returning.

Following procedures, the parole agent wrote a detailed report of the incident and the explanations he was given. He further recommended that the parolee not be violated since he did not apparently have any control over what had occurred. His report was sent up to the parole board for review. Their response was to violate the parolee and ordered him returned to prison for six months. I had also attached an evaluation of the parolee and a recommendation, which was part of the package sent to the parole board. In my evaluation, I pointed out that in the early part of the treatment, we had focused upon the emotional traumas and fears he had from his prison experience. It was evident that the efforts that the parole agent and I had expended on this parolee had been of no value to the parole authorities.

Two other brief examples of this trend are the violation of parole because a parolee's nineteen-year-old son became disrespectful and refused to turn down the television so it wouldn't disturb neighbors in an adjoining apartment. The father (the parolee), slapped his son on the side of his head. His mother (parents were divorced) was called by the son. She called police. They found nothing to report when they talked to the father and son. However, the parolee was violated after he reported the contact as per parole rules.

The second example is that of a paroled sex offender

165

who went to the hospital with his wife, where she gave birth to their baby. He was violated for having contact with a minor. This again represented the overall changes in social and political attitudes that was rapidly increasing the prison population.

In less than two decades we had abandoned efforts to reduce the high costs of prison by constructive use of inmate labor, and tentative efforts to rehabilitate inmates, and thus reduce the rate of inmates returning to prison. I use the term "tentative" to point out that the efforts were often small, scattered programs, not available to the majority of inmates. Briefly, there was a recognition that we needed to evaluate our efforts and learn more about criminal offenders through research. But all this came to a rapid end when one failure to rehabilitate a sexual offender was used to political advantage by politicos running for the highest offices in the nation, claiming that they would be tougher on criminals than their political opponents. The irony is that centuries of observations and prior decades of scientific studies have made no lasting impressions on our efforts to reduce the criminal population, and do little more than give lip service in preventing the creation of these social aliens.

Eight

The Continued Struggle with Evil and Blame

Mankind has long struggled with the issue of blame. Behind the humorous excuse offered today, "the devil made me do it," stretches a long history of struggle with human will. In the early middle ages bizarre or deviant behaviors in an individual were attributed to being outside of human will. It was believed that such a person had become possessed by a demon—unwillingly. Monks and friars wrote books of incantations, and devised other methods of ridding persons so unwillingly possessed of the evil demon who had supposedly taken up residency within them. Remedies were often quite direct and included shouting terrible insults in the face of the victim, aimed at the demon inside, or waving foul-smelling incense under the victim's nose. All these remedies were based upon the simplistic belief that if you made life for the demon living inside the hapless victim miserable enough, he would move out and leave the victim, who then could resume normal behavior. The more miserable you could make it for the demon inside, the quicker his departure, and the less apt to return. We can only guess the effects these treatments had on the person.

But as societies progressed, the concept of preventing problems came into consideration. St. Augustine wrote about ways to prevent such "possessions." As an example, he cited the case of a nun who had become "possessed" when she failed to bless a lettuce leaf prior to eating it. Unfortunately, according to the author, a demon was asleep on the lettuce leaf she consumed, and thus caused her unusual behavior. It is interesting to note that during the "treatment" with incantations and incense, the demon is alleged to have protested that it was not his fault that he had possessed the nun, as he was asleep, and had not been warned off by the nun with the appropriate blessing.

Ever wonder why when you sneeze today, someone around you says, "Gesundheit!" or "God bless you?" Again, go back to the same era. The belief was that when a person sneezed, his or her body was made vulnerable to entry by any nearby demon. Thus the blessing was intended to ward off such entry or possession! Any doubts about influences from the past?

Later, this way of accounting for human behavior did not satisfy some who saw individuals as having evil motivations on their own. Thus the leaders of the times began to shift away from the belief in unwillful possession, to willful compacts with the devil, and his demons. This greatly expanded the concept of blame. If you were a farmer and your cow became ill and died, who was at fault? You suddenly place significance on the crotchety old woman who lives a short way down the lane leading to your farm. You recall that on several occasions she has shouted epithets and displayed other unneighborly and perhaps illogical behaviors, all of which has made it clear that she does not like you for whatever reason. The bottom line is obvious in its connection. She bears you ill will, and your cow suddenly became ill and died. As a respected citizen of good standing, you immediately report this to the local magistrate. The woman is quickly brought in for questioning. If her answers do not suit her inquisitors, or can be interpreted by them as evidence that she is in cahoots with the devil, she is adjudicated to be a witch. That is, she is judged to have evil intent towards the farmer, and in her vindictiveness she made a willful contract with the devil, to wit, in return for her soul the devil would wreak vengeance upon her enemies. The penalty at the time was certain and swift public burning at the stake.

Thus, witches became of great public concern. The privacy and secretiveness of witches, and the evil they could bring upon anyone they took a disliking to, became a frightening prospect. It could happen to any unsuspecting citizen! Thus in this atmosphere of public fear, two Dominican monks came up with the answer on how such persons would be detected. "Malleus Malificarum" was the title of their treatise on the subject. They postulated that when the devil made a contract with the person, the devil touched his claw somewhere on the person, leaving a place where no sensation would thereafter exist. To find out who was a witch was just a matter of discovering that spot where no cutaneous sense existed. After successfully petitioning the Vatican, the two monks received a "white paper" which gave them "carte blanche" to travel about the kingdoms of Europe searching out witches. They would attend large public gatherings, fairs, market places, festivals, sticking unsuspecting persons with pointed objects. Small wonder that they became known as "The Prickers."

In keeping with social phenomena, any social problem that reaches public concern suddenly becomes widespread in its frequency of occurrence. Thus in some provinces in Europe upwards of ten thousand "witches" were burned at the stake within a period of one year. Perhaps we can characterize this as an early "war on crime."

In the differentiation between "good" and "evil," morality and crime has fluctuated throughout mankind's history. For example, sex with whom and how was of little concern to the societies of Europe during the Middle Ages. The "right of first night," children considered nothing more than miniature adults, mistresses if you could afford them, etc., made sex a non-issue. Even the Catholic churches in some areas sponsored houses of prostitution to serve the needs of nature. All this changed after the newly discovered Americas made their first major contribution to European culture—V.D. The inhabitants of the New World seemingly had developed antibodies or other immunities to the ravages of venereal disease, such as syphilis. However, when Columbus's sailors dallied with the locals on the voyage of discovery, they returned to the population of Europe a new problem.

Soon after the return of Columbus and his discovery of the "New World," other voyages were quickly undertaken. With wide acceptance of sexual activity, syphilis spread rapidly through Europe in the early 16th century. With no means of treatment, the terrible consequences of paresis and death were common due to the epidemic in some areas. When it became associated with sexual behavior, the beginning of sexual prohibitions occurred on a broad social front. Over time it became sinful, and then criminal.

In these United States we are the products of the past, both as a society and as an individual. When a society gets too wanton with few restrictions, it soon begins to suffer the consequences. Unfortunately, in remedying the problem societies tend to react by going to the opposite extreme of excessive prohibitions, without thought or reason as to possible consequences of that solution. All sociologists are well aware that societies progress painfully slow because they spend much time and energy moving laterally between one polar extreme to the other. Each of us grew up in a social context.

It is axiomatic that parents are the primary interpreters

of the social mores, customs and beliefs of society to their offspring. But there exists the reality that among parents there is again that attitude of "don't do as I do, do as I tell you," as well as, in larger societies, subgroups that do not adhere to the overall cultural mores and rules. Others outside of the family also add their interpretations of these mores and beliefs including teachers, ministers, hero figures, peers and others, as social exposure expands. We should not overlook a powerful new influence in our culture, the television and entertainment media which often have more access to a child/adolescent today than the parent. Thus there are often inconsistencies in these exposures, so as a child comes of age and learns to reason he must often resolve these inconsistencies as an individual. Imagine how much greater a task youth today are faced with in our very complex culture of diversified population, contrasted to small isolated societies wherein everyone held to the same customs, mores, and beliefs!

While our society continues to oscillate back and forth from question to question in what is acceptable and unacceptable in social behavior, it has made unprecedented progress in discoveries and inventions. There is excitement among many about the new age of technology and the possibilities that it opens up. But what are the social impacts? We are still struggling with this added dimension, how it adds to the influence of present and future children. I have already mentioned the impact of mass media in the form of movies, television and computers. The impact of television and computers has been quick and powerful. Recent surveys indicate that a school-age child in our society spends an average of five and a half hours viewing television each day. Now we are moving quickly to provide each child in school a computer. Some simple childhood math: eight hours for sleep, five and a half hours for TV, six hours in class, two and a half hours after-school activities equals almost a full day. Sorry, Mom and Dad, maybe you will see them some on the weekend. From this it would seem that parents are no longer a major interpreter of social behavior and mores. There may be cases where that is fortunate for the child, but those are exceptions.

In the not too distant past, the daily schedule was quite different. School days were longer, nine to four, with an hour off for lunch and half-hour recesses in the morning and afternoon. You had to be home by a certain time after school as specified by your parents. It was not a good idea to be late for dinner. Lots of sharing about the day occurred at dinner. After dinner, everyone helped with evening chores as assigned. Then homework, and then, hopefully, sitting with the rest of the family to watch television until appointed bedtimes. Somehow Mom and Dad influenced at least four hours each weekday, weekends, more. Friday or Saturday night, the family often went to the movies or outings together.

Well, we all are aware of the importance of the first five years of life, at least, some are. Maybe this is where parents can have the biggest impact in our society. Issues around day care for infants and small children have become important in our modern society. We set standards for licensed day care centers and workers. Parents are given advice on how to select good care for their pre-schoolers. So once again, the influence of parents on a developing child can be minimized. Fortunately, most parents that make time to be with their children, want to be with them, and arrange their lives accordingly.

Sadly, the demands, or maybe I should say the wants, of our present day society makes it very difficult for parents. It forces many to make difficult choices and decisions. Life has become much more complex in the past century in American society. But child development still follows its age-old course. From basic attachment in infancy, control of bodily functions during the toddler stage, the first flirtations with independence of the pre-schoolers, all successfully accomplished under the umbrella of "basic trust." The infant, toddler and pre-schooler needs to know that someone is there who cares enough to protect and comfort. That is, if I stand up and try to walk, you won't let me hurt myself if I fall. If I become frightened or startled, you will comfort me, and if I get an "ow ow" you'll kiss it and make it all right. When you tell me not to do something or go somewhere because I might get hurt or lost, you will prove that I can trust you to stop me, that you really care.

To establish this basic trust and answer all these non-verbal questions affirmatively takes lots of attention, and sometimes frustration, as children demand proof through what is called "testing the limits." If the parent remains consistent throughout with the "I care" message verbally, and more important, by actions, childhood becomes one of healthy growth, development, and learning. In this context, the parent also develops a most important leverage in their efforts to guide their child's moral, social and behavioral development; the child's desire to please the parent, to be like the parent, to make the parent proud of them! I have heard parents complain, "But I can't be with my child twenty-four hours a day!"

When a child has formed a bond with a parent, has established a basic trust in a parent so that the child trusts what the parent tells them, that parent goes everywhere with the child, not physically, but in the voice of the developing conscience. That child has the confidence to say "no" to a peer who wants to do something that the child knows the parent would not approve. Further, self-esteem grows as the child takes pride in fulfilling the parent's trust and faith. Oh yes, there will be failures and mistakes, but as these are dealt with in the context of caring and trust, the failures and mistakes become important lessons. After all, psychologists know that the primary means of human learning lies in learning from models ("monkey see, monkey do") and trial and error (learning from mistakes). More complex learning builds on these, cause and effect learning and conceptual learning with abilities to plan and anticipate outcomes.

Nonetheless, let's not underestimate the influence of peers. I have often admonished young offenders and others, "If you want to know where you are going with your life, take a look at your friends." None of us are totally immune to the influence of close friends and associates. So who is a child associating with during playtime? Are they children whose parents have taught them values and mores similar to those you have taught your child? No problem here, no conflict. Remember the key word, consistency. But we don't live in a consistent or perfect social environment. A child needs guidance and monitoring in their choice of associates. It is important to know where your child is, and who they are with, as much as possible. This concern can diminish as the child grows older and you have had the opportunity to observe the type of associates your child chose when left to his or her own choice. Again, the relationship you have established with your child has begun to extend beyond your presence. Vigilance is still a necessity of parenting as peer pressures arise.

As a child moves into adolescence, many problems surface. This seems to be a difficult transition for many youngsters and their parents. This is the time when the insecure parent is sorely tested and the authoritarian parent is driven to high frustration. "Because I say so!" is not a very satisfying response to teenagers or adults. And a teenager is trying to become an adult. The adolescent is between, that is, he or she wants to make their own decisions, but they also want parents to be there for them if anything goes wrong. But, most important, this is a vital stage in learning about decision-making. At sixteen, how do you learn about buying a car you are excited about, if the parent's response is, "No, you can't afford it. End of discussion!" Possibly the parent hasn't been too good about their own car purchases. After all, a youngster isn't going to learn much about reasoning if the parent is an impulse buyer!

Sadly, the advice about talking to their child, sharing some of their own thinking processes is incomprehensible to some parents. Those most lacking in communicative skills or are insecure within themselves are the ones most apt to rely on authority as the key ingredient of parenting. True, a parent should not relinquish their authority to the child, but it should not be in the forefront at any but critical times. Be secure in your own ability to reason! Even as adults, we have encountered the boss or administrator who has nothing to offer but authority. Such bosses or administrators are more of a detriment than a facilitator or problem-solver, and the results they achieve soon show it. So it is at home!

We cannot ignore once again basic learning. Remember "monkey see, monkey do"? As a small child, I remember some adults were shocked about the movie, *Gone With The Wind,* and the line, "Frankly, my dear, I don't give a damn." I understood because I had my mouth washed out at the age of six (I thought with soap, but it turned out to be baking soda), for exclaiming, "Got down truck" at a toy truck that rolled down a step. Later, in my youthful stint as manager of a theater, I had local nuns picketing the theater at the showing of the movie *The Outlaw* with its moving haystack suggestive of sexual activity. What do children see today in movie theaters and on television? Society has changed and will continue to change. In the process, it will place more or less burdens on parents.

Society reflects collective reasoning, but we allow those we elect to lead us and do most of the reasoning. We all, of course, believe that we are rational creatures. This brings to mind an anecdote that I had heard and always told at the start of the first lecture when I was teaching psychopathology. "It has been said that there has been three major revelations in the thinking of man. The first was the Copernican revolution when man found that the Earth was not the center of the universe. The second was the Darwinian revolution when man found that he was not totally unique, but shared much in common with the other creatures of the Earth. The third was the Freudian revolution, when man discovered that he was not a totally rational creature, but often driven by unconscious emotions and motives stemming from his past. A humorist summed it up this way: In the first revolution, man lost his world. In the second revolution, he lost his soul, and in the third revolution he lost his mind."

We often are moved by the desire to help the downtrodden or less fortunate. First, we attempted to offer more opportunities in hopes of raising everyone to higher levels of functioning within our society. However, we found that there were still many who were incapable of benefiting from the opportunities offered. So we changed strategy in our efforts to achieve local equality for all. We simply lowered social standards. Here again I offer a comment made to students and inmates who have complained about something being too hard. "If it is easy, then everybody has it already!" What will it benefit our society if a mentally retarded individual can obtain a college degree? All humans are not equal, not even in our justice system!

I always like the definition of self-actualization as the realization of one's own potentials. Those potentials have to be developed and encouraged within the capacity of the individual. I recall a student in one of my graduate-level classes who came in to complain to me that she felt her essay exam paper deserved better than the C grade I had given it. I listened to her reasons, and then I handed her a paper that I had given an A- grade, and asked if she minded taking the time to read it, and then tell me if she felt she had matched that student's effort. She did so, and then told me that she knew she did not put forth the effort she could have, and thanked me for my time.

Subsequently, she took two more classes from me and earned A's in both. I explained to students that if I gave away grades just to make everybody happy, I would be cheapening the efforts of those students who earned their A's. As a society, as a parent, as a teacher, we can reward achievement and encourage others to put forth their best efforts without cheapening the efforts of others who really give their best. I have seen young children burst into tears when they reach the age when they realize that a parent is allowing them to win a game, rather than allow them to put their true ability to the test. Once again, setting unrealistic standards for someone's age or abilities can be damaging and demoralizing. Society and parents must avoid these pitfalls. This requires more complex solutions.

In this chapter I have attempted, to the level of my ability, to give some of the basics that encourage the healthy growth of humans from infancy to adulthood. Herein I am guilty of one of the things for which I sometimes criticize others—oversimplification. The fact is that our society has accrued vast amounts of knowledge about human psychosocial development through careful research and suggestive studies, but sadly, uses very little towards training parents or teachers. Child protective organizations frequently make very damaging decisions for a child out of ignorance or fear of public opinion. We need to bring this knowledge together in a cogent manner that can help us improve as a society and as parents, teachers, professionals so that society can make more rational decisions. More punishment is definitely not the solution, and I have shared examples of why in the previous chapters and will share more in the chapters to come. I am hopeful that these examples show a clear contrast between what we term "normal" childhoods and the childhoods of the vast majority of our social aliens, the criminal offenders.

Finally, our continued struggle as a society with the source of blame is still evident. In our criminal justice system a person who has committed a criminal act can be found too insane at time of trial to participate, and sent to a mental facility until such time they are evaluated by doctors to be sufficiently recovered to understand the functions of the court. Other criminal offenders may be found not guilty by reason of insanity, if it is proven that at the time of their offense they were so mentally ill as to not comprehend the consequences of their act.

While these concepts were originally based upon our studies of the impact of severe mental illnesses, such as psychosis, they have in turn been misused by those legal and mental health professionals willing to distort them for personal advantage. They have expanded scientifically accepted concepts of mental illness to include mental health problems that do not impair the individual's thinking to the point of not comprehending what they were doing, even to the point of eating too many sugary Twinkies. Maybe we will again return to the concept that "the devil" is responsible for behaviors of the criminal offender. It is certainly evident that knowledge from past and present has very little impact on our dealing with criminals compared to emotions, and political and personal gain.

Nine
The Limits of Common Sense

As described in the last chapter, the struggle continues in the determination of willfulness and blame for individual behavior. Even though we no longer seek out witches to burn at the stake, we still struggle to place guilt before we pass sentences, including death penalties, upon those who commit crimes. Those who have studied ancient history can quickly recognize similarities. While we no longer struggle with deciding issues of whether an offender willfully made a pact with the devil, or unwillfully was possessed by an evil spirit, we struggle with issues of individual competency and other mitigating factors commonly found in criminal trials today. From florid mental illness to the consumption of sugar-laden "Twinkies," there is an unending stream of factors offered in mitigation of the will of the individual who has committed a criminal offense. The outcomes of some of these struggles have resulted in loss of faith by many in our judicial system and sometimes greater anger against miscreants in general.

Some of this anger is a natural outgrowth of the average individual's capacity for empathy for others. In a state of empathy for the victims of a crime, it becomes as if we ourselves have suffered a loss. The reaction to that loss is often thoughts, perhaps fantasies, about what ought to be done to the offender. The avenging emotions can bring forth primitive and brutal thoughts without limits or boundaries, devoid of any empathy for the person who committed the offense against another. In recognition of this darker side of our human nature, society has taken definitive steps to protect the accused from "vigilante" or "mob" justice. We recognize that strong emotions cloud and distort our ability to reason and be objective.

On the more "civilized" side we are taught, "there are always at least two sides to every story," or "a person should be presumed innocent until proven guilty," and that we should strive for "justice with mercy." These are very reasonable and civil admonitions and goals for our society. But again, emotions frequently result in these ideals being discarded. It is an old adage that the best way to get people to join and follow you is to find a common enemy. If you can't find one, you can create one. The most outstanding example in the past century is illustrated with the rise to power of Adolf Hitler. He convinced a "civilized" nation that they needed him to protect them from "inferiors" who were a threat to the good citizens, and a source of their problems. Toss in a little dish of flattery such as "super race" and Hitler promoted a deadly combination of emotions, a need for power to overcome "offenders," and a promise of leadership toward this end. The juggernaut was in place. As humans we are still searching for the perfect parent who will guide us and protect us from dangers, point out those dangers, and teach us how we should react to them. Add to that perfect parent list is the need to be assured that we are good children, acceptable above all others.

I recall in one of the cultural anthropology classes that I took in college, learning that every ancient culture for which we had any written or spoken record of their language, was a common set of words or phrases which they used to refer to themselves. These words or phrases translated into a common category: the Men, The People, The Chosen Ones, Children of the Gods, all implying that of the inhabitants of the world, they were the preferred ones. Many of us have witnessed the efforts of children for parental attention and, if possible, reassurance that they are special or the favorite child. We call it "sibling rivalry."

Since the end of the Cold War, we have been hard pressed as to where the most unknown lurking enemy might be found. However, our political leaders have quickly tried to help us fill this unifying void. One of those efforts has been the "War on Crime." There are certain requisites that must be accomplished when a war is declared. First, the threat of the designated enemy must be defined and amplified. Second, the enemy cannot be someone with whom we have empathy. Thus we must take steps to dehumanize the enemy. We have to see them as aliens, not capable of feelings like we are. Third, having made them aliens, and thus inferior, we no longer apply the standards that the civilized or socialized part of our being would apply to other equal beings. Fourth, we can permit ourselves to be non-empathetic and allow free rein to our vengeful anger, and exact increasing punishments without consideration for that enemy. Now, we good people can join with our generals and their soldiers and as one to wreak havoc, crush and annihilate the evil ones without compunction. This becomes plausible because we are joined in the common cause of self-preservation.

It is easy to see that the first step is the critical one. If there is not enough fear to motivate, there will be no response, nothing to join together or for which to seek or follow a leader. Those who rise as leaders are not ignorant of important weapons currently at their disposal. Such examples of these are statistics and statistical methods. I learned about these in undergraduate courses as well as graduate courses in college, and how to use them to critique scientific research. I later would have occasion to teach the subject myself. All of this made me acutely aware of how statistical results can be misused and distorted, made meaningless so as to result in erroneous conclusions, giving rise to the old adage that "statisticians don't lie, but some statistics do." Even Sir Francis Bacon commented, "There are two methods one can use to prove any point, quoting statistics and quoting scripture." Careful selection, ignoring the context, poor or inadequate sampling, extrapolating beyond the findings and treating that as factual, or reporting only part of the findings, are major ways you can make a false point with statistics. Statistical mathematics are complex and most people, including the majority of college students, are not cognizant of the potential for misuse and deliberate distortion. The other very important weapon of the potential leader is the media. The significance of this weapon has been clearly demonstrated and needs no further comment.

However, I would like to clarify one point. I have described both statistical methods and the media as weapons, a term that has negative connotations. We must all keep in mind that old adage, "there is nothing that mankind can conceive for its benefit that it cannot also turn to its detriment." So, in the late 1970s, political candidates had found their new springboard, the so-called "law and order" ticket. Their statistics stated that crime was growing at an alarming rate, spreading out from inner city ghettos to upper-class neighborhoods. Nobody was safe any more and if we didn't take quick and drastic action the bogeyman was going to get us! Much less attention was directed at context: population explosions, changes in economic prosperity, changes in social values and structures, changes in media influences and social expectations, all factors known to influence crime rates. Note the word "influence," and avoid the word

182

"cause." For here lies another statistical trap! Two factors moving in unison imply a correlation, not a cause and effect relationship, but that is not conducive to finding a quick and simple solution to increases in crime.

Once again let all voting citizenry "get in touch with the child within." When you did wrong as a child, you received punishment and you didn't do that wrong again. And if you were a good child, you knew you had the punishment coming, and when it was over, you returned to the good graces of your parents. Doesn't that make the solution to wrongdoing obvious? Punish the wrongdoer, and if the present punishment isn't stopping potential offenders, increase it! Simple, who needs to confuse the issue further?!!

And we don't want to overlook the deterrent effect on others! Remember when you were a child and your sibling got punished for something? You learned very quickly not to do the same thing your sibling did. So increasing punishment for defined offenses appeals to common sense. Common sense once convinced mankind that the world was flat! The politicians took advantage of our common sense, and we elected those who promised to be the best General in our "war on crime."

Money poured into this war effort. Like any war, sacrifices had to be made. Resources had to be taken away from other tax expenditures ("re-allocation of funds"). War production increased, we built new prisons at a rate never before imagined. At one point it was said that California alone had more prisoners locked up than any government entity in the world outside of Communist Russia! The number of soldiers increased tremendously as government made more funds available to hire police for our communities and guards for new prisons. Increased enticements such as pay increases and benefits helped recruitment to fill the ranks. It is paramilitary organization and therefore supervisory ranks are an absolute necessity to prevent maverick soldiers being unleashed on the citizenry. But it goes beyond this. It is axiomatic that as any organization increases in size, so does the administration of that organization, so a vast pyramid evolves. A great deal of paperwork and time is spent in planning and accounting for expenditures of time and money. Competition for promotions to higher salaried positions becomes intense, so mistakes take on larger significance. Mistakes, even relatively minor ones, can result in more accounting, more paper, and more staff. Financial costs escalate. But in a war, who cares?

We are now imprisoning more and more of the enemy by locking them in our new prisons for longer and longer sentences. To cut unnecessary costs, we eliminate "rehabilitation" programs. After all, you don't provide aid to the enemy, he is there for punishment, not "rehabilitation."

"Remember, the key word is punishment." How often I have heard that statement from correctional administrators! The war intensifies. New laws are passed by the hundreds to further the filling of prisons. Increasing penalties is a popular political response. As good citizens we often make the complaint that there is too much government interference in our lives, but hasten to contact our politicians when something offends us with "there ought to be a law. . . ." So there has been an increase in the number of things that were misdemeanors (with penalties such as fines, community work, jail time, and diversionary programs), becoming by law, felonies requiring prison time. It is inevitable that we build more and more prisons.

But those with an increased vested interest in the expansion of the criminal justice system as it currently exists insist that we are winning the war on crime and present statistics to prove it. Let us look at those stats critically.

Context: the past decade has seen the greatest economic expansion in our social history, impacting greater numbers in our society than ever before. Remember, one of those factors influencing drops in crime rates is general economic prosperity! Also, we are given inconsistent statistics showing different types of crimes receding and other increasing. But given an overall decrease in the frequency of crime in general, is it of any significance? If you have one thousand burglaries per year in a specific city area, and you reduce the number of burglaries in that same area the following year by five, the rate of burglaries has obviously decreased. In another city area employing the same crime-fighting methods, we are told that armed robberies have dropped from 250 last year to 210 armed robberies this year, but burglaries increased from 750 to 780. Given the same population size and make-up, what does this tell us about the efficacy of the new crime-fighting methods? In statistics, the term "significance" takes on a mathematical value.

As mentioned, there are many factors which have impacts on crime rates. But the important questions involve whether the impact is significant (i.e. better than chance), or just a transient fluke. Is the difference great enough to attribute causality or influence of import? And finally, is the impact significant enough to warrant the costs and sacrifices that have been made to achieve it? There are some who feel that any reduction in crime rates, real or not, justifies any sacrifice society can make. Most of these have made up their minds and any subsequent facts or findings will only raise their ire. Meanwhile, in our society we have created what some feel is a huge growth industry that is in danger of becoming self-perpetuating.

But before we rush to undo what exists, as was illustrated by the undoing attempted and partly accomplished at the California Medical Facility, let's take a closer look at costs and consequences. Just for a place to begin where we place our priorities is a question to be answered since there are never limitless resources. For example, would we get more for the dollars spent on preventing a child from growing up to be a criminal than for the dollars spent housing the adult in a prison? Prisons are costlier to build than schools and many times more costly to operate twenty-four hours of every day. Recent estimates give figures like $36,000 per year to house each inmate. To put that into perspective, a three-year sentence to prison costs $108,000, six-year sentences cost over $216,000 of public resources. We can easily calculate the costs of longer prison terms including life sentences. Punishment is a very expensive response! Obtaining a harsher penalty usually carries with it higher legal and court costs. Because of this, plea bargaining has become commonplace to cut costs. The cost of building and maintaining prisons, the costs of criminal prosecution, the costs of housing and caring for inmates, and the administrative costs can become a part of any careful effort to compare the cost-effectiveness of any alternatives to the "lock 'em up and punish 'em" solution.

Anyone who believes that going to prison is a deterrent punishment to the vast majority of our criminal population is extremely naive. If punishment is an effective deterrent, why do we have such high recidivism rates that have held fairly constant over the span of our "war against crime"? The generally recognized path of the career criminal has been mentioned, first incarceration in a juvenile detention facility by age twelve or thirteen, commitment to a detention facility for delinquent youths for at least a two year sentence or more by age fifteen or sixteen, first prison sentence by age twenty to twenty-three. Where is the deterrent?

Over past decades psychological studies of behavior modification approaches utilizing reward and punishment as methods of shaping behavior, it became apparent early on that what was generally chosen as punishment often had little or no effect. To effectively use a punishment and reward system, one had to carefully observe what was punishing or rewarding to the subjects of the study or treatment program. In the vast universe of what is meaningful to a person is varied and contradictory. That is, what is reward to one person can be punishment to another, and vice versa. Again, for those who promulgate the belief that going to prison is punishment to the habitual offender, and being released from prison is a reward for them is very ignorant of the facts. And yet there are still those who feel that increasing the length of prison sentences will deter criminals, and press for new laws to effect continued increases in our needs for more prisons.

Of course, there are always exceptions to even the general ineffectiveness of prisons in deterring repeated criminal activity in some individuals. There are a number of first-timers to prison that make it their last time. Most of these are the "non-criminally oriented" type, that is, those who do not exhibit the pattern of progression described, who inmates in prison refer to as "state raised," or for whom "criming" is an integral part of their lifestyle. These "one-timers" are usually persons who for the most part lived a law-abiding lifestyle up until they became involved in a crime due to some high stress incident, a so-called "white collar crime" wherein they obtained monies or property from others by fraud, or what is often called "a crime of passion."

Among the latter are, surprise surprise, one-time sex offenders of the non-violent type. To these types of offenders prisons are like the proverbial two by four to the mule, it gets their attention and awareness. But these types represent a small minority in our prison populations.

Nearly everything mentioned here about the increasing prison populations has been discussed in the reports of the National Criminal Justice Commission. Unfortunately, few people read these reports. Other writers have also discussed the rise of a prison-industrial complex paralleling the old military-industrial complex (see *The Real War on Crime* edited by Steven R. Donziger, HarperCollins, 1998). The important point is that as a society, we have allowed our political leaders to create a non-effective (in any positive sense), costly, self-perpetuating, often destructive or harmful solution to a complex social problem, thus following the frequent pattern wherein simple solutions to complex problems result in the creation of more problems than are solved.

Increasing penalties for crime and the construction of more and more prisons have had little real impact upon crime in our society. Recently we have been shocked by new types of violent crimes perpetrated by young people from seemingly ideal, stable families in middle class environments. Perhaps it is time to spend some resources to study the offender, rather than just committing more resources to punishment and revenge. In this type of effort, I have a deep sense that we will also have the side effect of improving our society as a whole.

We must also keep in mind that like any war, there is a long recovery period after the cessation of hostilities and adjustments to the irrecoverable losses. Attitudes are slow to change, many "wounded" will never recover. To make an effective change, we would have to replace emotions with reason, "common sense" with careful scientific proof, assumptions put to the test of effectiveness over and over. Earlier attempts described in preceding pages were hopeful, but too short-lived, underfunded, and exploratory. Effectiveness data was sometimes controversial and tentative. Since much of the data was destroyed and lost in obscurity, it could have provided us with some information about where to begin. Presently, the few efforts at "programs" offered prison inmates are quickly conceived, put into operation to prevent lawsuits, or satisfy critics and not evaluated for effectiveness in reducing recidivism. Many are best described as "window dressing." What is needed is a commitment to develop better effective solutions incorporating the ever-increasing knowledge of factors that shape human behavior. It can be said that we are all born with criminal potential. We are born self-centered, with no sophisticated reasoning, but emotionally reactive with no empathy for others, all factors found in most of criminal thinking. It takes almost two decades from birth to "civilize" us. What shaped the vast majority of us into law-abiding citizens? What factors caused us to become different from those thousands that fill our jails, our juvenile halls, youth institutions, and prisons over and over?

There have been efforts to get information over past years to this question. Poverty, crowded intercity areas, poor housing, broken families, school dropouts, drugs, sex and violence in the media, have all taken their turn as contributors to crime. From time to time, public resources have been committed to one or the other of these factors with little, mixed, or no results. Something is missing that makes each of the factors contributors or non-contributors to creating criminals. There is always the shining success case of a child who grew up in a minority ghetto in a crowded urban area, from an economically deprived family in a crowded tenement, who lacked all the modern niceties of life and became a model citizen and successful. The general reaction is that these factors can't be that important, then, in causing crime. Back to another important distinction in the study of causes, the distinction between contributing factors and essential factors. Simply stated, without the presence of essential factor(s), contributing factors do not always have the predicted impact.

Therefore, while we know with reasonable certainty that the factors cited all contribute to criminal behavior, some essential ingredients need to be present for them to affect some individuals. Why have these essential factors not been defined and remedies brought forth? Perhaps it has, but been rejected and avoided because it is too threatening in some way. As a psychologist in private practice helping individuals towards confronting factors in their lives that are causing them grief or blocking their personal growth and happiness, or preventing them from realizing their own potentials, it is common to encounter resistance, avoidance, or denial. Therefore it is not illogical to assume that society can also be resistive against confronting emotionally and psychologically difficult issues especially if it requires looking inward instead of outward. Therefore, issues that have been brought up in scientific studies, reports by commissions and news events, have not had the same public impact that has resulted from the "war on crime," and its simplistic notion that containment and punishment will solve the problem.

After all, it reinforces the notion that the problem is "out there," and has little to do with good people, and thus the solution is equally impersonal and taken care of by someone else.

It is noteworthy that locating sites for new prisons is not an easy matter. Sites for prisons are easier to establish if they are removed from population centers, and can be touted to nearby residents as a boon to the local economy. "Not in my backyard," is an often heard protest. After all, it is more pleasant if we keep these unpleasant reminders or negative implications out of sight and out of mind. Let someone else deal with it, it's "not my problem."

But the necessity for criminal laws and ways of dealing

with offenders continues generation after generation. True, the average citizen never worries about criminal laws. They conduct their lives according to moral codes or "common sense," the origins of which they seldom give much thought. As humans we are reluctant to accept any possible responsibility for wrongdoing. From time to time we have tried to write off all responsibility with the comforting thought that criminals are just born that way. This approach was often put forth by theorists with much public appeal for the notion. Even professionals jumped aboard until scientific data could find no substance. "Constitutional psychopathic inferior" was one of these theories that caused many (like Billy in an earlier chapter) to suffer the taint of inferior beings, while relieving the rest of us from any responsibility. Then there was the XYY chromosomes and once again these monstrous aliens who committed violent and repetitive murders were outside of any relevance to the rest of us humans.

I would like to take the reader through a process of how the aliens we call criminals come to be, and by omission, how we as a society share the blame. It was my intent in the previous chapters to provide hints from direct experiences and observations in dealing with the lives of criminal offenders, trying to understand how these offenders became aliens to our society as I encountered them. What follows is a common template that evolved.

To begin, there are some significant factors that arrive at birth and become manifest thereafter. Among these are physiological factors that manifest themselves in hyperactivity, learning disorders, and attention deficits. Surveys indicate that these problems are present at significantly higher rates among the prison population as compared to the population at large. Again, not all children who suffer from these problems grow up to be criminals, making these somehow possibly contributing, but not essential, to later criminal behavior.

Many of you are familiar with studies that have supported the idea that early environmental stimulation gives infants and toddlers advantages in early brain development and learning. As you will see, it is in contrast to a broader, presence in the developmental backgrounds of offenders, i.e. neglect. Closely associated to this is the concept of early attachment, as initially brought to attention by studies in the 1930s and '40s and more recently developed by other researchers. While I am trying to avoid making this a scientific treatise, I feel it important to refer to influences that have impacted on my experiences and observations.

Most criminal offenders, like the rest of us, have very little recall of their infancy and toddler years. Much of what they report about this period of their lives are things told to them later by family members, such as the young offender's report that when he was restless or cried as a baby, his mother would blow marijuana smoke into his face to quiet him. This, and other stories of being given a little alcoholic drink as small children, all proved to be the stories from family members who claimed to have witnessed such occasions. I have talked to numerous women who have insisted upon having babies, offering reasons very similar to those offered by a child, that is, wanting a new doll. So as to the very early years of most criminal offenders, we are limited about their actual early development. I have found that a large number had little or no recollection of their fathers, and for good reasons. They never knew who their fathers were or their parents divorced within the first four years of their existence and did not maintain any contact.

There is another problem encountered in attempts to obtain early childhood and even later information from some criminal offenders regarding their childhood experiences, a desperate sense of loyalty or identification with parents.

Joey provides an outstanding example of this. Only after his father's death could he allow himself to question or examine his relationship with his father. This is particularly true in cases where a child is brought up with a brutal parent. Another example was that of a young man from whom I was trying to obtain information about his childhood in an impoverished family. Every mention of the father contained an assurance to me of the virtues of the father. These frequent protests made me suspicious, but it was not until one day when he was talking about his mother's efforts to get some food for him and his siblings that he suddenly broke into tears, sobbing out that his father was a brutal drunk who only showed up to beat his mother, and force her to give him the money she had earned taking in washing and ironing. Interesting too was the fact that this young man's father was recently deceased, and the young inmate expressed guilt about saying bad things about his father. It is not uncommon among both criminal offenders and clients in private practice to respond to the first question about their childhood with, "Oh, I had wonderful parents!"

However, I have not encountered this nearly as frequently among criminal offenders. Stepfathers, mothers' boyfriends, stepmothers, and mothers can be sources of anger whose depths are surprising, even to the offender himself. The cases of Steve and Joey illustrate this contrast.

This seems to be a good point to begin laying down the template for creating an alien. While we have only anecdotes and impressions of their infancy and toddlerhood, we have good reasons to believe that inconsistency was already a part of their experience. Good care alternated with neglect, based not upon the child's needs but the impulsive emotional needs of one or both parental figures. From my work with delinquent and criminal offenders I have become convinced that one factor occurs throughout their developmental years—inconsistency. Whether it is in physical care, guidance, moral learning, or, more important, reassurances that they are cared about, inconsistency becomes apparent. I consider this to be an essential factor.

So in constructing our template for creating aliens, let us remember that we must take inconsistency into account. Having discussed that, let us proceed further. Very often, by the time the child reaches school age or soon after, he has received a label from others which begins to impact self-image. If the child encounters different goals and values and behaviors at school than those he learned at home, problems and labeling can begin. Let us call our developing young alien Johnny, for convenience. At home, Johnny has already learned some powerful lessons. Just to cite a few, Johnny learned from the adult male of his household that the most effective way to get your way is by aggressive actions. Johnny has learned this very effectively through both example (modeling), and the process called "identification with the aggressor" as a recipient. In this process he also learned some choice language, some rewarded by remarks such as "isn't that cute?" In addition, Johnny is starved for attention which is a hard to come by commodity at home. Among the kinder labels he is likely to receive and maybe has already received from home, are "problem child," "troublemaker," "bully." What if there is some unusual physical feature about Johnny? Other children are quick on labels, "crip," "four eyes," "bones," "fatty." In a paper I wrote long ago I gave the example given me by two teachers of a little boy with a pituitary condition. Other children delighted in using him to be the "monster" in their playground games, feigning shock and fear at his appearance. We don't have to go to that extreme. Let us just choose one not so obvious problem, dyslexia, or attention deficit disorder. Now, there is only a problem when Johnny is called upon to read in the class exercise, or explain back to the class something the teacher just taught. His fumbling and stammering efforts are met with classmates' snickers and laughter, and the teacher's admonition that he needs to pay more attention in class or try harder. Comments from classmates later are simple: "dummy," "stupid." Very assuredly Johnny is not developing a feeling of being like his classmates or even any affinity for most of them, envy maybe, but no affinity. Complaints at home fall on deaf ears and at best elicit the stern reminder that he has to go to school. At school his only relief and support comes from a small group experiencing a similar alienation process. They concoct their own labels for the majority of the other students, "lames," "stooges," "pets." Johnny and his group band together and reassure each other that they have something over the others, that they "know where it's at," that the majority of students there are just "jerks" who go along with the teachers and are the "real dumb-dumbs." The essence of true alienation, "them versus us," has begun. Any rules, laws, mores, etc., followed by them is rejected by Johnny and his group. But wait, what about at home? The adults at home are busy or at least preoccupied with things more important than Johnny's social problems.

Again, significant (not essential) numbers of parents of criminal offenders are or have been alcohol or drug abusers, and drunken fights in the homes of children who end up in prison is fairly commonplace. Ask a delinquent why he had rather go to juvenile detention than go home and you will often get reasons like, "the old man comes home drunk all the time and wants to fight." "My mom's got a new boyfriend and I don't get along with him because he is drunk or high a lot of times." The home environment has made "hanging out" with other aliens preferable. Late in the alienation process, some parents do notice and try to intercede, but too late and with too little in their favor. Johnny and his fellow aliens have long given up on adults, parents, teachers, etc. "They say one thing and do another." The inconsistencies experienced over the years have become convincing that "all authority is untrustworthy and it's a dog eat dog world, man!"

Yes, when Johnny began to have confrontations with authority, juvenile officers, teachers, etc., his parents did finally react. Punishment received at home quickly revealed that Johnny's wrongdoing was not the focus. Rather, parental displeasure is often focused on how he had inconvenienced them. Example, "Do you realize I had to go down to the school and talk to the principal?" Or, "You caused me to have to take off work to go down to Juvenile Hall to pick you up!" There is probably not a juvenile justice who has not heard parents complain that they "just can't do a thing" about their wayward child. "Juvenile beyond parental control," rules the juvenile court, and off to a group home or other long-term detention center goes the miscreant, often with a parting admonition from the parent, "See what you got yourself into, I warned you it was going to happen sooner or later."

Well, now our Johnny is off to "alienation school," to further the process. He is no longer contaminating our nice neighborhoods or being a problem in our schools. He has been "taken out of society," to receive further indoctrination by fellow aliens. "Them versus us" get a real clarification now.

There are those often cited warnings that are seen during this stage of development. Destructive behaviors that appear to be motivated by a sense of power and excitement. Destructive fire setting and other dangerous destructive acts, cruelty to animals seem to carry expressions of resentment and power, extreme rebellion, mastery and excitement that may be aimed generally or specifically. One multiple murderer I became acquainted with recalled the pleasure he received from torturing and killing the pet cats of his mother and destroying his older sister's dolls. Significantly, his victims were all females, with one exception. He harbored a deep resentment towards his mother for leaving his father and moving to a distant state when he was about to start school. The house his mother rented had only sleeping facilities for mother and older sister. A small room in the basement became his bedroom. The most horrible memory of this era was having to pass by the roaring furnace with its flickering flames each time he went to and from his basement cubicle. His imagination created fearful images among the flames and flickering shadows. In time his resentment grew as mother and sister, comfortable in their bedrooms, brushed off his fears of the "furnace monster." At school he was teased about his shyness and the fact that he was physically larger than his classmates, further fuel for his misery and resentments. There was no contact with his father after mother's divorce and departure to other locales.

The happiest memories and respite from his miseries were occasional summer visits to his grandparents' farm where he enjoyed hikes in the hills above their house. He also enjoyed helping grandfather with chores and was rewarded by grandfather with a rifle so he could shoot squirrels in the woods on the hill above the house. On warm afternoons he liked climbing up the hillside and sitting in the shade of a tree where he could see grandma sitting in her rocking chair in a window knitting or crocheting. He could also see grandfather doing things in the garden and around the barn. Sometimes just idling away time, he would sight his rifle on grandma sitting in her favorite window. This was the summer of his fourteenth year.

One day he saw grandfather come out of the house and get into the car parked in the carport and drive down the driveway to the main road. The boy assumed that grandfather was making one of his usual trips to the nearest store in town for something. As the car disappeared he went back to sighting his rifle at different targets, especially grandma. "What if I pull the trigger?"—a thought that began to repeat itself in his mind until it happened. He admitted he didn't like grandma because she bossed him and grandfather around a lot, but he hadn't planned to shoot her. He ran into the house to where grandma was slumped in her chair, blood all over her dress. She was dead!

What to do? Grandfather would be angry at him and would be deeply grieved to find grandma dead. The thought of grandfather's grief was foremost in his mind when he heard grandfather's car pulling into the carport. He ran and hid behind the kitchen door as grandfather came in with some bags of groceries. Before grandfather walked towards the door to the room where grandmother was slumped in her chair, the boy leveled the gun and fired into his grandfather from behind. Grandfather did not have to grieve for grandmother.

The boy went to court and was committed to the State Hospital for the Criminally Insane until he reached maturity, after which he was to remain until he was deemed no longer a danger. While in the hospital setting he was compliant, proved to be bright and was able to attend classes within the facility. In time he was released to the community and was scheduled for annual psychiatric examination for three years. At the time he was being interviewed for one of these evaluations by a designated psychiatrist, the head of his second female victim rested in his refrigerator freezer in the apartment where he lived. Years later he communicated to me the peak of excitement he experienced each time he could see in his female victim's facial expression, her realization that she was about to die. His adult killing spree included nine young women, his mother's best lady friend and finally, his mother. He served as one of my clerks in prison until I had to replace him due to his insistence on doing things his way rather than established procedures.

This is undoubtedly an extreme case, but it illustrates the development of a deep-seated hatred and rebellion that became acted upon in stages. As a preschooler, his world was suddenly and inexplicably torn apart. He had evidently felt some affinity and support emotionally from father. In his eyes, mother took him away from father and plunged him into a situation of terror and misery in which he received no emotional relief or support. None of this would encourage the development of attachment and empathy. His experiences at school furthered his resentments and feelings of being alone. Indeed, he exhibited that third warning signal, he became a loner. That is, no close friends, little or no participation in social events, keeping his own counsel. Then there is the acting out against the cats and dolls, expressions of his deep resentment and antidotes for his sense of powerlessness. We get the idea he felt some feelings of acceptance and worthiness from grandfather, but these were in danger in his perception of grandmother. We can extrapolate from this that the final discovery of the ultimate excitement of the power of life and death became the key to pleasure in a hostile, alien world.

So we can have two paths of overall social alienation, affiliation with others who share Johnny's distrust of adults and rejection by the mainstream of peers, or isolation from everyone, thus keeping one's own pain invisible to others. Isolation from others is dangerous in that it allows the development of ideas and fantasies that are not corrected or questioned by others with healthier ideas. Over the years I have become conditioned, when reading news accounts of horrendous offense by a youth, to look for the adjective "loner" in the descriptions from those who were fellow students or neighbors of the offender.

So far, in our construction of a template for major factors contributing to our prison populations are certain parental and peer factors. As already described, there are the juvenile halls, group homes, and youth prisons that thoroughly promote and prepare our hypothetical "Johnny" for his criminal career. Just in case he might on occasion exhibit some controls, we need to add alcohol and drug addiction. Indeed, these addictions sometimes are sufficient unto themselves in many cases. I recall doing an evaluation on an inmate whose records indicated that he was raised by well-educated parents who appeared to have "spoiled" him with material things. As an adolescent he did well in school, hobbies and sports, but also liked to hang out occasionally with ghetto "street kids." He even completed college degrees resulting in a doctoral degree in psychology. Sadly, he became involved in drug use while in college, graduating from marijuana to cocaine. Later he began shooting amphetamine and cocaine mixtures and using alcohol to an excess, which ended his short career as a psychologist. He began doing burglaries and other offenses to support his addiction, another variant in the much more common template for criminal offenses.

It is apparent there are several paths that lead to prison besides the most trodden one of direct abuse and neglect. I have occasionally after giving a talk on criminality, had someone comment that I seem to put the blame on parents. Once again, instead of focusing on blame, we need to understand the factors that contribute to an infant growing up and becoming a criminal. That infant is not an alien from outer space, but an earthly human molded into an alien by the mainstream of our society. Before we can develop better solutions than we have currently, we need to better understand the problem so that we can prevent it.

In the next chapter I will explore even more the impact of parenting, and its importance to all of us psychologically. As a researcher, I attempted to explore some manifestations of this among adult criminals with some significant results. As with much scientific research, the results can often lead to more questions. Science is a frontier where we struggle to push forward with more knowledge into the unknown.

Ten

Early Creation Factors of Alienation

I am sure some who read the title of this book mistook it for a sci-fi novel. No, it does not refer to aliens from other planets, rather, more specifically to aliens within our own culture. In every culture the parents are the primary interpreter of the culture to their children, the accepted modes of behavior, the moral values and beliefs, the do's and don'ts of manners in relating to others within the culture. These cultural mores are very powerful in determining what is acceptable and not acceptable. Over generations there are gradual changes in some of the cultural mores, but the essential core remains.

Throughout history it has been clear that intolerance, and the rejection of cultural differences, has resulted in wars, and sometimes the annihilation of smaller cultures by larger, more dominant cultures. Subcultures are small groups who harbor some beliefs and behaviors not practiced by the culture within which they exist. So long as they do not offend the major cultural tenets, these subcultures are tolerated. However, if a subcultural group violates major cultural tenets, they often face violent reactions and are persecuted and driven into hiding or fleeing to isolated places.

The prison culture is one such subculture. It is important to recognize that adherence to the cultural mores of the culture within which you are raised and spent much of your life is essential to a healthy survival. It is fundamental to human nature that those thoroughly indoctrinated into a particular culture strongly believe that theirs is superior to others. In Chapter Two I described prison culture, and the mores and demands that hold sway in that environment. Over subsequent years of working with criminal offenders both in and out of prison, I began to realize that the impact of that culture was so powerful as to overcome some inmates who were motivated to make real efforts to break their past criminal patterns, to return to prison.

I have described the early factors that begin the alienation from society outside of prisons. Remember such factors in the homes of these future aliens such as abuse, neglect, modeling and encouragement by parents of violence, drug abuse, rejection by members of the dominant society, a building resentment and anger towards all authority, who represented that dominant society. Early rebellion frequently resulted in negative encounters with an increasing array of authority figures such as teachers, police, judges, and others. Juvenile halls often became a major training facility for strengthening this alien culture. There they discovered others with whom they could share their angry feelings and negative experiences and, most of all, their general resentments. In this evolving culture they learn a major value lies in being strong and surviving, the purpose of all cultures—survival! Do what you have to do is a guiding principle. The basis of early cultures were adaptations to their environment. The culture I am about to describe is also an adaptation to an environment.

Juvenile halls are segregated places. Boys in one part of the facility, girls in another. Each has a few cells and series of dormitories. There are also some limited recreational facilities, dining rooms, and day rooms. The settings are very stark with barred windows, holding cages with furnishings that are hard and often bolted to the concrete floors. Stark concrete walls nearly everywhere.

There are adults whose job it is to maintain order and to counsel youngsters on the rules they are supposed to follow. This is usually referred to as counseling, and some of the adult employees are sometimes referred to as counselors. The training and experience of these counselors has varied over time in these facilities for "wayward children." Some facilities have a degree of segregation by age groups. The offenses these youngsters have committed are varied. Those with a violent nature are often housed in the cells, while the less violent live in the dormitories.

Newcomers frequently are shy and cautious, especially if it is their first time in such a place. After their initial session with the adult counselor, they begin the process of exposure to their peers. After initial sounding out and acceptance or rejection by more experienced peers, begins the establishment of the role the newcomer will occupy among the other residents. Since the vast majority of these youngsters have experienced rejection and ridicule by peers outside the juvenile halls, many are pleased to discover the common experiences of their peers inside and the acceptance received. Here their anger and resentment toward all authority figures is reinforced by those whose values are close or the same as their own. The feeling of acceptance here becomes of great importance.

The peer leaders are the larger, more aggressive youngsters who tend to gather groups of followers. Under the watchful eyes of the adult counselors, peace is usually maintained. Nonetheless, rivalries frequently surface, fights occur, and disciplinary cells are filled. Adaptation to this environment, like others, demands adherence to cultural beliefs and values. Authority figures are the enemy, so have as little contact with them as possible. Tattling is strictly forbidden and can result in rejection, and possibly violence from peers. If you are one of the lucky ones that receives goodies sent in by family or friends outside, you can buy lots of favors by sharing. If you see something you want, take it if you are strong enough. You have to be tough to survive without friends, and therefore it's wise to belong to a group.

Some children adapt well to the juvenile hall environment and often return. Some even find it a safe haven from violent home environments and the physical or sexual abuse by parents. The frequent fighting between alcoholic or drug addicted parents is more frightening than the fights in juvenile halls that are usually quickly stopped by the counselors.

Budget restraints dictate the availability of programs for children in juvenile halls. Even if some efforts are made at this level, most of the children are resistive to becoming involved. Resentment and mistrust of adults and the shortage of highly trained counselors or psychologists prevents much in the way of individual evaluation and attention to individual needs. The result is too often the soon return of those children released, back to juvenile hall for repeat offenses. A pattern is now evident. These children are well acquainted with the beliefs and mores that allow them to adapt comfortably within those confines, compared to home.

As these children mature into adolescence, their crimes tend to become more serious. Instead of a few months in a juvenile hall, they now spend long terms, even years, in state youth authority institutions. The lessons learned for survival in juvenile hall are reinforced with greater intensity. Learning to fight is very important. If one were unwilling to fight and fight hard, one had to team up with a protector. Gangs form around many of the stronger and aggressive boys. Even then, you have to fight if ordered. Quiet, unaggressive youths suffer great humiliations. With the sex drive running high at the adolescent age, that leaves two options among this group perceived as weak by their peers. If they appeal sexually to one of the stronger youths, they might become the exclusive sexual slave to that boy. The other option is to become a sexual commodity of one of the stronger youths who would then loan the passive youth out for sexual favors to others in return for other favors and allegiances.

Giving oral sex and receiving anal sex becomes a daily duty to their "protector" or "owner," daily humiliation and expressions of contempt are a daily diet for them. But since they had experienced rejection and contempt from their peers in free society this was not so bad, because here they were protected from physical harm by their "owner" and sometimes even given favors. They were integrated thoroughly into the "inside" culture. As they crossed the age barrier into adulthood, this is the culture they took with them. Prison inmates refer to these youth facilities as "gladiator schools."

By the time they have completed their stints in these youth facilities, the graduates have become thoroughly adept at the inmate language. It often resembles "jive talk" or "hip talk." However, it takes on different meanings. Just as other youngsters develop language codes to baffle adults or to exclude non-accepted peers, these delinquent youths develop their own special language that sets them apart from the dominant culture and authority figures. Use of this special language often gives a delinquent youngster the first feelings of acceptance after years of rejection from members of the outside culture, and further enforces their integration and sense of belonging with delinquent and eventually adult criminally oriented offenders.

Alienation from authority is strengthened. Beatings by frustrated guards or others assigned to watch over these youths are not uncommon since the more aggressive youths would also try to humiliate or attack them. Frequent throwing of urine or feces at guards occurs. It is like living in a war zone for all concerned. The sexual activities among the inmates of these facilities are often ignored with the attitude that at least they aren't fighting or causing trouble.

Another factor that the vast majority of these youthful inmates have in common is the lack of early guidance and education that results in mature reasoning. Cause and effect reasoning is almost totally absent. Everything negative is someone else's fault. They are extremely self-centered and often oblivious of their surroundings. It is this immaturity of thinking that results in their getting caught for their crimes and the childlike excuses they are prone to give when caught. Grouped together in these youth facilities, they train each other on how to reason and what is socially acceptable. They now are well integrated into a culture that is foreign to that outside of these facilities.

Within a few years, the majority of these youths will find their way into adult prisons where they adapt quickly to familiar customs. True, the prisons are larger, housing thousands, and are to many intimidating at first. But the familiarity with the prison culture soon overcomes the fear of the larger population and the huge cellblocks and they begin to feel at home.

Many prisons now have large dormitories with double and sometimes triple high bunk beds. While most beds in prison are narrow steel bunks, isolation cells usually have concrete slabs. Steel and concrete are a large part of the visual environment. The physical environment in a prison is a very harsh one. Activities within a prison have become more and more limited within prisons in California. The growing prison population in California has resulted in increased building of more and more prisons, which in turn fill to beyond capacity. Thus spaces for programs to rehabilitate or even occupy inmates in useful activities have been filled with more bunk beds. It has resulted in California having the largest prison population in the world.

It is a common notion among those in our society that allowing inmates positive outlets for their time and energy is nothing more than "mollycoddling" inmates. Athletic or exercise facilities, personal property items provided by family or friends, such as small television or typewriter, limited by prison policy, provide needed outlets for inmates. Gone are most educational and job training programs that might expose an inmate to a culture outside of the prison culture. What does this leave? In the prison culture it results in "dead time," that is, empty time with boredom. However, this is short-lived as the prison culture provides for exciting activities. Prison gangs and individual rivals blossom forth in warfare and riots. It should be noted that in our free society, directing and channeling our needs for excitement is well provided for in acceptable activities.

Given the austerity, violence, and boredom within the prison environment, many of us wonder why so many inmates when they get paroled soon return to prison for a new offense or violations of their paroles. Remember that cultures initially form as an adaptation to a physical environment. Once adapted to surviving in that environment, the individual now becomes comfortable with the familiar. He or she knows what is expected, how to gain respect from associates, and what not to do to lose that respect. When such a person is taken out of their familiar environment and placed in another unprepared, where he is rejected by others and often described as "scum" with no or few skills needed for survival in that culture, it becomes very frightening. I will share with you some of the letters and conversations from some who have had the experience.

A letter I received from a young man under thirty years

of age who had spent most of his life in the facilities described, clearly illustrates the continued struggle. This man had done very well in his therapy program, and was highly motivated to turn his life around and never return to prison. He successfully completed his parole and had moved to another state. In the letter, he brought me up to date on his life. He had finally married and both he and his wife worked at good jobs. They had a car and were in the process of decorating their house. "I'm just starting to feel human again . . . haven't touched no booze or drugs. Had no desire to even when things were tough. I had to see if I could really make it. The only thing that bugs me is that Joint feeling, it's hard to explain, it's kind of scary. Like sometimes I get lonely for it. Maybe that's why so many don't make it."

He went on to tell how he didn't feel on the same level with the "free people." "I don't know if it's below or above, I just want to get away." He further concluded, "I mostly blame the Joint for this feeling and I hope I can overcome it some day.

"The tensions out here are greater than those in prison. The biggest one is responsibility and the gnawing thought of the easy way out. In prison you don't have much choice, out here the door swings both ways. Another thing is to be conditioned to tensions in prison, the close association with others, where out here you can get away and yet you have a feeling of loss, the tensions of interpersonal relationships. But you can divide the bitter and the sweet and you'll find a little more sweet for the price of freedom."

He asked me to share what he said with the inmates in my treatment groups. Subsequent letters revealed that he slowly won the struggle to adjust to the new culture so different from the prison culture in which he was essentially raised.

Many others were unable to adapt in free society. Some

struggled for some time, but succumbed to overwhelming emotions. One bright, well-read individual wrote me a six-page letter vividly describing his emotional struggle to try to find his place in a new culture. He described his loneliness, not being able to identify with other human beings, the need "to understand the meaning of life or of being wanted." In the end he quoted from a sociology book he was reading, "If a person cannot function properly in one society or country, he should find one where he can function properly." Over time I had occasion, many times unfortunately, to interview returnees to prison after high expectations of success. They reported the difficulties they had sleeping at nights, awakening because they missed the night sounds of prison, loneliness for their prison companions, fear of unfamiliar people, failures to gain employment due to prison background, and fears of their employers when they did gain work. The solution was the same. "Buy a ticket" back to prison with a new offense or violation of parole rules. They all claimed to feel more relaxed and safer in prison.

I can't resist reporting a little irony here. Follow-up studies over some years had consistently found that parolees who were released to supportive families did significantly better on parole. However, some law enforcement chiefs from larger cities convinced legislators that too many inmates were being released to their cities. As a result, a law was passed that parolees had to be released back to where they committed their offense. Thus, the vast majority was released to areas where they had no positive social connections, another rejection by the outside culture.

So often the majority of their lifetime spent adapting to the values of juvenile, youth and adult "correctional" facilities and obtaining acceptance and respect of this inside culture, is there any question what a powerful impact it has on the inmate over the years? Add to that the rejection, contempt and unfamiliar demands and often early abuse heaped upon them by members of the outside culture, it poses a powerful obstacle even to real efforts to "rehabilitate" those who have never been habilitated to the outside culture. Thus, the biggest obstacle to reducing recidivism is the prison culture itself. To appreciate this fact, imagine if you were taken out of familiar surroundings and away from long-time associates, and suddenly set down in the middle of a foreign culture away from any supportive contacts. You are given a few dollars and some rules to follow, but you have a basic understanding of the language. Many of the people in the strange culture do not seem to want you around, and may treat you with a degree of contempt. You have only two choices, to overcome your fears of the strange, unfriendly surroundings, or use whatever means available to return to your past familiar surroundings where you felt more secure.

To most citizens in our free society it is unimaginable that anyone could learn to feel more safe and secure in the harsh violent settings of our youth and adult prisons. But it is covered in the old adage that as a whole we humans are comfortable with the familiar and fearful of the unfamiliar. As humans, we have some basic needs in common: the need for nourishment, both physical and mental, the need for attention and recognition, need for acceptance from others, need to feel someone cares about us and will protect us, and the need for guidance.

With regards to physical nourishment, our society generally responds with help to a malnourished infant or child. Sometimes this requires that the infant or child be removed from neglectful parents. On rare occasions an infant is discarded in a garbage dumpster, unwanted by the natural parents. More frequently a small child suffers from mental malnourishment by alcoholic or drug-addicted parents or parents who feel they have better things to do than coddle a small child. Sometimes there are prenatal problems caused by alcohol or drug abuse or other harmful habits, particularly by the mother while carrying the fetus in her womb.

As the child matures, the child demands attention by crying or some other behaviors. "Look at me!" becomes the goal of more and more behaviors, and the need to feel acceptance from the parent for certain behaviors takes on added pressure. Sibling rivalry for fulfillment of these needs to feel special, or the chosen one among siblings, often occurs. If a child cannot fulfill these needs via positive behaviors, it often finds it via bad behaviors. Differentiation between acceptable and unacceptable behaviors depends on which gets rewarded the quickest.

The need for acceptance grows stronger as the child gets older. The search for someone who cares follows almost in tandem. In the outside world the child is increasingly exposed to little friends or some adult who may provide this in the absence of the parents. A nice neighbor next door, or a sympathetic teacher may provide some sense of acceptance and caring. There are times when this acceptance and caring from others outside the home offsets the negatives within the home to a degree that may benefit the child's later development.

The need for protection is also a very powerful force, and underlies the child's early needs for guidance. I have an example when teaching child development classes where a parent takes a child out to play in the front yard. The parent instructs the child to play on the grass and not go near the street. Shortly thereafter the child heads for the street. I have two examples of how a parent could respond. One way would be to tell the child that it had been told not to go into the street, that it might get hurt. "But if you want to go in spite of my warning and get hurt, don't come crying to me."

The message to the child is confusing. One message is that there maybe is no danger in the street, and another is that the parent doesn't care if I get hurt. Another response would communicate that there is a danger in the street and the parent cares. "If you do not stay on the grass and away from the street, I will bring you inside and not allow you to play." This type of response assures the child both that there is a danger in the street and that the parent cares enough to guide and protect him or her from unknown dangers in the world outside.

Our developing aliens from our free culture rarely find fulfillment of early needs of being cared about, of trusting guidance. They, like all children, continue to test the limits of hopefully caring adults. But our budding aliens usually received inconsistent or indifferent responses. The lack of guidance and the fulfillment of the other needs of childhood leads to behavior problems that result in a stay in juvenile hall. Even though a little frightening at first to some, this often results in getting some attention, albeit negative, from irate parents and other authority figures. They discover other children who share their rebellion and welcome them into their developing alien culture.

While most of us in the dominant culture disapprove of the delinquent behaviors and mores of this developing criminal culture, we need to remember that as humans we share in their underlying needs. But as they become more integrated into the institutional criminal culture, the need to survive takes greater precedence. Once they learn to survive that culture, other needs also become fulfilled. Ironically, within youth and adult prisons there is the structure and guidance they didn't get outside. Counselors and guards, as well as their peers, provide for these basic needs. Although trust of others is hard to come by, evidence of care, although fleeting, and often superficial, is there in the form of food, housing and medical provisions. To be sure, there are dangers present as in all cultures. But once one learns how to avoid or minimize these dangers, survival becomes easier.

It should be noted that in all societies or cultures there are multiple ways of dealing with the stresses of life. Many learn to deal with stresses constructively, such a recreational activities like sports, hobbies, and family activities. They have enough self-confidence and social awareness to confront and resolve problems that confront them. However, there are many who habitually take what is called avoidant responses such as alcohol and drugs, constantly changing environments, and other ways of resolving problems. Yes, going to prison can also become an avoidant response for those who have adapted to prison culture, and lack the skills and support to adapt to free society. These avoidant responses are a big hurdle to face in habilitating criminal offenders.

Eleven
Those Rejected by Both Cultures

One of the most powerful human drives is sex and it has often had strong impacts on the histories of all cultures. The age in which an individual can participate acceptably in sexual activities continues to be arbitrary, even in present day cultures, including our own.

A brief review of this subject from our knowledge obtained from cultural anthropology and historical accounts illustrates how we humans have dealt with our sexuality. For example, early South Seas Islands cultures had elaborate ceremonies referred to as "puberty rites" which clearly marked the demarcation between childhood and adulthood. Passing through these ceremonies often involved painful circumcision type cuttings. At the close of the ceremony the newly designated adult was totally treated as an adult, and had rights to all adult privileges. The determination of when this ceremony took place was when the child showed physical signs of pubescence, usually between twelve and fourteen years of age.

In many cultures throughout history, sex between adults and children was and is accepted, and it is known that adults who prefer such liaisons sometimes travel to these cultures for the purpose of indulging their preferences. Even different religions and cults vary in how they deal with this topic. Over history, how leaders and nobility handled the subject varied from abstinence to the right of the first night, wherein the local lord could demand the right to initiate the children of his serfs into sex.

Today, in the United States, the age of consent varies from state to state. Also, we are ambiguous in our attitudes about sex. A few decades ago, dress codes required strict modesty, no suggestive or revealing clothing. Gradually over time as movies and television became major sources of entertainment, the previous restrictions have disappeared. From the aforementioned shocking line of Clark Gable in Gone With The Wind, "Frankly, my dear, I don't give a damn," to the present anything goes in terms of sexual utterances, descriptions of sexual anatomy and behaviors can be constantly heard and even seen. Sexual scandals among media stars get wide publicity and increased viewer attention. What few restrictions still exist are under attack as censorship in our culture.

In contrast, sexual offenses against the umbrella of the law are usually harshly dealt with regardless of any mitigating circumstance. The types of sexual variances in the behavior of humans is seemingly endless. As in general human experience, intense emotional experiences often cause lasting emotional and psychological fixations within the individual. These causative experiences commonly involve experiences so foreign to all other learning and experience in life that the individual finds it difficult to incorporate, and thus develops disturbing psychological defenses in attempts to cope with the emotional trauma. Such severe traumas have long been known to happen among soldiers in wartime, sometimes referred to as "war neuroses."

Sexual emotions among humans are very intense. The so-called sexual drive usually begins with the advent of puberty, but can be strongly influenced by earlier exposure to sex. Sexual aberrations can occur as the result of something or some person taking on a sexual meaning. The resulting sexual excitement can in turn result in subsequent attempts to duplicate the experience. (I will discuss other human behaviors that emanate from the desire for excitement later.) An example would be a young male, usually shy around girls, but nonetheless sexually interested. He obtains access to female panties and uses these to further excite himself during masturbation. Sometimes the excitement can be increased by stealing women's undergarments. Some will find it exciting to wear these undergarments while masturbating.

Our shy male adolescent, perhaps forced to deny his sexuality, via parental prudish or religious attitudes, may turn to a common known expression of genital exhibition. Early feelings of powerlessness can result in an increase in sexual excitement via control of the sexual partner, sometimes resulting in rape. In short, there seems to be no limit to the variants of human sexual expression and sometimes cults and clubs that cater to them.

However, there are two types of sexual behaviors that are harshly responded to in our culture. One is sexual acts against the will of another, and the other is sexual acts involving children under the legally specified age of consent. Forcing another person into a sexual act stems from a variety of underlying factors as already noted. Rape can occur sometimes directly from the disinhibiting effects of alcohol, or the increased aggressiveness brought on by illegal drugs. The act involves a lack of sensitivity to the victim, the unique meaning (sometimes symbolic) the act has to the perpetrator, or an extreme sociopathic orientation characterized again by the attitude that "I can take what I want when I want it."

The sexual molestation of a child has a very surprising span of motives to most citizens in our culture. A significant number of child molesters were themselves sexually molested as children. The circumstances under which their own childhood sexual molestations occurred influenced the meaning it had to them. Many of these stemmed from such circumstances as growing up in a home lacking expressions of affection and attention. Their adult molester showed them the affection and attention they so craved, and the sexual acts took on the meaning of a secret, special bond. Most professionals know that probably a majority of such early sexual molestations are never reported. Many of these include a failure on the part of the adult to demarcate the roles of parent, adult, or close relative to the child. The adult, in such cases, actually feels a deep affection for the child. The negative impact on the child is when the child matures enough to realize that this is "unnatural" behavior. Now the child is in serious emotional conflict between the affection and love experienced, and the sexual pleasure and unnatural acts involved. As therapists and others know well, the victims of this conflict often blame themselves for what happened. In some cases, this guilt can result in serious consequences, including suicide.

The type of child molestation described above is usually limited to one child rather than multiple victims. Also, the adult does not initially seek out the child for sexual purposes. Since the sexual activity often stems from efforts to resolve some of the adult's unresolved emotional conflicts, this type of child molester usually responds well to psychotherapy. They represent the majority of the convicted child molesters that I had to evaluate and treat.

Unfortunately there is a small number of another type of child sexual molester that represents to the general population in our society that stereotype of all child molesters. This small group of child molesters is referred to as "child predators." These are the ones who go out and grab children they don't know, or entice them to go somewhere with them.

218

They are extremely dangerous, and at a seminar on child molesters conducted by a FBI psychologist it was emphasized that these are the ones that needed to be the focus of law enforcement and public alert. While this group represents an estimated less than three percent of all cases of child molestation, due to public hysteria about child molesters in general, efforts to focus on the small group is diffused by grouping them with all child molesters.

These sexual predators of children and youth are focused on the excitement of the search, the capture, and their sexual gratification. The element of power and control over the child adds to their excitement. All of these elements overcome any recognition of the child as a human. Rather, the child is just an object that is sometimes disposed of afterwards. At our current level of knowledge, there is no "rehabilitation" or effective treatment for this group of child molesters, and therefore these individuals should never be considered for release back into society.

Another dangerous group of sex offenders are the serial rapists. Again, power and control over their victim are essential elements contributing to their sexual excitement. Once again, some of these type of sex offenders expand their behaviors to include superfluous violence, to torturing their victims, and even to killing their victims. Why some rapists carry their sexual behaviors so far is once again dependent upon the personal meanings they attached to these behaviors earlier in their lives. This represents another group that poses a serious danger to society and needs to be subjected to a lot more scientific study.

The broad range of human sexual expression is seemingly limitless, and often shocks or puzzles most of us. Among these are those who reject the birth sex and insist on hiding their birth sex, or even surgically changing it. It is true that there are some individuals born with genitalia of both sexes, and are referred to as "hermaphrodites." But the much larger number is suffering from what is sometimes referred to as genital or gender dysphoria. Males, so affected, commonly resort to sex hormone treatments to enhance female characteristics. A few even resort to surgical alterations.

Needless to say, some of these gender dysphoric men end up in prison. At the California Medical Facility we had a separate housing unit for these individuals. A question of major medical concern was whether or not extensive use of hormone treatment should be suddenly terminated in prison. As coordinator of clinical services I was asked if I could come up with some ideas on the subject. I interviewed some individuals who had undergone both hormone therapy and genital alterations from special medical facilities across the nation. I obtained the addresses of two of the best known such facilities, and sent requests to them for the guidelines they used to determine when to provide such treatments. After receiving and studying these guidelines carefully, I came up with a set of guidelines for our staff to utilize in determining when to continue or not continue hormone injections at CMF. The staff decided that since I had done such extensive research of the literature on the subject that I should be the one to evaluate and recommend whether or not hormone treatments be continued. I admit that I was not pleased having this added burden, and gave it a lower priority so that I often received complaints from the inmates involved over delays in their evaluations. This task expanded to the point that I was also called as expert witness a couple of times for the Superior Court.

For those of you who are curious about the criteria adopted, here are the basics: 1) Medical staff require medical documentation of prior treatment for sexual dysphoria prior to imprisonment. 2) A persistent desire on part of individual to identify as a female in early childhood by feminine behavior, talk, play, and fantasies. 3) Lack of interest in their own penis as evidence of their sexual identity or as an organ for erotic behavior with attempts to hide penis from sexual partners. 4) History of working in jobs traditionally occupied by females, while posing as a female. That is, the individual had attempted to live as a female for at least two years. Prostitution alone does not qualify. 5) Assumption of a female lifestyle, with actual steps towards sex change through hormone treatment and use of surgical procedures such as castration and vaginoplasty. 6) No evidence of any psychiatric emotional condition that might impair cognitive function. 7) Evidence that they have a knowledge of the literature on the subject of sexual dysphoria and its treatments and potential dangers. 8) Medical staff include in their referrals for considerations, risks, or other potential negative consequences for discontinuation of hormone medication. I recommended that all medical, psychological, legal and ethical factors involved in dealing with this unusual subpopulation needed a highly coordinated set of guidelines. As a result of these guidelines, there were two inmates transferred to a women's prison, and a few court cases resolved.

One example is that of a thirty-two-year-old subject I was asked to evaluate. He told me that at age seven or eight it became noticeable that he preferred to play with girls than other boys. At age nine he began to put on items of clothing belonging to his sisters, particularly brassieres. At age twelve he had his first sexual experience involving a nineteen year-old male. As a teenager he was teased a lot by his peers for his feminine appearance. He experienced his first ejaculation at age fifteen and later began openly cross-dressing after dropping out of school. Sexually he preferred to be the receptive partner in sexual intercourse and experienced ejaculation via prostate stimulation. He claimed that he wanted surgery to remove his penis, but his mother talked him out of it. At age eighteen he began taking hormone shots from a doctor in Southern California.

He held jobs as a female, both in a restaurant and in a convalescent hospital. He further claimed to have worked as a female dancer and model for private parties. His records showed an arrest for prostitution. The offense resulting in his prison sentence involved standing on a corner dressed as a female when a sailor stopped, and subject entered his car and went with the sailor to a motel room. While "making love" our subject removed the sailor's wallet and took his money. However, the sailor caught him and our subject pulled a knife on the sailor and escaped with the money, only to be caught a short time later. He was convicted of armed robbery.

I have attempted to introduce the reader to the broad and often bizarre span of human sexual behaviors as encountered in our society. Most citizens have not heard of or encountered these extreme sexual expressions. The human sexual drive as noted is very powerful. Couple it with other human drives for control, affection, and other powerful meanings, and sex can result in extreme expressions frequently found in serial killers.

Even within the prison culture sexual offenses are ranked lowest on the social totem pole. Most sex offenders lie about their offenses to other inmates, claiming they were sent to prison for property offenses or even physical assault on a male. Offenses against children can result in beatings or even stabbings by other inmates. Some sex offenders have to be housed in protective custody if their actual offenses become known to other inmates. How their offenses become known to other inmates can occur when an inmate assigned as a clerk in a custodial sergeant's office accidentally overhears a comment or catches a glimpse at an offense roster. On rare occasions a correctional officer, for some personal motives, reveals to other inmates an individual inmate's true offense.

In both our dominant culture and the prison culture, sexual offenses are among the most severely punished. The few that continue to re-offend with additional sexual offenses after release from prison once again is testimony to the power of sexual fixations!

Within the prison culture ironically exists a double standard borne out by the same powerful human sexual drive. Rapes are common in prisons and juvenile facilities, as noted in earlier chapters. Sexual servitude and gang rapes among same-sex populations in institutional settings contrast with the looking down upon sex offenders as lower on the social caste system in prison. Power and a macho image take precedence even in the expression of the sexual drive. Thus the irony is that the same factors that frequently result in forcible sex offenses are the same factors that result in most sexual liaisons in prisons. Any suggestion that the dominant male involved in sex with another male is homosexual could result in the death of the inmate making such a suggestion. Anger, power and sex are a potentially fatal combination in institutional settings and once again characterize the most dangerous of the aliens among us.

As I was writing this chapter, news reports were coming in about some horrendous cases of repeat sexual predators who had kidnapped and murdered some young children after sexually molesting them. The reactions to these reports were enhanced by the news that the worst of these predators have been arrested before for sexually molesting children on several occasions, and managed to avoid prosecution by jumping bail, plea bargaining, and by moving elsewhere without registering or by assuming new identities.

Once again, emotional reactions by politicians ignore previous knowledgeable experts including the FBI psychologist already cited. Politicians want to pass laws creating huge data banks on all sexual offenders, exposing all of them to public exposure that could have devastating consequences upon them and their families. Again, this will diffuse law enforcement efforts to monitor large numbers of sex offenders who pose no threat, rather than placing intense focus and control over those who do. These numbers of dangerous sexual predators could be further reduced by further restricting their release from incarceration, from not being allowed to post bail when apprehended, and subjected to intense evaluation. Once again, prevention via early evaluation and treatment of youngsters who commit unusual sexual behaviors would help reduce later sexual crimes.

Just as politicians rode the bandwagon on the "war against crime," by playing on the emotions of the public, sexual offense will also be clumped together, and politically expedient reactions will result in costly destructive solutions, rather than rational evidence-based ones. Hopefully, more people in our culture are beginning to recognize that current political figures are taking us further and further from laws that benefit our society as a whole.

As mentioned before, our cultural mores are under continual changes. From movies, television, and computers, our children are exposed to more and more explicit sex. The simple swear word "damn" to every swear word or phrase ever used is heard repetitiously on numerous movies and television programs. Sexual scenes have seemingly become a must in many movies and television shows. I have seen full frontal nudity in a few popular movies rated for parental guidance or those ages eighteen or over.

Perhaps the most alarming contributor to the increase of sex offenses against children and adolescents is the computer. Presently, children receive training in computer operations at a young age, and many are provided their own personal computers. As repeatedly occurs, anything we humans can come up with for our benefit can also be turned to our detriment. Thus young people can get on computer "chat lines" with strangers. Many of these strangers turn out to be adults looking for sex with young girls and boys. The excitement and curiosity of these youngsters can lead to indulging in the viewing of sexual activity by both the adult and the youth on computer screens. Some go further and arrange to meet together for the purpose of specific sexual activities.

This rapidly growing type of sexual offenders is amazing in that many of them profess that they see nothing wrong with such behavior. I must confess that I am dating myself when I say that I am glad to have retired from treating sex offenders prior to this new social phenomenon. It represents another burden on parents who are trying to be responsible parents in today's culture. There are reports that some youngsters secretly prostitute themselves to earn money for things they want to buy. The battle between freedom and responsibility continues!

Twelve
How Bad Can It Get?

In Chapter Ten I described the beginning of a trend based on the political advantages of the "get tough on crime" philosophy. The ignorance of lessons learned from history has continued. Administrators of prison systems, youth institutions and prison wardens continue to be those with political connections, rather than those knowledgeable and experienced with the total operation. Civil Service evaluations are no longer relevant, and many such systems have been essentially eliminated.

In California we continue to build new prisons as our jails and prisons are bursting from the pressures of more and more returns to prison, and as confinement is seen as the solution for even the most minor offenses. Over the past decade the increase in violent offenses has risen. Movies, television shows, video games and computers have exposed our children to more and more violence and sex. One can see school children walking to school in clothing similar to that worn by female prostitutes two decades ago, boys wearing low-slung pants with midriff and more exposed. Teenage language is openly sexual. Adolescent gangs have increased in number as well as their level of violence. Social tolerance has increased to the point that many wonder if all social limits are disappearing.

However, there have been signs that the pendulum may

change direction soon. Some public schools are trying to set dress codes for both teachers and students. More parents are becoming aware that they need to monitor what their children watch on television, and the use of their computers. With the return of liquor advertisements on television, the sometimes thin line between personal responsibility and censorship is coming into debate, as well as the termination of an unwanted pregnancy versus the death penalty. This takes us back to what is happening in our prisons.

Recently there have been reports of abuse by guards in Youth Authority facilities and adult prisons. Prison violence has increased as facilities become so crowded that many programs (as much as most were mere window-dressing to impress the legislators) have been completely shut down. The reason is that all available space is occupied by tiers of bunk beds. Medical care of inmates has deteriorated to the point that numerous cases of deaths have resulted. In the California prison system the investigations by federal investigators proved the level of medical care was so bad that a federal judge has taken charge of the medical program of the California Department of Corrections, and vowed to restructure the entire medical program.

Similar problems are occurring in the few mental hospitals remaining, following closure of many of them during the time of Governor Reagan's administration. Jails are packed with mental patients awaiting evaluation since mental hospitals are filled beyond capacity. Again, the level of care provided has been found to result in deaths of a number of patients.

Another by-product of the trend toward increased punishment and fewer paroles is the increasing number of elderly prisoners. This population requires more intense medical care and once again bolsters the costs of medical services in our prisons. Another unanticipated cost of doing away with rehabilitating type programs in favor of punishment.

In the climate of worldwide war with terrorists and the constant news of deaths of innocents and loss of family members, the desire for a kinder world is beginning to surface. Reactions to news of child abuse and children in need of better social guidance have resulted in increased resources aimed at advice and training for parents in guiding children and helping them with various problems. Local juvenile detention facilities are expanding programs to identify and treat the problems that have resulted in the delinquent activities of their wards.

Nonetheless, there are still destructive, counter-productive holdovers from the past. Recent horrible news stories about sexual abuse and murders of children committed by known sexual predators have stirred up public emotions. The fact that these were known predators who had previously been arrested for crimes against children and had been allowed to escape at times with minimal or no consequences, clearly indicates vital omissions in law enforcement and our courts. Some of the predators simply moved to other states after posting bail, or had changed their names and moved away without required registration.

I was dumbfounded, as I am sure many people were, after reading about the prior records of their repeated offenses against children. These individuals were clearly in that less than three percent of all sex offenders previously discussed, that need the focus of our laws. Rather, they tend to fall through the cracks in the laws that lump all sex offenders together. This diffusion overwhelms our law enforcement, parole agencies, and sometimes the courts.

Once again, politicians have begun a repeat of their costly, destructive and ineffective approach to their previously declared "war on crime." They are proposing blanket laws on all sex offenders that will have extremely destructive impact on the vast majority of sex offenders of the past, who have gone through treatment and evaluations and have since established themselves as good citizens and who have families dependent upon them, as well as businesses. Who will feel safer when someone in that nice family next door that you have known for some years has to post a sign in front of his house stating that a sex offender lives there?

Maybe the offense occurred two decades or more ago when he was drinking, or otherwise failed to set boundaries in his or her expressions of affection. As is well known, the human sexual drive often overcomes good judgment. The ones that need our focus are those who repeatedly sacrifice others to fulfill their pathological sexual pleasures. Don't muddy the waters with gross over-inclusiveness!

The prescription programming of the 1960s and 1970s had demonstrated that prison populations could be reduced. There were indications that good educational and vocational treatment and even arts and crafts programs could have an impact on reducing recidivism, as noted in previous chapters. Changing the focus to increased sentences, avoiding "mollycoddling" of inmates with such programs and privileges have further packed prisons and the high cost of maintenance. The cessation of using prison labor to produce products for use by the State has also furthered the cost to taxpayers who support the multiplying prisons and other state facilities.

Politically controlled parole boards have become another source of waste. Decades past, paroles were based upon reports of prison staff concerning how well the inmate had carried out his prescription program, and the evaluations of clinical professionals as to his/her suitability for return to free society. At the present time in California such evaluations are usually ignored. Many inmates have begun not attending their parole board hearings because they are aware that no matter how positive the evaluations given by staff over years, they will not receive a parole date. In fact, for many the parole hearings have become demoralizing to both them and their families, because the hearing consists of having their offense read to them with questions about details of their crimes. No questions or comments about their changes in thinking, values, or the good reports from prison evaluations. It is very apparent that political expediency overrules the knowledgeable opinions of prison staff and professionals. The inmate who many years ago was sentenced under the rehabilitation law, wherein he was given a base term after which, when judged to have been rehabilitated to the point they were no longer considered to be a threat to free society, could be released. But over the years after they were sentenced under that law, the laws have been changed. So the trend that followed by administration and legislators was one of "why spend money on efforts to rehab inmates?" and just build more and more prisons.

Currently the situation in our jails and prisons and mental hospitals is creating dangerous conditions in our society. As I read the daily news today, there was a lengthy article about a woman arrested weeks ago for a "smash and grab" burglary of a local business, who posted bail and was released. Two days later she was arrested again when valuable stolen property from another business was found in her possession. Again she posted bail, but later found to have committed other burglaries, and to be using credit cards stolen in home burglaries committed prior to her initial arrest. She was released on her own recognizance on these crimes. The reason given was that the local jail was almost full, and the few beds left were reserved for more serious offenders.

Such conditions are widespread and contribute to more multiple crimes. Due to the lack of sustained rehabilitation efforts, when convicted offenders are later released after serving their increasingly lengthy prison terms, many quickly return to prison for new crimes or parole violations. A vicious cycle has been created and a growing alienated culture has become a growing threat and burden to our free society. It should be clear that there will be no quick, easy solutions, and certainly no perfect solutions!

Alcohol and drug addictions are high contributors to crime. Yet we are ambiguous about our efforts to resolve these well-known factors. At one point in time, the advertising of alcoholic beverages was restricted, to protect our youth from becoming enamored by alcohol use at a young age. Recently again, such ads have returned to the media. Government has focused on trying to eliminate marijuana use, even though the drug has been demonstrated to have medicinal use in relieving pain of cancer victims, and could be limited by requiring a physician's prescription to obtain.

While focusing government resources to illegalize any and all use of marijuana, one of the most potent, addictive, destructive of human life drugs, methamphetamine, has been allowed to reach epidemic proportions in its use in our culture. For decades another highly addictive drug has been freely and legally available. The catastrophic impact on human health has had little effect on its accessibility. The drug, nicotine, is a drug that, some studies have indicated, ranks along with heroin in its addictive powers. The damage it does to the human body has been documented heavily over the years. To force its removal from tobacco products would possibly eliminate or seriously reduce the industry and government has its priorities as illustrated above.

Recent reports of some arts and crafts programs for delinquent youths have clearly indicated that when youngsters discover that they have some positive talents, they tend to stay away from further antisocial behavior. Once again the

231

wheel has been invented. Recall the high success rate of arts and crafts programs in the prison described earlier! But that became history, and we have a tendency in our culture to have a disdain for history, and thus repeat it.

Perhaps headlines and newspaper articles over the past few years can present a strong picture of how bad the prison situation in the California prison system has become. In 2002, the author in the State Assembly of the "Three Strikes" law touted it as a proven deterrent. In a press article he wrote, "Nearly half of all convicted child molesters are returned to prison within three years of being released." He further stated that child molesters are "among the most prolific and recidivist criminals in our society."

Another newspaper article almost a month later reported a study of the re-arrest of former inmates of prisons in fifteen states, including California. The article contained the statement that, "Convicted car thieves and burglars were more likely to be re-arrested than those who had served time for murder or sexual assault." Later in the article was a statement by another person that emphasis should shift from tougher sentencing rules to rehabilitation programs. However, law enforcement groups disagreed.

Another news release a few months later in 2002 brought attention to a bizarre experiment the CDC wanted to do on mentally ill inmates. Prison officials wanted to house some fifty-two mentally ill inmates for six months in solitary cells specially designed with thick walls and sound baffles, no windows or other sensory stimulation. Fortunately, a judge ruled against such an experiment. Maybe if past scientific research on the effects of sensory deprivation had been reviewed, the prison administrators would not have contemplated such a torturous experiment. But then they were a new operation and did not want to hear anything about the past.

Another article at the same time involved the legal question of "ex post facto," that is, twice being sentenced for the same offense by changing the terms under which an inmate was convicted. As mentioned in an earlier chapter, many murderers were sentenced under a rehabilitation law, that is, after serving a designated number of years they could be considered for parole if there was sufficient evidence that they had completed rehabilitation programs and had a good behavioral record while in prison. The Parole Board then made the final decision. The governor at the time, Gray Davis, had vetoed the parole board's decisions for release of over 150 qualified inmates. It was later decided, after numerous back and forth rulings by the courts, that the governor should have that power.

As I was finalizing this book, California newspapers were flooded with articles about the crisis currently facing the CDC and the scandals that have come to light. Proposals and counter-proposals for solutions are being bounced back and forth. Included among these proposals is the construction of two hospital-like facilities for mentally ill and chronically sick inmates. Again, history repeats itself. Remember in an earlier chapter I worked for years at the California Medical Facility before incoming politicos turned it into "just another prison," and began eliminating the treatment facilities and programs?

Other articles address the problems associated with the powerful correctional officers' union, the CCPOA. Even during my stint as supervisor of clinical research in the 1970s, they were powerful enough to get the administration of CDC to order me to stop a project aimed at weeding out unsuitable officer recruits. Present news reports that the CCPOA is spending five million dollars on political campaign television messages supporting a candidate for governor of the state. The present governor has angered the

CCPOA for statements he made in a speech some year and a half ago, to wit, "For many months, you could not pick up a newspaper without reading about a youth dying in prison, or codes of silence, or abuses of force. I want to put the corrupt people in our prisons on the same side of the bars."

All of these currently discussed issues plaguing the California prison system are not new or unique, but also affect other prisons throughout our nation. We tend to go in circles and fail to learn from the past as I hopefully have illustrated in past chapters. Over the past two decades we have certainly made progress in maintaining aliens in our culture. The question still remains as to how bad will it get, or improve, as we enter this new cycle.

Thirteen
The Maturation of Adult Offenders

As mentioned in previous chapters, we humans are born totally self-centered, driven by impulse and wants. We have to be socialized, enculturated, taught to control our impulses and wants, and eventually how to think or reason. Of course, this all requires models of behavior, caring and guidance, limit setting and teaching about the world around us by adults in our lives. This maturing process ideally involves good parents, teachers, and peers. Unfortunately, this is not the process experienced by the vast majority of our criminal offenders.

We have given illustrations of the immature thinking of many criminals giving rise to clinical staff comments about thirty-year-old inmates whose reasoning resembles that of a pre-adolescent at best. In explaining their offenses, they reveal that they think their explanations are perfectly logical and acceptable. Given the fact that most of them have associated for many years with others who share their immature reasoning, one can understand this continued immature thinking. And again, the old adage that if you tell a story often enough, you yourself can come to believe it.

Add to this self-centeredness and how it is expressed at this very limited level of reasoning. There is no differentiation between "I need" and "I want." In the maturation process guided by the equally immature peers, there is a lack of impulse control. In contrast, those who grew up with parental discipline and guidance that taught them to express their emotions according to time, place and person, according to our culture, they learned to exercise self-control. In the alien culture of our criminal offenders, acting on impulse is very common, closely resembling the behaviors of children. Thus "I want" is frequently followed by "I take." If someone gets in the way, since they are not supposed to keep you from fulfilling your want, they are pushed aside one way or another.

Consequences? Among criminal offenders that is something that others suffer when they interfere with your wants, and is only considered after the fact. Cause and effect relationship in behavior is not something that occurs when acting on impulse. After the fact, cause and effect is only used to explain the consequences the other person suffered because they didn't do what they were "supposed" to do. Once again, it is the type of explaining we have all heard from children who have transgressed against another child.

As stated previously, every culture develops methods and mores for dealing with our basic needs and emotions. Learning how to control our anger, and express it harmlessly, how to share feelings of sorrow, happiness, and love in positive ways, how to satisfy needs such as hunger and sex in acceptable ways have been the result of caring parents who have translated the dominant culture in which most of us have been raised.

The alien culture in juvenile and adult penal facilities, like all other cultures, provides the methods and mores required for that environment, albeit on a much more simplistic and, some would term, "primitive," level. It must reflect and sanction the very immaturity of reasoning and overall limited knowledge of its members. "Enculturation," the process of absorbing one culture into another, is a more accurate description than "rehabilitation" in describing efforts to help these aliens to become productive members of our dominant free culture. Yes, there are a few who were habilitated to our culture, but who took a wrong turn at some point due to individual reasons. These are the minority of inmates who appear to have come from "good" families. For this minority group, the term "rehabilitation" can be accurately applied. In my work with such individuals, I have found that exploring their relationships with their parents is often surprising but very effective in getting them to recognize what changes they need to make in previous thinking and behavior. These individuals are usually "first termers," those experiencing prison for the first time.

But what about those offenders who are now continuing to trigger the expansion of our costly prisons, those thoroughly entrenched in the alien culture of prisons? We know from the limited and short span of "rehabilitation" efforts that some are salvageable, that is, they can be helped to break their criminal patterns and live successfully in our free society. However, this can be risky. Helping the individual probe into their childhoods and the sources of their emotions can sometimes be dangerous even to the trained psychotherapist. This is particularly true of those with violent histories. Attempts by the therapist to bring about what is termed a "corrective emotional experience," that moment when the anger and resentment is suddenly triggered in a manner that reveals to the individual the source of their lifelong battle with free society.

Another risk is knowing when an inmate is making an earnest effort to better understand themselves, and when they are merely trying to extract a favorable report for parole consideration. This risk is minimized by well-trained, knowledgeable therapists and professional review committees, and includes reports and observations by experienced correctional staff. But the final risk is borne by the free society when a person is released from prison after habilitative efforts, and then re-offends. Past research surveys clearly indicate that such failures were very significantly fewer among those who had undergone habilitative efforts than those who had not. Once again, we need to support research efforts to help us learn from these failures.

I have shared with you excerpts from letters and comments from some inmates who were in my treatment caseload that returned to prison out of their fears of free society. Being largely on their own in a strange environment, with only minimal external control, caused them to actively, in some cases, seek out a return to prison. But of equal importance is why some did not, and the reasons to which they attribute their success. I recently opened two storage boxes filled with letters I received over the years from inmates who I had in my treatment caseload many years past. I am sure that my former staff colleagues received many such letters, also. The two most frequent statements contained in those letters were, "You were the first person who ever listened to me," and "You were the only person who really cared about me." These two statements alone say a lot about why these men grew up feeling so alienated.

It is true that these inmates had done lots of harm to others and left many victims in their wake. I have talked with some of their victims and their family members, and there is no undoing some of the terrible sorrows they suffer. But, as said before, to really find out how they came to do the things they did, in short, to understand the criminal mind, one has to set aside pre-judgment and listen. It wasn't always easy, but myself and the very skilled professionals with whom I worked over the years learned a great deal, and in the process were able to help some of these aliens become successful members of our society.

Many of those who entered the psychotherapy programs soon became encouraged to get involved in educational, vocational, and art programs. This further allowed them to discover their potentials and find pride in personal accomplishments in constructive activities, rather than negative acting out. As mentioned, I have received letters from many of those who were in my treatment caseload who became well-known artists, musicians, and successful in various vocations. But the biggest obstacle was and still is breaking from the "correctional" or institutional culture. Another fact that should be noted is that no matter how many successes any rehabilitative efforts achieved, only the failures gain media and public attention, which in turn is taken advantage of by politicos. We need to recognize that there is no perfect solution to any social problem, that humans are so complex that multiple solutions are often needed.

The problem of teaching inmates to reason more maturely is directly connected to the alien culture of our juvenile and adult prisons that serve to perpetuate immaturity in thinking. In addition, as we have illustrated, it fails to prepare many parolees for the transition to freedom.

To counteract this alien culture, we need a multifaceted approach. Throughout their lives, the feelings of rejection and shame from free society has caused them to find superficial pride in their antisocial behaviors, and acceptance by their equally antisocial peers. I use the term "superficial" because I found in their conversations with me, beneath many of these facades, deep perpetual feelings of shame. Suicides in jails and other delinquent and adult facilities occur as a result of shame and hopelessness. Recall that frequently the records of the past behaviors of murderers contained incidents of attempted suicide, and some dramatic serial offenders have reportedly have left pleas for police to catch them and stop their repetitive crimes.

The importance of feeling cared about, and listened to about their feelings and problems, the acceptance by respected peers, and encouragement from teachers and other admired authority figures escaped the childhoods of the vast majority of criminal offenders. Instead, there was no caring by parents, no acceptance by respected peers due to their antisocial behaviors, resulting in being called contemptuous names by others, feelings of rejection by authority figures, and thus nothing to build an essential feeling of self-pride in positive accomplishment.

It should be noted that it has long been known that a larger percentages of the youth and prison populations have learning problems, such as "attention deficit hyperactivity disorder," which no doubt added to their problems from early childhood. Such early problems in school can sometimes be traced back to classroom events resulting in early disciplinary problems and name calling by peers, leading to early resentments and feelings of alienation.

It should be no surprise that as these youngsters grew older, more and more of them turned to alcohol and addictive drugs to escape the emotional pains in their lives. Alcohol is a major disinhibitor. That is, those emotions and impulses that are usually restrained or inhibited are released. Under the influence of alcohol, the anger and resentment comes to expression, often resulting in violent behaviors. Some drugs provide escapes into euphoria, that leads quickly into repetitive and addictive abuse. These escapes result in a disruptive lifestyle that becomes more and more self-defeating. Sadly, many youths begin the use of these drugs to be accepted as a part of a group of peers. They convince each other that they can stop using these drugs any time, scoffing at reports of a drug's addictiveness.

But currently two very destructive drugs that have gained widespread abuse among all social levels are cocaine and methamphetamine. The latter has spread in epidemic proportions, according to numerous surveys and reports. It initially replaced much of the use of cocaine due to its easier and cheaper access, becoming known as the "poor man's cocaine," since it produced similar effects. Methamphetamine can be made easily from over-the-counter ingredients "cooked" into white powder and crystals. It is usually snorted (sucked up through a straw inserted in the nostrils), and sometimes mixed with water into a fluid and injected into a vein. The cooking process is also dangerous, as the fumes can sometimes explode, severely burning anyone close by. A police officer shared with me the account of a raid on a residence known to be a source of meth. As he and fellow officers entered the residence, they saw on the coffee table in the living room syringes, white powdery substances in little rows. Also, there were small cellophane packages of the substance nearby on the table. Standing next to one side of the coffee table were two little girls who turned out to be ages three and five. In the kitchen were the parents, who were obviously cooking up more amphetamine. It is not hard to guess which was more important to these parents, the drugs or the welfare of the two children. Illicit drugs, especially meth, have become a very serious national threat to all social levels of our society.

In my work with criminal offenders over the years I have seen illicit drugs displace alcohol as a primary catalyst to crime. Adults who began use of these drugs at a youthful age frequently show signs of early physical problems such as loss of teeth and appearing much older than their chronological age. Adding to this is the impact on the brain that results in mental hospitalizations and imprisonment. Drug abuse is another factor that prevents normal maturation both physically and mentally. Bizarre and grossly immature

241

thinking becomes the end product of long abuse of illicit drugs.

In this chapter, I have attempted to summarize the major factors that contribute to the expansion of our youth and adult prisons, and facilities for the criminally insane. It is obvious that no single solution will be successful in solving such a complex social problem. Of two major approaches, prevention and rehabilitation, the former holds the greatest promise currently of reducing the crime rate that threatens our safety and increasing tax burden. However, rehabilitation should not be abandoned since it, too, can salvage many lives and reduce the need for more prisons. Mature thinking can benefit all of us!

Fourteen
Some Possible Solutions

Over the years I was invited to address several social organizations such as Parent-Teachers Associations, community clubs and other groups involving parents and others concerned with the raising of children. In the meetings I often asked, "What do you want your child to learn?" Most parents at one point or another have made comments about things they wanted their children to learn. Unfortunately, many had not given thought as to how they were going to teach their child those valuable lessons. As noted, early childhood is where the foundation is set for later learning, and is a time of golden opportunity for parents who want their children to learn the essential lessons that will be the building blocks to a good life. Here we are discussing parents who care about their children and are able to make the sacrifices needed to raise children. Perhaps it would be of help if we had high school classes on early child development and healthy parenting.

We also, however, must deal with the children who have parents who do not care about the children they produce. Even worse, those who resent children and abuse them need to be discovered early for the sake of the child. Sadly, government priorities have resulted in severe cutbacks in public education. Most of these cutbacks have reduced the number of school counselors. Well-trained child guidance counselors are in the best position to access the students who are showing problems in school adjustment, both in behavior and learning. The sources of these problems could be discovered early, thus preventing many children from ending up in juvenile facilities. Children with learning difficulties could be helped instead of being made fun of or ostracized by classmates. Children with behavioral disorders could be evaluated to determine the source of maladaptive behaviors and remedies sought. A caring adult who elicits trust from a child has often prevented a child from taking a wrong path in their lives.

For those who do not respond to these initial efforts, and enter our juvenile halls, there needs to be programs aimed at further evaluations and the setting up of programs to counteract the behaviors and attitudes of these children. To provide needed constructive environments in these facilities, personnel need to be carefully screened and trained. Staff should protect the residents from preying on each other, and not in turn abuse them, out of their own frustrations. Too often today, some staff of juvenile facilities obtain vicarious thrills at residents preying on other residents.

Sadly, not all parents are prepared for parenthood. It has been said that most accidents occur in the bedroom. Add to this the problem that many that become parents will pass on the attitudes and frustrations from their own childhoods upon their children. And tragically, there are those who become parents who are totally irresponsible and should never be parents. Due to their irresponsibility they will produce children whom they will neglect, or brutalize, in taking out their own frustrations and need to express their sense of power. Unhappily in our own present culture we have become increasingly violent and perceive punishment as the solution.

Revenge is another one of our human traits that we continue to struggle to control, as a society through our laws, and as individuals in our internalized feelings as beliefs in mercy and forgiveness. I am very aware that when I hear or read in the news media about some horrific crime, my initial response is one of how revenge could be taken on the perpetrators at once. But when I begin to think about the factors that began in their childhoods, and what the future holds for them, I feel saddened as I see the effect analogous to a stone tossed into a pond of water. The alienation process began in the childhoods of many of the perpetrators and becomes the stone that is tossed into the pond of our society, resulting in a terrible ripple effect on their victims, family members, friends, and even our society at large. All of this is greatly enhanced when the direct victim of a crime is killed or permanently crippled in some way.

What is the solution to this perpetual problem? Increase the penalties for crimes, a vast majority in our society will answer! In spite of centuries of evidence that this does not solve the problem, there is still the common belief that punishment will deter humans from committing crimes. Even politicians elected or appointed to high office are discovered to have succumbed to the temptations of committing crimes. These highly regarded individuals have two important factors in common with the occupants of our prison. The first is weak personal ethical standards. The second is the belief that they are too clever to be caught in their crime. So much for the deterrent effect of punishment.

However, punishment does have a very strong impact on our society, the impact of financial costs. Very few members of our society are remotely aware of the high cost of punishment, and the sacrifices that are required. While one hears about the objections to doling out welfare to needy families, and the occasions when some members of society take advantage of such aid, very little is said about the costs of providing "three hots and a cot," and medical care to those housed in our prisons.

The earlier that we intercede with programs that involve caring and attempts to counteract the early negative influences, the more likely we are to have a major impact in reducing our crime rates. School counselors and improved environments in our juvenile facilities are vital solutions. Early rejection and ostracism followed by what present prison inmates refer to as "gladiator schools" or "prep schools for prison" (as noted in an earlier chapter) needs to be counteracted by more constructive efforts. I see this as the most effective solution to reducing the population of our prisons.

But there are even broader-based solutions that are needed in our society. These are influences outside of the loving, caring parental home. We pride ourselves in our freedom which gradually expands as we grow toward adulthood. Ideally, we learn to set limits on our freedom as we learn to consider the right of others.

Hopefully we learn what we call morals such as the basic rubric of "Do unto others as you would have them do unto you." This defines a basis for social and behavioral interaction between people. It also sets limits to acceptable behaviors. This provides another dimension to our basic human self-centeredness by setting limits to the behaviors taught to children by responsible parents. But as the child encounters life beyond the purview of parents, these limits can come under other pressures and exposures.

Over the past fifty years there has been an immense change in social values in our society. This is reflected and often influenced by increased media access. Individual rights increasingly replace social responsibility. More and more homes have greater access to cable television and computers. While there is no doubt about the vast benefits available in this new technology, there is also an increased burden placed upon parents to protect their children from the negative influences also contained in these products. Constant depictions of sex as a recreational activity without responsibilities, except occasional cautions to protect against unwanted pregnancies and sexually transmitted diseases, are common. Add the excitement of video games that give instructions on how to commit a crime and winning the game by not getting caught. These are just other factors that make it more difficult to raise socially responsible children today.

It has long been known that an individual is shaped not only by parents, but the community that surrounds that individual. For example, raising a child in a gang-ridden, high crime neighborhood makes it very difficult for even very caring and responsible parents. Surviving among peers is a very important determinant in what the outcome will be. Peer influence and community support are determinants as to which culture the individual learns to belong. Thus, it is not surprising that poverty and the need to survive is a large contributor to crime rates. But before those of us who are more fortunate become too comfortable with these statistics, recent studies have indicated crime rates among youths in wealthy neighborhoods are increasing. Recent surveys have found that the drug methamphetamine has reached epidemic levels in its use in this country, and spans all socioeconomic groups.

Alcohol and drug abuse have long been major contributors to our prison population. However, the effects have increased to the extent that one observes in news reports daily violent activities, some of a bizarre, but fatal outcome. Another contributing factor is the increase in youth gangs, particularly involving children of immigrants who have had problems integrating into our overall society. They experience problems similar to the problems encountered in the childhoods of those who enter our youth and adult prisons. Solutions to this problem are much the same as solutions needed for all alienated children and youths.

Again, the solutions encompass educating children to the dangers of alcohol and illicit drug use. To be effective, these messages must be consistent, and not counteracted by conflicting messages. A major example is the messages given out by purveyors of one of the most dangerous of drugs, nicotine. The aging process on the human body and the major contributions and direct causative effects it has on a broad spectrum of human illnesses and deaths is tolerated as long as the marketing of the drug is accompanied by warnings of the hazards on one's health, and references to methods of overcoming the addiction. This is analogous to a father warning his son not to smoke while the father puffs on a cigarette.

While there are organizations that warn youths about the dangers of alcohol abuse, television advertisements show young people gaily partying with drinks in their hands, extolling the taste of their product then a text underneath briefly appears the message, "Drink responsibly." How effective are these messages that are obviously directed towards a segment of our population who has not yet fully matured? The messages received by our youths are not consistent. We need more consistency between the messages given at home, at school, and the broader community.

Money as the root of all evil has been an adage in human society for centuries. However, it can also be used to the good. Compare the costs of a jail or prison cell to the cost of a classroom, or the salary of a prison guard to that of a schoolteacher or school counselor. Most taxpaying citizens will have a surprise coming! Because of security needs, prisons are very expensive to build, requiring high walls and fences topped with coiled barbed wire, steel gates, and cell doors controlled by electronic openers, high guard towers with good observation and communication equipment, just to mention a few.

The setting up of productive work programs and habilitation programs can also reduce the "revolving door" problem, as well as result in more earlier paroles. The word "effective" is key, since just setting up programs, often just for "window dressing" for the public, is not effective. Follow-up on the effectiveness of the programs in reducing recidivism is very important, not only developing more effective programs, but in teasing out factors that make these programs vulnerable to exploitation.

Another solution to reducing youth and adult prison populations is the reduction of political influence in favor of knowledge. Returning to the original concept of parole board members being representative of the cross-section of citizens at large is one step in the right direction. However, the need for knowledge and experience about criminal offenders is paramount. There should be members trained in evaluating offenders, and there should be a return of a well trained and experienced professional sitting with each parole board panel as a consultant.

The current use of the present parole board is a total political function and operates under the counterproductive and highly costly policy of being "tough on crime." Over the past two decades legislators have passed legislation that caters to special interests and, in California, allows for one of the largest and fastest growing prison systems in the world. There are no perfect solutions to the problem of crime, just as there are no perfect solutions to any other social problem. There will be failures and mistakes, but with an increasing search for better solutions, these failures and mistakes can be reduced. Where to most effectively spend our resources should be our goal as a society.

In the next chapter I will try to give you some illustrations of some of the failures I have experienced in the years of dealing with criminal offenders and the reasons for these failures. Remember the analogy of the auto salvage yard!

Fifteen
Too Damaged for Salvage

In earlier chapters I have given examples of prison inmates severely damaged by their childhoods, that, with help of trained professionals and good programming in prison, were able to turn their lives around. But there were also tragic cases that were not salvageable for various reasons. While we can learn a great deal from the successes, we also need to learn from the failures. I hope to use the words of these individuals to allow the reader to see the inside of their minds, and the thoughts that preceded and affected their behaviors. I must warn that much of this may be very repugnant to the average person.

I will call my first example Robert, and give you his childhood background. He was referred to me for psychotherapy for his acute depression and emotional instability. I had done a psychological test to assess his ability to benefit from therapy in terms of his intellectual level. He was of good normal intelligence with a high level of comprehension. I began seeing him on a weekly basis in August of 1984. He was housed in the acute treatment unit at the California Medical Facility, and was being given psychotropic medications. From his prison records I had reviewed his background, which like many other backgrounds of violent offenders revealed a childhood of horror and abuse.

Mother left the father when our subject was about age

251

two to three, with his younger brother who was six months old. They were subsequently moved back and forth between their parents. At age five the subject's father had mother watched, and found out that she left the children alone for long periods of time and had her declared an unfit mother. The boys went back to live with their father. Shortly afterwards father married a woman who was a schoolteacher, The father and the stepmother fought physically, frequently. The boys thought it was their fault since the fights were often over their behavior or grades. Robert wasn't doing well in school. The stepmother divorced their father when Robert was in the sixth grade. Robert became infatuated with matches and started some small fires.

Father began trying to palm the boys off on relatives and friends. Robert was very hurt and felt rejected, as he had loved his father very much. However, when father would get drunk, he would become very mean to the boys. He liked to scare the boys, sometimes threatening them with knives, telling them that he had brought them into the world and could take them out. Other times he would load a gun and tell how he was going to kill their stepmother, the boys, and himself. He would then put the boys in the car and go and watch for the stepmother until he sobered up a bit. Father would sometimes use a little AC/DC generator to punish the two boys. Starting when Robert was age seven, the father taught Robert, and later his younger brother, how to steal things. This became worse as father began drinking heavily and frequently. Robert began missing school and running away, at age ten. Father approved of him dropping out of school in the ninth grade. Beginning at this time, father began having sex with one of the boys each night. Robert was getting into more serious crimes, and occasionally taken to juvenile hall. At age sixteen he began using marijuana and LSD. He was sent to Provo State Hospital because it was felt that he was "dangerous, uncontrollable, no conscience, and full of hate and fear." He remained in the hospital for two months for observation and evaluation and was subsequently released.

Some of the crimes that had resulted in Robert getting sent to juvenile halls were of a serious nature. For example, at age nine he had attempted to stab another boy with a screwdriver. He moved around a lot and was frequently the new boy in school, getting teased and beaten up. When Robert was age seventeen, he was serving time in the California Youth Authority for burglary of a gun store for guns. While he was serving his time there his father died. The father had health problems for a number of years. Robert reported a bitter memory of him and his brother being picked up by police and taken to jail while his father was in the hospital. Robert was about age twelve at that time.

Robert's younger brother began sniffing glue and taking drugs at age thirteen. Robert's drug abuse increased to the use of LSD (about 25 times), PCP (one time), and methamphetamine, and cocaine frequently. When Robert's younger brother was twenty years old, he committed suicide by shooting himself in the head. At age twenty-six, Robert was charged with four counts of assault with a deadly weapon, four counts of attempted murder, and two counts of receiving stolen goods.

The events leading up to his crimes reveal how severely impaired Robert was at the time. He had married and both he and his wife were using cocaine. The following is Robert's version of what happened and why: Late one evening he drove to a location with the intention of making some money to buy some cocaine for him and his wife for that evening. He planned to prostitute himself, which he had done several times previously. He always hated himself for it, feeling shame and guilt afterwards. But he could not think of another way to get money quickly. He met another hustler who suggested they go to a bar to find "tricks." Robert was quickly approached by a man who offered him eighty dollars to go with him to the man's apartment. After the man fellated him, Robert drove back to his own apartment. There he spent some time cleaning his guns so that he could be ready in case he was attacked by "niggers" or the CIA, who might come to get him. He was feeling very guilty about his hustling, and was thinking that his father was right when his father called him and his brother queers, faggots and fuckups. Subsequently he went to the bar where his wife worked. After the bar closed, a group of the dancers, Robert and his wife went to the bartender's apartment to have a party. They snorted and injected cocaine there. Robert felt uncomfortable around people and asked his wife to leave with him. She insisted that her female friend come with them so that she would watch while he had sex with her. However, Robert became afraid and refused, feeling that "demons could take control of his body while having sex and make him into a homosexual." They took more drugs and the women went to sleep.

Robert began to hallucinate that his father was talking to him. He became agitated and depressed and went to a nearby park to "talk to Dad," who was telling him he was a queer and a fuckup for spending money on cocaine. He later returned to his apartment and started telling the women about his father's voice. Both his wife and the girlfriend became angry at him, screaming that he was crazy. The girlfriend gathered up her belongings and tried to get his wife to leave also.

Shortly after the girlfriend left, the police arrived in response to a noise complaint by a neighbor. The wife answered the door, and assured the police that the arguments were over. When the police left, Robert began to feel fearful that his wife's girlfriend was going to send the "niggers" to get him. He strapped on three guns. He and his wife continued to argue and Robert threw her out of the apartment. Again, the police returned. He answered the door and his wife barged in ahead of the police officer. Robert claimed that he was convinced that his father was standing dressed in shorts and tee shirt telling him he was a queer and a fuckup. He felt that he had to kill his father to stop him. The next thing, he had a gun in his hand and the officer was running away. The noise of the gun made him realize what he had done. He had shot at the police officer four times!

What followed was a scene of chaos. After the police officer ran out of the hallway through a fire exit, and out on a second story balcony, Robert ran after him, but could not see him. He then returned to his apartment and got his ammunition satchel. His father had taught him to be ready to shoot it out if anyone threatened him. Robert then ran out of the building, down the steps, and into the park, because he knew the place would shortly be crawling with cops.

He jumped over a fence into someone's backyard. There were two dogs in that yard, so he jumped a wall into another neighbor's yard. There he ran into a gate he couldn't get open. He then kicked the back door to the garage open and entered the garage to hide. However, the big front door of the garage was open. A woman came out and he yelled at her to get back into the house. Her husband ran out right after her. She yelled at her husband to stop, saying he's got a gun. Robert started to lower the gun in his hand when a helicopter went overhead. While he was distracted, the neighbor man grabbed his arm and gun. While they struggled, the gun discharged twice. Another neighbor man joined the struggle, grabbing Robert from behind. One of them got his 357 Magnum away from Robert. Robert tried to get his 38 out but it slipped and fell onto the driveway. One of them kicked it away. Robert remembers them hitting him, and he thinks he said a lot of crazy things. Robert told them, after they tied him up, to kill him or he would kill them, that life was unfair and he was tired of living. The victims of his outburst of violence were two male neighbors, one of their wives, and the police officer.

After Robert was arrested, while in the interrogation room, he found a pocketknife in a drawer. He used the knife to slash his left forearm which required fifty-three sutures to close the wounds.

Following transfer to the county jail, Robert attempted to hang himself in his cell, but was found in time by an officer. Two weeks later on Father's Day, he again imagined hearing his father's voice and inflicted lacerations on his upper left arm. When discovered, he was rushed to a medical center for suturing of his wounds and observation. When returned to jail he was placed in restraints.

In later psychiatric examinations Robert was asked if he had ever tried to kill his father. His answer was very revealing of Robert's internal emotional conflicts. He stated that following an argument with his father in 1973, he had pulled a pistol on his father and threatened to shoot him. He had thought about it many times, but realized that his father was the only person who cared for him despite his abuse and brutality.

While incarcerated in jail, he was beaten up several times and his cigarettes stolen. This increased his suicidal thoughts and hallucinations. He experienced repeated nightmares that he was losing control of his bowels, constantly expelling feces until his insides were coming out and wolves were following him and eating his guts.

Robert was convicted for his offenses and sent to the California Medical Facility for further evaluation and treatment. He had at that time a sentence of just under twenty years in prison.

In August of 1984 Robert was referred to me for psycho-therapy for his acute depression and emotional instability. I saw him in individual sessions until early December of the same year. When he failed to come in for his appointment at his usual time, I sent out a call for him. When he arrived at my office, he informed me that he had been taken before the unit screening committee, and referred for transfer to another prison for continuation of treatment. In this session he appeared to be back to where he was when I first started working with him, talking suicide and violence.

I wrote a memo to the chief psychiatrist of the acute treatment unit protesting the manner in which the transfer recommendation was handled. I told him that I was appalled that staff involved in the treatment of these seriously disturbed inmates were not consulted when decisions regarding these inmates were being considered. I pointed out that the time spent treating this inmate to date had been essentially wasted, and that I was concerned about his possible response, since it was conservative to say that this was a very dangerous young man who should never be paroled without extensive psychotherapy and evaluations.

While the decision to transfer this inmate was made by the politically appointed administration described in an earlier chapter, the chief psychiatrist was able to persuade them to postpone the transfer. I continued seeing Robert on a weekly basis with periodic staff evaluations. However, events in the facility continued to interrupt treatment continuity, which slowed progress. Again, I had to write a memo to the chief psychiatrist about Robert's combination of medical and psychiatric problems. Numerous medical orders in his chart had never been implemented or were delayed for long periods of time. We had been trying to get him on the psychotropic medication, lithium, for over four months. A major part of the problem was the changing around of staff so that there was no continuity. I had had to send this inmate to psychiatric lockup on occasion, as a result. Again, I pointed out that Robert was a very volatile individual, and without some coordinated effort, it was impossible to make headway in his treatment of this case.

Later, in 1985, Robert returned to court for re-evaluation of his sentence due to his mental status at the time of his offense. Subsequently, I received a letter from him from the jail in Southern California. He was apologetic that he had not been able to contact me before he was sent out to the jail. In his letter he stated, "We had such a good session and I had a list of questions for our next one." After assuring me in the letter that he was doing fine on his medication, he said, "I still have those re-occurring dreams where Dad is trying to beat me up and screw me! I hate that, and the dream always ends up with me killing him. I wish we could talk right now. My inner conflict about Dad is where a lot of my problems lie." Two weeks later, I received another letter from Robert. Again, he stated, "You never miss what you've got until it's gone. I'm talking about our sessions. We were just getting down to business and I'm called back to L.A. court!" Later in the letter, he mentioned his nightmares. "Medication is not helping. It is extremely depressing and I can't understand why I'm being haunted even eleven years after he died." I responded to his letter with as much encouragement and suggestions for him as I could.

In early 1986 I received a letter and a court subpoena from Robert's attorney to testify in Robert's hearing. The attorney had been appointed by the State to represent Robert in this sanity phase retrial. He informed me that the prosecution was contending that Robert was malingering and not suffering from any mental illness in spite of previous evaluations and juvenile records. Further, the prosecution had obtained prison records and claimed that there was no evidence of mental illness, and therefore Robert was just fabricating. This was the reason that I was being subpoenaed by the court to testify and to bring relevant documents.

Fortunately, the case was settled after Robert withdrew his plea of not guilty by reason of insanity. He was resentenced with a reduction of two years in his sentence due to time spent in jail. Two months later I received another letter from Robert. This was the last time I heard from or about him. Here is his letter:

"Right now I feel fucked! I want to die or escape from this place of existence. Fuck this class. Fuck this prison, I don't care about being free. Fuck my wife. I don't love her, we don't get along. Fuck my kids. I don't want to care any more. Fuck me! I'm tired of being sad and hurt. Life is nothing more than pain 4 me. I don't care about anything in this life or even want to. Life has always been fucked up for me and always will be. The grain is set. Hopelessness, Depression, Hate, Sadness, Loneliness, Misery! I don't want to care or even try. These feelings have always been with me and always will be with me like a recurring sickness . . . My Mental Disease. Why Me?

"A part of me wants to survive (Ego?) and a part of me wants to die and with dying my memory will be erased. Thank God! Fuck this life and all its ramifications. Life means nothing more than Pain, Frustration, Anxiety, Hurt, Sadness, Loneliness, Struggle, Sickness, Old age, Disease, Strife, Death. If I could commit suicide I would. Right now NOW!

"I don't want to hurt anyone anymore, only myself. I am beyond help, beyond any chance or hope of rehabilitation or realignment or health mentally or spiritually. Why live? Why try? No reason of any real importance. Please let me forget. Let me die! Only in death will I find freedom of this bullshit on this planet. My fascination with death must be met!"

This is the last word I received from Robert, as I said. I hope that he received fulfillment of a wish he had expressed in an earlier letter to me while he was awaiting trial, the wish that he would be sent to a mental hospital.

I have attempted to present an example of an inmate sent to prison so damaged in life as to be beyond our current abilities to salvage. I will now try to analyze the factors that resulted in this damage, and what interventions might have prevented its terrible outcome.

At a very early age, the parents of the subject separated. The children were bounced back and forth between the parents. The important factors of idealization and identification during these early stages of childhood mental and emotional development, have been described earlier. In this particular case, it is highly probable that the two little boys received considerable positive attention from the father, in contrast to the mother, who was found later to leave them alone for long periods of time. It is not uncommon during early childhood that a parent is enamored by the cuteness and cuddliness of a small child, and will spend positive time and give affection to their children. By the age that the two boys were returned to live full time with father, it is probable that a close emotional bond had been formed and both boys idealized and identified with the father.

The physical fighting between the father and step-mother added another dimension to the identification with father—fight for what you want. Note that the fights often stemmed from arguments over the boys, their grades, and their behaviors. Father defended, and thus supported their misbehaviors and lack of motivation for school. The step-mother left with the boys firmly convinced it was their fault. A serious sign of severe emotional problem arises at this time in Robert's childhood, infatuation with matches and setting fires. This has long been known to be an early symptom of emotional disturbance in a child. Father began to withdraw his emotional support of the boys, and began to abandon them emotionally. Both boys were very hurt by this as they had formed a close bond and idealization with him. At this time the father began to get drunk and became mean to the boys, scaring them, threatening them, and brutally punishing them at times. Also, during this period of childhood, their idol with whom they identified began to teach them antisocial behaviors, as the father's drinking became worse. With this model, it is typical for a child to mimic the behavior of a parent.

Another warning sign for Robert appears. He is a loner in school, getting into fights, and finally, with father's approval, drops out of school. Then comes the greatest trauma for the young brothers approaching the beginning of adolescence with the demands of developing and resolving the issues of identity. Father begins having sex with one of the boys each night. The physical and emotional trauma now brought upon the two brothers was very overwhelming. Their model was now avoiding his emotional problems with alcohol, and antisocial and perverted behaviors. It should be no surprise that the boys turned to illicit drugs to escape their emotional problems. They had no one to turn to for help as father had socially isolated them over the years. The extensive use of the drugs they turned to for relief had permanent adverse impact on their future adaptation and mental abilities.

Remember the essential task of adolescent and early adult development. What kind of person am I? What are my abilities? What do I want to do with my life? These are among the questions we all face during this period of our lives. With good role models, good peers, and encouragement, most navigate these issues successfully.

But what did Robert and his younger brother have for

help during this span of their lives? By adulthood they were firmly alienated from any society. Their mental status was so distorted that they were unable to adapt to the cultures of juvenile halls, youth facilities, prisons, etc. Robert's younger brother resolved his issues in his early twenties with a gunshot to his head. It was still an open question as to how Robert might resolve his issues.

Less severe adaptive disabilities can still occur without mental insanity becoming a factor. The next example I wish to share is one in which criminal behavior was the only way of life for this man who also identified closely with his father. I will call this the case of Michael:

Michael was the youngest of four children, and the only boy. His parents divorced when he was two years old. The records describe the mother as promiscuous and alcoholic. Following the parents' divorce, Michael spent his early years in various boarding homes and boarding schools. Again, the records indicate that when Michael was living with his father he was pretty much on his own, without guidance or supervision. Father was in the oil business, and moved around a lot. Thus, Michael changed schools frequently. The father liked to carry guns around, and managed to get himself deputized as a reserve deputy officer, which allowed him to carry a gun legally. This also allowed Michael's father to throw his weight around and get into fights. In previous evaluations, the father was described as "undisciplined, amoral, and a somewhat violent man."

Michael's criminal history began when he was fourteen. Attempts at probation and forestry camp placements failed. Finally, he was sent to a Youth Authority facility for grand theft, auto. There again Michael made a poor adjustment, creating disturbances, agitating racial incidents, and became involved in forced sodomy. He also accumulated several escapes and escape attempts on his record. Staff described him at that time as very insecure, and covering it by aggressiveness. He was paroled to a married sister of his, but after six months he made contact with some former friends he had made in the Youth Authority. This began a whole new series of crimes including assault, forgery, and burglary. He also began to use narcotics. During this period of time, Michael's father was having financial difficulties, and increasing health problems, culminating in the father committing suicide.

Six months later Michael was sent to prison for an armed robbery he committed with another Youth Authority parolee. Thus, at age twenty, Michael began an eighteen-year prison career, broken only by a later escape. Three years after entering prison, he was given an additional term for possessing a homemade stiletto. This was found on him following an incident in which another inmate was stabbed in the abdomen and legs. The other inmate also had a prison-made weapon. A few years later, Michael was sent to work in a prison conservation camp. He and another inmate escaped and were apprehended three months later, and convicted of assault with a deadly weapon, and robbery. However, while awaiting trial on these offenses, Michael again escaped, was caught, and charged for escape from jail. The next eight years in prison were marked with frequent disciplinaries, including fights with other inmates. Because of his behavior, he was housed in a maximum security area of Folsom State Prison.

Michael's behavior began to finally level off with only one disciplinary in 1969, and a good work reports from his supervisors. In late 1970 he was transferred to the California Medical Facility to participate in a special program there called the Stress Assessment Unit. This program was aimed at evaluating inmates for their stress levels, assessing how they responded to stress, and attempting to teach them how to better deal with their stress. Michael failed the program after two times through the program. Understandably, he was not recommended for parole. He was transferred into worker status at the facility, but later managed to get himself into the general psychotherapy program. He was referred to me, and I subsequently saw him for several individual sessions in addition to weekly group therapy. However, it was not easy for Michael, who had by now spent lengthy time in prisons such as Folsom and San Quentin.

Group psychotherapy presented a threatening breach to the inmate code of "doing your own number," and not revealing yourself in any way, especially your emotions. He made an attempt to stick out these anxiety provoking sessions, not because he felt he needed them, but rather because "it is required of me to get out."

In general, Michael remained much the same as described in previous reports over the years. He was very self-oriented, rigid in his thinking, and nonconforming to standard expectations. He was quick to condemn others if they did not conform to his expectations explicitly. Like other long-term criminal offenders, he continued to project what happened to him upon others. On the positive side, Michael had participated in job skills training programs, taken college extensions classes, and had done well holding down a clerical position, wherein he came into direct contact with custody and treatment staff. Based upon the dramatic behavioral changes Michael had made over the past few years, he was given a parole by the board.

Soon after his parole I began receiving letters from Michael. As with the example of Robert, I will share pertinent contents of Michael's letters to let you see into the process of the thinking and reactions that resulted in his failure on parole:

"Well, I shall have five months of freedom under my

belt on the 23rd. Man, the sole adjective that can be used to describe my predicament when I first 'surfaced' is bewildered. Long prison terms beat hell out of a man. . . ." "I had to learn to dial phones, ride buses, make love, everything, all over . . ." "I used to do an awfully lot of things well. My almost twenty-year term, along with the really bad beatings I received from police, took an enormous toll upon my person. The 23rd, supra, will also be my 39th birthday. I live with one genuine fear. That the police may some day frame me. I'm simply getting by on short dollars now that the longshoremen are out on strike. If some white male American with enormous proportions commits a crime, I am suspected automatically. Cops haven't rousted me recently—knock on wood!"

Michael goes on to talk about some health problems he is having, his thoughts about moving to a ranch in the mountains owned by an old family friend that had offered him work. He spends the bulk of the letter talking about all the injustices he sees around, living as he does in an impoverished area of San Francisco. Nonetheless, he inserts periodic comments about policemen, "who delight in smashing heads and collarbones with nightsticks, and parole boards who make men serve, say ten years for a second degree burglary, are worse than the 'criminals.' The persecute prosecute. No social do-gooder this writer, but Doc, there's as much wrong on the 'good' side as the bad." In the letters, Michael calls himself the "San Francisco Cowboy."

The above is highly significant in revealing Michael's thinking processes that preceded the storm of letters I began receiving from him, beginning about a week after the above letter. It began like this, "Dear Doc, Well, here I sit . . . no excuses nor recriminations, but wowee! I must be crazy! I am charged with twelve felony complaints (thus far)—two counts kidnapping, four counts robbery, and six counts of attempted murder on policemen in this county. I am really down for the count of nine, but am calm and relaxed. I could always handle the bad (beatings, years in the hole, etc.), but man, simple everyday living beat hell out of me, your prohibition/touring car gangster in the space age. Man, I just did not fit in anywhere. I realize that I had serious charges before and had to serve a lot of time, but they kept me too long. I really loved even the bad days of freedom. I've been in bad health and was seeing a doctor. . . . He was an M.D. and a hell of a nice person, he finally talked me into seeking psychiatric help a day or two before my arrest. . . . I asked him to write to you and explain that I was at least trying. I certainly left prison with good intentions. I will be OK now, though it appeared as though I'd need a bit of patching up. I suffered serious rib injuries and my hat size is about fourteen."

Michael continues on in the letter thus, "It seems as though they have dug every crime up ever committed in this county and filed them on me. I'm far from popular here—the main allegation being that I took 40–50 shots at police with an automatic rifle. I'm 'Dundee,' I guess, but why? Doc, I have to concede that there' s something to that old psychiatric mumbo-jumbo. I was too divorced from freedom to ever be a person when I first got out. I gave it a heck of a try, Doctor Mattocks, give me that much.

"Here's a prime example of too too many years in. Now I expect to be buried in Folsom, which is a waste, but I realize that I have serious crimes charged versus my person. If I go through CMF as a parole violator or parole violator with a new term, I would like to speak with you and for a change level with you."

A newspaper account described the crimes Michael committed as beginning as a simple traffic stop by three officers on Michael's car for an illegal U-turn on a highway. Two shots were fired, hitting the police vehicle, and a high-speed chase began. Other police units joined the chase and three officers received cuts by glass as their car was struck by bullets from the fleeing car, before it finally crashed into a retaining wall.

Michael wrote in one of his letters that he heard the testimony in court that, "my codefendant and I were stopped for a traffic violation and that I just started shooting with a .30 M1 carbine and that I fired between thirty and sixty shots into policemen and police cars before I got into a 100 MPH wreck, crashing through a roadblock about a half-hour later. Genuine and absolute madness."

In a subsequent letter, Michael gave me another piece of information when he revealed that while out of prison and before his new offenses, he had gone to the "Silver Serpent." That's an old term for the hypo needle. In his letters he made attempts to analyze why he had such a penchant for violence and crime. Michael was an avid reader and spent much of his time reading. One point he made in a letter was a very astute observation, "Do some of us need the security of a narrow cell and a world of arbitrary limitations? I've become trapped in odd loyalties and hatred has often kept me going. When one can really hate well it sometimes overcomes loneliness and depression."

He went on to say, "I only used to be comfortable around thieves in the 'can,' then I met the treatment staff and got liking you, Doc. Maybe that corrupted and confused me."

Several years later Michael was again paroled from prison. Once again I receive a letter, this time he had been out fifteen months. He stated that this time he must be "habilitated, or something." He stated that he had been working on film jobs as a bodyguard for several stars. He claimed that he had cleared ten grand in three months appearing at the side of a well-known movie actress. This was the last time I heard directly from Michael. His physical health had continued to plague him, and I was told that he had disappeared and was never seen again.

As with Robert, Michael's parents divorced when he was about two years old and spent most of his early years in various boarding facilities. Even when he lived with his father, the boy was very much on his own. The father was very obviously a violent, undisciplined role model for Michael. Although intellectually bright, Michael learned no self-discipline. The only time any limits were placed upon his behavior was when he was locked up in one of the "prep schools for prison." He was totally alienated from the outside world. He had failed school, had learned no marketable skills, and had strong hostility towards authority. Michael liked gangster movies and shared with me on one occasion his fantasy about standing on the running board of a prohibition period touring car, spraying bullets from a machine gun.

Both of these cases illustrate the importance of early role models, the importance of setting limits on a child's behavior, and teaching, both by words and actions, social values. It is notable how these two examples deal with the concept of responsibility. Robert took extreme responsibility resulting in repeated suicide attempts, and other self-destructive activities. However, he both internalized and externalized his hostility, a phenomenon previously noted in murder cases, wherein suicide attempts have been noted prior to the killing of their victim.

In the case of Michael, he also struggled with why he continued to commit such outlandish crimes. Here he was so long involved in a social learning environment that taught that whenever something didn't come out the way you wanted, it was someone else's fault. Even as he tried later to indulge in some self-examination, the focus always returned to what had been done to him, rather than what he had done to trigger others' response to his behavior.

Both of these cases represent much damaged individuals who continued their paths in absence of early or consistent intervention. Nonetheless, these types of cases continue to exist and some totally reject any efforts to help change their thinking and behavior. There are those who will do what Michael did, that is, go along with the program to obtain parole from prison. In both examples described, seeds were planted in their therapy exposure, but sadly in infertile soil. It is important to recognize that in both of these men, illicit drug abuse also played a determining role. The drugs severely damaged them both physically and mentally, and the results were most probably irreversible.

We must acknowledge that many factors come together to create what some call the "criminal mind." Ongoing research is needed to determine the impact of each of these factors, and their contribution to the criminal population so that we can develop methods to counteract and prevent their destructiveness to our society.

In the next chapter, I hope to describe some of the currently known factors and cite evidence of the impact of certain efforts to counteract these factors. Again, we are not looking for the perfect solution, just better solutions.

Sixteen

Other Possible Solutions and Issues

I hope that I have given you, the reader, some ideas and examples of the complexities and enormity of the problem faced by our society in dealing with criminals. As has been noted, there has been no lack of simple solutions suggested over the past decades. The results have been an increasing creation and maintenance of aliens from our culture.

Numerous factors contribute to the increase in this problem. One of them, as previously mentioned, is the normal human desire to "get back" and seek revenge against those who violate our basic values involving human life and property. We can readily identify with the innocent victims of crimes and want retaliation. It is easy to imagine the suffering of the innocent victims of the crime, and wonder what kind of mind would someone have to have to do such things to other humans.

A major consideration in our search for solutions to crime problems must be the victims of crimes, their families, and friends who suffer also. For this reason we need to place a strong emphasis upon prevention. The old adage that an ounce of prevention is worth a pound of cure, perhaps can be changed to a ton of cure, with more effective efforts.

We also need an increase in awareness. Crime reports are a constant attention grabber in our news media. Rarely, if ever, in the past or present have we heard about how those released from successful treatment and training programs in our jails and prisons, who have been able to turn their lives around, and become good citizens. One failure from programs attempting to change serious behaviors in individuals gets the focus of attention, while the hundred or more successes receive no mention. Once that individual is convicted, as noted in an earlier chapter, the funding for the program is often ended, and the exceptional failure is sentenced and all is out of sight and forgotten. Therefore our desires for revenge and our limited attention works against seeking more constructive solutions.

Cycles of wars and interludes of peace also affect our concerns about how we deal with criminal offenders. When our attention is focused on the terrible events of wars, and the brutalization against innocents, we become satiated with the inhumanities that occur. For a time following a war's end, as noted, there is a trend towards peace and helping the less fortunate. This tends to even penetrate into our prisons, and give concerns about how inmates are treated in our youth and adult prison facilities.

Also, we need to be aware of the steady changes in our overall society. As has been said, children are not only raised by their parents, but also by the community. In decades past, that was limited to small communities and neighborhoods for the majority. However, with the increase in our technology the "community" has expanded to nation-wide and beyond. Economic changes have seen a change where both parents work outside the home and tend to spend less time with their children. Many children spend the major portion of their time with televisions and computers. Therefore, children in our present society are exposed to many aspects of life that require they make decisions on their own, often without parental guidance or awareness.

The increase in youth gangs has become an increasing

problem in our urban areas especially. All children seek acceptance. Thus, children who feel unaccepted at home or school are prime recruits for youth gangs. Another human need, excitement, is also provided by gang membership. After a gang recruit completes some daring tasks demanded by gang members, he or she is accepted into the gang and provided continued excitement from drive-by shootings, tagging, beating up non-members or members of rival gangs, stealing, and other illegal activities. When a gang member is arrested and interrogated by police, they often refuse to talk, only saying that the gang is their family and they won't harm their gang family.

Add to these facts the increasing alcohol and drug problems that confront our world. The constant promise of new thrills, and the want for acceptance by a social group combine to pressure more and more children youth and adults to experiment with the deadly potential of alcohol and drugs. The illusion of being in control and denial, combine to mask them from the consequences of their addictions. While this is one area where we have increased the number of treatment programs, we know that there are failures and later relapses. Since many are forced to participate in such programs, there are those who will pretend to participate with no intention of stopping their use of alcohol and drugs afterwards.

It is very essential that we learn from the past in seeking solutions to the problems of crime. Wars are very costly as most of us know, either by history or from current experience. The 1980 Declaration of War on Crime has been very costly and ineffective in solving the problem. For those who have doubts, I would refer you to a book, *The Real War on Crime,* edited by Steven R. Donziger, published by Harper Perennial, a division of HarperCollins Publishers. This book was published a decade ago in 1996 and provides an excellent background and describes the consequences of the politically driven "war on crime."

Again, the impact in California has resulted in an increase in the number of prisons from twelve to thirty-four, with pressure to build more. No impact on the crime rate can be traced to the mania for more prison construction and the increase in the lengthening of prison sentences.

Before any effective solutions can be implemented there has to be a removal of politics from prison administration to be replaced by knowledge and experience. Prior to the late 1970s, the administration and professional personnel were highly experienced in their field. The Director of Corrections had begun his career as a Correctional Officer. Over the years he had promoted up through the ranks to become Director via Civil Service evaluations of his experience and knowledge. Civil Service Boards were made up of individuals knowledgeable in their respective fields. The candidate for promotion was orally interviewed and reports of job performances were reviewed. Candidates were then ranked accordingly for possible promotion. It was when this Civil Service procedure was eliminated and replaced by political appointments that CDC and other state departments began to become adversely affected, and expanded into large bureaucratic, ineffectual and destructive masses.

What is needed now is more constructive methods to deal with our crime problems. These methods must also demonstrate their effectiveness. In short, that means it can't just sound good, but it must prove that it does good. Over the past few years, there have been articles appearing about small programs which have demonstrated success in helping delinquent youths change their behaviors in positive ways. Sadly, those isolated reports are little noted due to constant reports of sensational crimes occurring daily.

From the case histories I have presented in previous

chapters, it would seem clear that efforts at prevention would be the most effective way to reduce our prison population. Intense studies of the various types of criminals, exploring their thinking and their developmental histories, can produce valuable information about how we might develop preventive measures. In the case history samples in earlier chapters of this book it is easy to imagine interventions that could have prevented such tragic outcomes. It is also important to note how the need for intervention went unnoticed so that we can now develop awareness of early signs that a child needs help.

Equally obvious in the examples given is the fact that some parents were lacking knowledge of the developmental needs of their children, and that they often took out their own unresolved issues upon the child. They were lacking in the fundamentals of child rearing needs for parental guidance, and the setting of examples by their own behaviors. We all require education and training to perform adequately in our jobs. Therefore, it would seem logical that we need education and training to perform the most important job of all, being a good parent.

There will always be those to whom responsibility will remain an unknown concept. Impulsive, unprotected sex, or the need for general validation may result in unwanted, abandoned babies, and abortions, legal or otherwise. Some are deposited in a dumpster, or the door to a hospital, whichever is more convenient. Here the partial solution might involve free sterilizations, or more drastically, require sterilizations for those who have demonstrated that they cannot be responsible to raise or support children.

Added to this is the problem of the parent who will sacrifice their children to the depravity of their spouse in order to preserve their marriage. This is vividly illustrated in the case of Steven presented in Chapter Five. The mother in that case did no try to protect her children from the beatings and horrors perpetrated by the stepfather. Even when her oldest child was taken to the hospital for injuries inflicted by her husband, she supported his stories about how the injuries occurred. My staff encountered many such cases wherein a parent failed to intercede when their child was physically or sexually abused by their spouse or live-in companion.

It is clear that there are lots of problems that we, as a society, need to consider in attempts to prevent the terrible tragedies that result in so many victims. When reading reports about the crimes committed by the offenders, it is difficult, if not impossible, to imagine what led them to do the terrible things they did to innocent victims. Commonly our focus is on the crime, our condemnation is on the perpetrators of the crimes, and our empathy is for the victims of the crimes. Little thought goes into how the crimes might be prevented in the first place.

So far there have been numerous suggestions over the past decade of possible solutions that could have impacts on reducing crimes in this country. There have been a few isolated implementations, but other priorities have prevented widespread efforts. Since poor parenting has been a heavy contributor to our crime rate, the inclusion of high school classes in child development and parenting would seem helpful in increasing the rate of good parents, maybe even helping some to postpone becoming parents, or not becoming parents. The responses I noted in a previous chapter from university graduate level students were eye opening in revealing the lack of awareness of the sensitivity of preschool children to their parents' emotional tones and behaviors. It is obvious that better training for the most important job that one can undertake, parenting, is very needed.

As children enter preschool and grammar schools,

some begin to exhibit signs that portend future serious problems. Learning problems, poor social skills need to be picked up and remedied as quickly as possible to prevent a growing negative impact on the child's development. Such problems, if neglected, can be quickly increased by name-calling from others, bullying, and social isolation. These all contribute to the process of alienation from school, and even society at large. Seeking to belong in some way can result in troubled youths banding together with the bully in school to enhance their feelings of worth by picking on others.

At the other end of the spectrum is the social isolate. This individual may shun others or form a close alliance with only one or two friends who also remain aloof from others. Over the years, I have noted that the young perpetrators of violent acts in schools or other locales are often described as "loners." Again, a reminder that the delinquents and adults who commit violent crimes are characterized by deep, boiling anger and feelings of alienation from mainstream society.

Among the possible solutions to these problems, having more highly trained school counselors who can diagnose the child's problem, and come up with remedies. To further aid in these efforts, more school monitors would be needed to observe and note problem behaviors in hallways and on playgrounds at schools. Children and teenagers should also have access to school counselors to discuss problems they are having. This could have the added benefit of reducing suicide rates among youths.

Another vital problem that needs serious attention in drug abuse. Presentations, beginning in grammar schools, graphically showing the impact of drug abuse, and the power of addictiveness, could reduce early temptations to try substances out of curiosity, or the urging of peers. It should include the fact that use of alcohol and drugs becomes a way of running from facing problems and learning how to solve problems, and thus has serious impact on both brain, behavior, and body. These presentations should be powerful enough to leave lasting impressions on young minds, hopefully before they have any personal experience with mind-altering substances.

Since we know that there will always be crimes, we also need to consider developing methods that will reduce the populations that end up in our juvenile halls, youth facilities, and prisons. Programs made available back in the 1970's were very successful at reducing the prison populations in states that offered them. These were the programs aimed at helping those who were motivated to get professional treatment to resolve emotional problems originating in their childhoods, helping many to discover that they had abilities and talents that enhanced their pride, and feelings of acceptance by members of mainstream society. In this book, my goal has been to give examples of the successes of these programs. Also, I have offered examples of the failures.

The failures are important to our efforts to reduce crimes. We need to conduct intensive studies of these failures in order to accumulate information that will further help us to understand how we can improve our preventative and habilitative efforts. We need to not allow radical elements such as those back in the 1970s who blocked efforts to use inmate volunteers for research purposes, that benefited the inmates as well as the rest of us. It would seem much more beneficial and humane to study inmates for information that will lead to improvements in preventive and habilitation rather than executions via the death penalty.

Whatever solution is attempted will cost money. However, the potential savings over current methods are enormous, and can be reduced further. The building and staffing of a prison is extremely costly due to all the expensive security structures and highly paid staffing required. Most taxpayers would be shocked if they were able to compare the costs of construction and maintaining housing for three thousand inmates of a prison, with the costs of construction of school facilities for three thousand students and the needed staff for both.

Other comparisons are worthy of consideration. A prison guard requires a high school diploma, and extensive training in police academies and/or prison training programs. This training commonly takes twelve to sixteen months. During this training the individual guard is considered for probationary employment. That is, if he or she does not pass any of the training requirements, they can be dropped from employment as a prison guard. When accepted as a full-time guard, they begin to receive full health and retirement benefits.

Schoolteachers have more extensive requirements in education. Usually they have to complete five to six years of college to become credentialed as a teacher. Due to cutbacks in funds for schools, a teacher is often required to buy supplies for their students with their own money. After getting tenure they also receive medical and retirement benefits. The process leading to tenure has sometimes been compared to on-the-job training.

In comparing these requirements for prison guards with those of teachers, one should also compare their salaries. Both belong to unions that try to protect their interests. Prison guards do have to pay higher union dues than teachers. However, the salary raises over the years surpass those of teachers. In California, it has been reported that the union to which prison guards belong is one of the largest contributors to political campaigns for governor of the state. One of the justifications for their subsequent raises and higher salaries has been termed "hazard pay," referring to the hazards they face in their duties as prison guards. Again, threats and shootings in our schools have increased. Children caught coming into schools with weapons, threats made upon teachers and other students, all have made teaching in some of our schools more hazardous. Also, note the high number of deaths and injuries suffered by police, sheriffs, and highway patrols as compared to prison guards. The point is that there are high risks in many jobs and professions that do not receive higher salaries and benefits as a result. Just another factor to think about in considering the costs of our jails and prisons.

Yes, there will be added costs to staffing our schools with highly qualified teachers and professional counselors. However, the construction of more jails and prison facilities will place higher burdens on the taxpayers, and take more monies away from education, health programs and other benefits to the general public in this nation. The past treatment and habilitation programs described herein were very cost effective by reducing recidivism rates, and even some violent incidents within prisons.

There is one other factor that I have mentioned before that is worthy of further elaboration, that is, our criminal justice system. Over the past decades there has been a phenomenal proliferation of laws in our nation. As noted, many are written in such a manner as to be subject to later interpretations. The right to a quick trial is rarely enforced as crowded court schedules, delays by attorneys requesting postponements, and prolonged investigations can result in years before some cases some to trial. After coming to trial, even further delays occur, placing stress on citizen jurors at times to make decisions to get over the extended time demands on their services.

It is quite well known that the wealth of the defendant is a major factor in the conviction process. Several notorious and widely publicized cases over the past years have brought this to public attention. District Attorneys, as political offices, need to win cases that will impress voters of their abilities. Hired attorneys for the defendant usually charge by the hour. The more impressive their record of winning cases for their clients, the higher that hourly rate. And then, there is the court-appointed attorney for the defendant. That attorney is often paid a fixed salary from the judicial budget. Frequently these are attorneys that are accruing experience in the field of criminal law, in order to move up in their profession. At this point, I will leave it to the reader to decide which of these attorneys are most likely to spend numerous hours searching through voluminous law books for technicalities that might be used to win a case.

These differences in level of defense, and the inequities in sentences for crimes, are major inequalities in our legal system. Determining the harshness of a sentence often falls to a judge's discretion. Judges have their own biases based upon what the crime entailed, and their impression of the perpetrator. Attorneys often attempt to take their case before a judge that they feel might be prone to rule in a certain manner due to their past experiences with that judge.

And then there is the jury selection process which has changed considerably over the years. From merely trying to eliminate from the jury anyone who professed any type of bias that might color their judgment of the facts presented, the selection process has changed to the point that lawyers actively try to seek out prospective jurors that will rule in their favor. From my own personal observations of our justice system, I believe that term "justice" no longer applies. These massive defects in our legal system also serve to further alienate those who pass through our courts and often experience firsthand these inequities. They use these factors to further justify their own criminal behaviors. I have often heard inmates use examples of judicial "crimes" to excuse their own criminal activities, with the phrase, "everybody does it."

Throughout this book I have attempted to share with the reader my own direct experiences in evaluating and treating criminal offenders, my experiences and observations from within the California prison system for a span of forty years, and my direct observations of our legal system. From all of this I feel that I have learned a great deal. Even though I had a broad academic background, I learned from some unique opportunities presented me. It has left me with my own optimisms and pessimisms. I am optimistic that the prevention programs I have discussed carried out on a broad scale could reduce our prison populations. I am convinced that continued research and evaluations will also increase their effectiveness. The same is true for rehabilitation programs in our prison facilities, as demonstrated by the results achieved in the 1970s in the California Department of Corrections.

However, I must also confess to pessimism about two very major factors that have negated past efforts, and probably have a large impact on any future efforts. Both of these two factors are so integrated and inseparable that any possibility of change is improbable, or will face large hurdles at best.

While I may be perceived as painting all lawyers as bad, I want to say that I have known some very fine lawyers among my friends. As the saying goes, "there are few rotten apples in every barrel." This is true for every profession, including my own professional field. Thus we all need to be judged by our behavior, not by mere words. Like all societies, our society is in the process of changing. What these changes are like will be where we place our values, how we assess our responsibilities, and how we treat each other.

I would like to close on a positive note. Since history often repeats itself, I detect that the prolonged war in Iraq will have citizens again wanting something more positive. In the past, as noted before, there has been a tendency to try to help the less fortunate, including our youth and adults in the prison programs. I have recently noted reports of reviews, exposes, and improvements being made in some of these facilities. As we all travel down the road of life, we will alternate between our need to care about others and our need for power and revenge!

Bon Voyage!!

Epilogue

Over the past two and a half decades, prison conditions in California have become an increasing burden on taxpayers, almost tripling the number of costly prisons. Under the battle cry of supporting a war on crime, politicians won votes by convincing voters that they could reduce crimes by increasing punishments. Once again, centuries of evidence that punishment alone will not stop criminal behaviors was ignored.

Political expedience replaced knowledge and experience. Administrators of California prisons, who had moved up to their positions via experience and knowledge by way of passing civil service exams and interviews, were replaced by political appointees. These new appointees further illustrated their ignorance about prisons by announcing that they did not want to hear anything about the past of what went on in prisons before, that they were a new operation.

No longer is the input of professionals considered at parole hearings. Parole hearings have become a sham in most cases to the extent that increasing numbers of prison inmates have refused to attend their hearings, knowing that any evidence of positive changes over the years will be ignored.

Efforts to help motivated inmates to make positive changes in their lives have been abandoned. Small token programs have been established by CDC only when trying to stave off takeovers by federal judges. The results have been that prisons in California are jammed beyond capacity. The current governor's solution has been to ship inmates from California prisons to prisons in other states, and to build more prisons in California. Abuse of prisoners is only occasionally revealed due to the secrecy imposed by prison administrators. However, violent acts by inmates are published quickly. It has been a long known fact that inmates who do not have constructive outlets will resort to increasing riots and other violence due to "dead time."

A recent news report about the increased usage of illegal drugs in prisons made brief passing mention that some prison guards smuggle in drugs to sell to inmates, but goes on to emphasize that non-custodial employees such as cooks and other non-members of the Correction Officers union make huge amounts of money in this illegal activity. The money received is often provided by friends and family members of the inmates. Since prison guards have the greatest access to inmates, one can draw their own conclusions as to which prison employees are most involved. In my experience, the vast majority of the custodial staff was there to do their jobs and did it well. The old adage that there are few rotten apples in every barrel applies here. Of course the larger the barrel, the more rotten apples.

Perhaps the biggest factor resulting in the gigantic mess facing CDC today is that politics has replaced past knowledge, and has stifled any efforts to expand knowledge as to how to reduce the need for so many prisons. Increasing numbers of news media articles have, over the past two years especially, exposed the terrible conditions in our prisons harmful to both inmates and the public. Sadly, politicians have created and maintained the costly and tragic conditions in our prisons so long and to such an extreme, the remedies will take a long time and be costly to all of us!

If the system continues, we will suffer more and more.

Currently, prison guards, thanks to the power of their union, with their high school diplomas, receive higher salaries than schoolteachers, and college professors according to recent news articles. Our courts are so backed up that it takes years for cases to come to trial, thus skyrocketing legal costs paid for by taxpayers. It would certainly be less costly to learn from the past and research more effective prevention and rehabilitation programs than to continue down the path of political expediency. How much are you willing to pay to just lock offenders up and throw away the key?!